A 52-WEEK BIBLE STUDY

ENCOUNTERING
God's
Love

FROM GENESIS
TO REVELATION

Randy & Rozanne Frazee

HarperChristian
Resources

Table of Contents

The Story of Jesus (Matthew–John)

The Story of the Church (Acts–Jude)

The Story of the New Garden (Revelation)

The Art Gallery and the Mural

Two of the most famous works of art in the world help us understand how the long, sweeping story of the Bible—seemingly a narrative only about God and ancient people with strange names—connects to your story. To view the first painting, you must travel to Paris, enter the renowned Louvre Museum, and walk past painting after remarkable painting by some of the greatest artists who have ever lived.

You climb stairs and move from one cavernous room to another until you finally spot it: *Mona Lisa* by Leonardo da Vinci—the most famous painting in the world, and the most valuable, reportedly worth $700 million.

After several minutes in front of this famous masterpiece, you stroll through the museum, stopping every now and then to study other paintings that catch your eye: *Supper at Emmaus* by Rembrandt, *Liberty Leading the People* by Eugène Delacroix, *The Virgin and Child with the Infant Saint John the Baptist* by Raphael. Each one is completely different, having its own unique tale utterly unrelated to the *Mona Lisa* story. By the time you leave the museum, you will have stood in front of dozens of exquisite paintings, each with a different and distinct story behind its creation.

To view the other famous work of art, you must catch a flight to Rome, grab a taxi, and use your best Italian to ask the driver to take you to the Vatican. Upon arriving, you walk across a magnificent plaza, buy a ticket and go through the Vatican Museum, and finally enter the Sistine Chapel where you look up to see the breathtaking work of Michelangelo.

You get to the center of the room and tilt your head back to look at arguably the second-most famous painting in the world—*The Creation of Adam*. As you shift your gaze to the right, then to the left, you quickly realize that the story behind this painting doesn't sit alone in a room by itself like the *Mona Lisa*. No, it is connected to three hundred other characters.

The Louvre and the Sistine Chapel—two different venues for creative expression—both display astounding art. The Louvre tells thousands of unrelated stories. The Sistine Chapel, on the other hand, tells only one. The *Mona Lisa* hangs in an art gallery; *The Creation of Adam* is a part of a mural.

A VIEW FROM THE LOWER STORY

To better understand this story, we will need to view it with a dual lens. Just as if we were wearing bifocals, through the lower lens we will gaze at the individual stories from the Bible in chronological order. Think of these individual pieces as our Lower Story.

The Lower Story reveals the here and now of daily life, the experiences and circumstances we see here on earth. In the Bible there are the individual stories of people like Adam and Eve, Abraham and Sarah, David, Esther, Jesus, Paul, and Peter. As we probe these stories, they offer unique lessons for living.

A VIEW FROM THE UPPER STORY

But God has a higher agenda than our individual stories of survival and comfort. When we rise above the here and now, look beyond the daily grind, and view each of these stories in the Bible from God's perspective, we see something much bigger.

This is the Upper Story. As we view the Bible through this lens, we see that God has been up to something amazing from the very beginning. He has a vision, a big idea, and it is all good news for us. When we look at the Upper Story of God—his magnificent mural—we discover where we fit in, because this story was created to deliver one singular message:

God loves us and wants to be in a relationship with us.

The Bible is more like a mural than an art gallery.

GOD'S STORY . . . MY STORY

That is the journey we are going to take together. We are going to take a look at individual characters of the Bible in chronological order from Genesis to Revelation and discover Lower Story lessons for living. But we are also going to look at these stories from above and see how God is weaving them together to tell one epic love story. A look through both lenses will be extremely helpful as you seek to connect your Lower Story to God's grand Upper Story. That is the goal of this fifty-two-week journey we are taking together.

1. What do you hope to receive from this study?

2. When you hear the phrase, "God loves you," what emotions are stirred in you?

3. What do you think about having the ability to share God's story with others by the end of this study?

4. Consider asking three people to pray for you as you embark on this journey. Write down their names here.

Let me give you a huge clue about God's story. It does not unfold as the kind of linear story we are accustomed to, where things keep moving forward. God story is like a circle. This amazing adventure ends where it began. Read the first two chapters and the last two chapters of the Bible, and you'll see they are almost identical. God's vision in the first garden is ultimately restored, and in the end, a new garden appears.

SHARE THE STORY

One of our goals in this study is not only for you to see God's grand story and your role in it, but for you to be able to tell the story to others. So, each week we are going to equip you, little by little, to tell this story to others to encourage them that they, too, are characters in this epic story that God deeply loves.

Five Movements of God's Story

As you read through the pages of the Bible, you are going to encounter five movements within God's story.

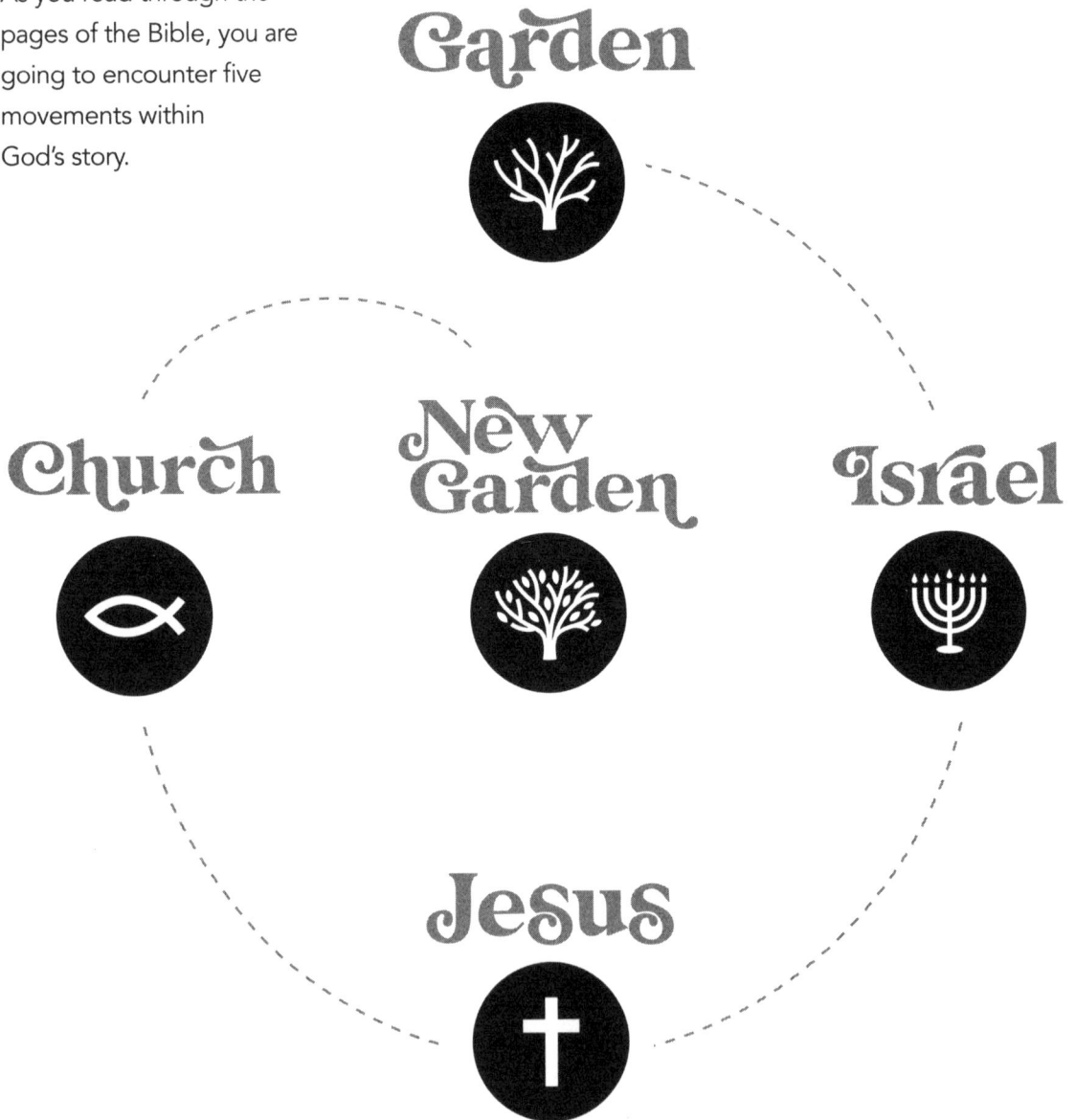

Garden

Church

New Garden

Israel

Jesus

The Story of the Garden (Genesis 1–11)

In the Upper Story, God creates the world of the Lower Story. His vision is to come down and be with us in a beautiful garden. The first two people reject God's vision and are escorted from Paradise. Their decision to disobey God introduces sin into the human race and keeps us from community with God. At this moment God gives a promise and launches a plan to get us back. The rest of the Bible is God's story of how he kept that promise and made it possible for us to enter a loving relationship with him.

The Story of Israel (Genesis 12–Malachi)

God builds a brand-new nation called Israel. Through this nation, he will reveal his presence, power, and plan to get us back. Every story of Israel points to the first coming of Jesus—the One who will provide the way back to God.

The Story of Jesus (Matthew–John)

Jesus left the Upper Story to come down into our Lower Story to be with us and provide the way for us to be made right with God. Through faith in Christ's work on the cross, we can now overturn Adam's choice and have a personal relationship with God.

The Story of the Church (Acts–Jude)

Everyone who comes into a relationship with God through faith in Christ belongs to the new community God is building called the church. The church is commissioned to be the presence of Christ in the Lower Story—telling his story by the way we live and the words we speak. Every story of the church points people to the second coming of Christ, when he will return to restore God's original vision.

The Story of the New Garden (Revelation)

God will one day create a new earth and a new garden and once again come down to be with us. All who place their faith in Christ in this life will be eternal residents in the life to come.

The Bible as One Continuous Story of God

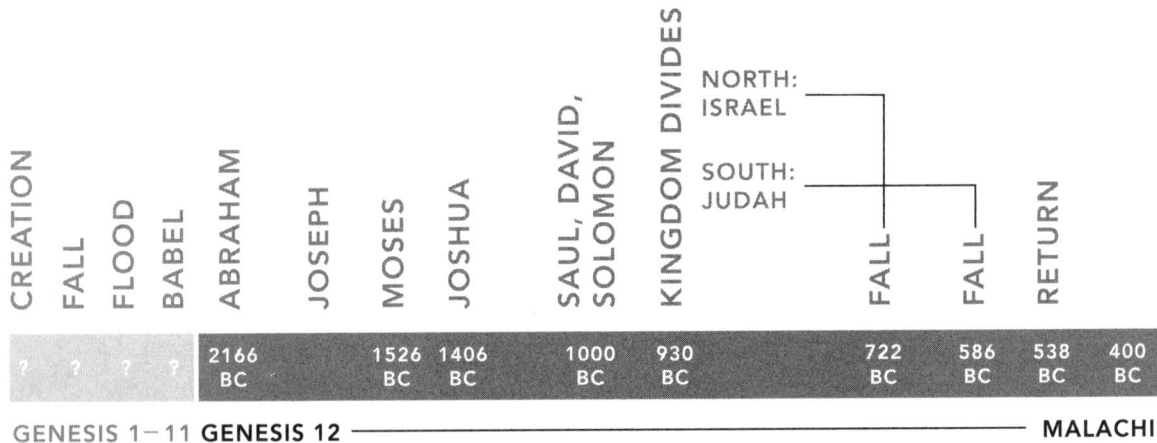

				ABRAHAM	JOSEPH	MOSES	JOSHUA	SAUL, DAVID, SOLOMON	KINGDOM DIVIDES	NORTH: ISRAEL / SOUTH: JUDAH	FALL	FALL	RETURN
CREATION	FALL	FLOOD	BABEL										
?	?	?	?	2166 BC		1526 BC	1406 BC	1000 BC	930 BC		722 BC	586 BC	538 BC	400 BC

GENESIS 1–11 **GENESIS 12** ———————————————————— MALACHI

JESUS' BIRTH
JESUS IN TEMPLE (AGE 12)
JESUS' BAPTISM
CRUCIFIXION & RESURRECTION
BIRTH OF CHURCH
PETER
PAUL'S CONVERSION
PAUL'S JOURNEYS
DEATH OF PETER AND PAUL
JOHN EXILED TO PATMOS
JOHN WRITES REVELATION
US!
2ND COMING
GREAT WHITE THRONE

| 5 BC | 7 AD | 26 AD | 30 AD | 35 AD | 67 AD | 95 AD | 2000 AD | ETERNITY |

MATTHEW ——— JOHN ACTS ———————————————— JUDE REVELATION ———

God Wants to Be with Us

The Story of the Garden

CREATION

   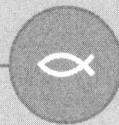 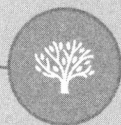

GENESIS 1–11

CREATION · FALL · FLOOD · BABEL

🌿 **READ THE STORY** | Follow this reading guide if you want to pace yourself this week:

○ Day 1: Genesis 1:1–25

○ Day 2: Genesis 1:26–31

○ Day 3: Genesis 2:1–2

○ Day 4: Genesis 2:3–17

○ Day 5: Genesis 2:18–25

A VIEW FROM THE LOWER STORY

The first chapter of Genesis is like a page out of the Trinity Construction work log, except it reads more like poetry. The sequence and pattern are simple, but almost too overwhelming to take in. On days one, two, and three, God painted the places of the earth on the canvas. Then on days four, five, and six, he put objects in each place to fill this space. Here is how the week breaks down:

DAY 1	DAY 2	DAY 3	DAY 4	DAY 5	DAY 6
Light/darkness	Water and sky	Land	Sun, moon, stars	Fish and birds	Animals
(verses 3–5)	(verses 6–8)	(verses 9–13)	(verses 14–18)	(verses 20–23)	(verses 24–25)

With the end of each day of creation, God stepped back, took a look, and recorded in his journal, "This is good." But while the creation of the heavens and the earth and the other one hundred billion galaxies or more is impressive, it is not the point of the story. Mount Everest. The Grand Canyon. The stark beauty of the Sahara. The cascading elegance of Victoria Falls. Combine these and thousands of other jewels of his creative powers, and you're not even close to identifying the core passion of God. Those are just the display cases to highlight his real work of art.

The pride and joy of God's handiwork, the point of it all, is revealed in Genesis 1:

> Then God said, "Let us make mankind in our image, in our likeness, so that they may rule over the fish in the sea and the birds in the sky, over the livestock and all the wild animals, and over all the creatures that move along the ground." So God created mankind in his own image, in the image of God he created them; male and female he created them.
>
> Genesis 1:26-27

A VIEW FROM THE UPPER STORY

So, we know what God did. The big question is, why? Why would God step outside of his perfect Upper Story and come down into our Lower Story?

The *real* point of Genesis is so amazing it's almost unbelievable: God wants to be with us. The God of the universe has created a place to come down to be with us. He no longer wanted only to enjoy the perfect community he had as the Trinity (Father, Son, Holy Spirit). The Ultimate Author of this grand story wanted to share life with us.

"In the beginning" God came up with a plan to perfectly connect his Upper Story with our Lower Story. He literally desired to bring heaven down to earth—first to create a paradise and then man and woman in his own image, and then to come down to take walks with them in the cool of the day.

When God (Father, Son, Holy Spirit) created Adam and Eve in his image and stepped back to take another look, he not only said it was good, like he did on every other day of creation, but he said it was *very* good!

GOD'S STORY . . . MY STORY

1. Read Genesis 1:1–25. Several verses begin simply with "God said." In what ways does this impact your view of God and his authority?

2. Read Genesis 1:1–25. Each day of creation ends with the phrase, "and there was evening, and there was morning." Does that seem backward? What do you think this means?

3. Read Genesis 1:26–27. God says, "Let *us* make mankind in *our* image" (emphasis added), seemingly referring to the Trinity. Then he tells us it was both Adam and Eve who were made in the image of God. What do you think this means?

4. Read Psalm 8:3–4. The number of galaxies God created is somewhere between one hundred billion and two trillion. How does that make you feel?

5. Psychologist Dr. Allan Schore defines joy this way: "What I feel when I see the sparkle in someone's eyes that conveys 'I'm happy to be with you.'"[1] When God looks at you, he says, "You are very good." How does this make you feel?

---

[1] Jim Wilder and Michel Hendricks, *The Other Half of Church* (Moody Publishers, 2020), 52.

SHARE THE STORY

Memorize the five movements of the story along with the books of the Bible connected with each. See page 11.

The Story of the Garden (Genesis 1–11)

The Story of Israel (Genesis 12–Malachi)

The Story of Jesus (Matthew–John)

The Story of the Church (Acts–Jude)

The Story of the New Garden (Revelation)

We Got a Big Problem

The Story of the Garden
ADAM AND EVE; CAIN AND ABEL

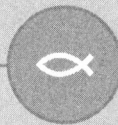

GENESIS 1–11

CREATION | FALL | FLOOD | BABEL

🎵 **READ THE STORY** | Follow this reading guide if you want to pace yourself this week:

○ Day 1: Genesis 3:1–6

○ Day 2: Genesis 3:7–20

○ Day 3: Genesis 3:21–24

○ Day 4: Genesis 4:1–12

○ Day 5: Genesis 4:13–26

A VIEW FROM THE LOWER STORY

In the midst of a flawless environment that God had created, something shifted. When God gave Adam and Eve this perfect home in the garden, he also gave them something else: *freedom*. Rather than force them into a relationship with him, he gave them the freedom to choose whether they wanted to be with him or go it alone. To provide a way for them to accept or reject his divine vision, God set two trees in the middle of the garden. One was the Tree of Life, which bore fruit that when eaten would sustain life forever. The other was the Tree of the Knowledge of Good and Evil. Eating from this tree would signal to God that Adam and Eve had rejected God's offer.

According to Scripture, a serpent—a creature we later learn represented Satan,[2] the very force of evil—appeared before Eve and told her that if she and Adam ate from the

---

[2] Revelation 12:9, 15; 20:2

forbidden tree, they would be like God. Of course, this was a lie; they were already like God, made in his image. However, this made good sense to them, so they ignored God and ate from the Tree of the Knowledge of Good and Evil.

The tree lived up to its name. Evil was deposited alongside truth in the DNA of Adam and Eve. At the core of this evil, which is called "sin" throughout the Bible, is selfishness. God looks out for others; evil looks out for self. Selfishness is the root of hatred, jealousy, violence, anger, lust, and greed. Adam and Eve were covered in it.

Adam and Eve were banished from the garden. The sin nature within them had no place in the perfect, loving community of God. God would meet with them outside the garden, but they would not be allowed to reenter until the problem of sin was reconciled.

After they left the garden, Adam and Eve began their family, only to witness the pain of a brother killing his brother. This signals to us that the sin nature birthed in Adam and Eve was transferred to their offspring. Because we are the offspring of Adam, we, too, are conceived in sin and act it out in our relationships with God and each other.

A VIEW FROM THE UPPER STORY

While this is a tale of great tragedy and loss, embedded in this story are two clues—two pieces of good news from the Upper Story.

The first clue from the Upper Story comes at the sentencing for sin. God declares to the serpent:

"I will put enmity
between you and the woman,
    and between your offspring and hers;
he will crush your head,
    and you will strike his heel."

Genesis 3:15

Clearly, many women have an adverse relationship with snakes (four times more than men), but there is much more. This is the first clue from the Upper Story that God is coming for us to redeem and restore us. The offspring, or seed, of Eve, not Adam, is a reference to Jesus.

Satan will bruise his heel (the crucifixion),
but Jesus will bruise his head (a fatal blow
defeating Satan once and for all).

Second, when you read the story, you notice the first thing that Adam and Eve did was to cover themselves. Immediately upon eating of the fruit, they recognized they were naked and felt vulnerable. Now that they had the knowledge of evil, they pondered how another might take advantage of them, so they covered up.

When God found them hiding, did you notice the first thing he did? He replaced their fig leaves with the skins of an animal. Why would God do this? Well, certainly animal skins are more durable than greenery, but there is so much more. God is giving us an important clue. What is it?

The true covering of our sin will require
the shedding of another's blood.

This is the second clue of many in the Bible that lets us know that God is working out a master plan to get us back into the garden because of his great love for us. The first clue is all about *who* God the Father will use (Jesus); the second clue is *what* God will use (the blood of Jesus).

GOD'S STORY . . . MY STORY

1. Genesis 3 never refers to the serpent as Satan. Read Revelation 12:9, 12:15, and 20:2. Why would God allow Satan into the garden?

2. Read Genesis 3:8. Why do you think Adam and Eve hid from God? Are we still doing this today?

3. Read Genesis 3:15. Why is the seed, or offspring, of Eve mentioned but not the seed of Adam? (See Luke 1:35.)

4. Read Genesis 4:3–5. Why do you think God accepted Abel's offering but rejected Cain's? How does this inform our offerings to God today?

5. Read Genesis 4:8 and Romans 5:12. When Cain killed Abel, it signified that the sin nature birthed in Adam and Eve is transferred to their offspring at conception. What do you think about this?

6. Read Genesis 4:6–7. Sin is like a predator ready to pounce on us if we crack the door to wrong. How do we rule over this temptation? (Compare with 1 Peter 5:8–9.)

7. Read Genesis 4:23–26. Sin is intensifying through the offspring of Cain and yet the chapter ends with people calling on the name of the Lord. What is this about?

SHARE THE STORY

Share the five movements of the story with at least five people this week. See page 11 for help.

The Solution Is Not in Us

The Story of the Garden

NOAH

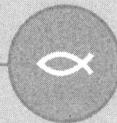

GENESIS 1–11

CREATION · FALL · FLOOD · BABEL

🌿 **READ THE STORY** | Follow this reading guide if you want to pace yourself this week:

○ Day 1: Genesis 6:5–22

○ Day 2: Genesis 7

○ Day 3: Genesis 8

○ Day 4: Genesis 9:1–19

○ Day 5: Genesis 9:20–28

A VIEW FROM THE LOWER STORY

As the population on earth grew, it became clear that when given a choice, men and women choose evil over good. According to the Bible, God saw that mankind had become so wicked that "every inclination of the thoughts of the human heart was only evil all the time" (Genesis 6:5). Reformed theologians call this the doctrine of total depravity—a doctrine suggesting that human beings inherently will choose evil over good, that we are unable to "be good" all the time on our own, leaving us unfit for God's community.

Here is the most mind-boggling thought contained in the pages of the Bible: Even in our state of blatant selfishness, God wants us back! Plan A is obvious. Start over with the best guy the human race had to offer. His name? Noah. It is one of the few times in the Bible that the most likely candidate is chosen. A tsunami from the sky fell for forty days and forty nights. Noah and his family, along with two of every kind of animal,[3] boarded the massive ark on dry land.

In the Lower Story this is all about faith. Hebrews 11:7 says this about Noah:

> *By faith Noah, when warned about things not yet seen, in holy fear built an ark to save his family. By his faith he condemned the world and became heir of the righteousness that is in keeping with faith.*

Some suggest from this verse and Genesis 2:4–6 that there had never been rain falling from the sky before. And yet he built an ark in the middle of dry ground. It's hard to act on something you have never seen . . . and when you do, people think you are crazy.

The ark was a football field and a half long and four and a half stories high. It was roughly half the length of the Titanic. The Titanic held 3,547 passengers; the ark contained over fifty thousand animals and eight people.

Simply put, this is crazy faith.

A VIEW FROM THE UPPER STORY

The Upper Story sends us another important message.

After one hundred and fifty days the water was gone. Only Noah and the residents of the ark survived. One of the first things Noah did was to plant a vineyard. Probably at the first harvest, Noah drank too much and passed out in his tent. One of Noah's sons disgraced him by not only looking at his nakedness but bringing his brothers back in to see it. Maybe you do, or don't, see this as a federal offense. One thing we know for sure is that the problem had not been resolved. Plan A failed. Even though Noah was a "good" man (our very best man), he and his children were carriers of the sin virus.

You would think that this would be the end of the story—that God would finally give up on us—but he didn't. He couldn't. Regardless of what Adam and Eve and Cain and Noah did—

---

[3]   Genesis 7:2–3: Noah collected seven pairs of clean animals and birds and one pair of unclean animals.

regardless of anything we have done—God still loves us and wants to be with us. God's Upper Story has not changed. He still wants to do life with us in a perfect, loving community of unified fellowship.

If the "start over plan" wasn't successful, then there must be another way. This leads us to our Upper Story clue:

The solution to getting us back
will not come from even the best of us;
it must come from another.

Keep reading.

GOD'S STORY . . . MY STORY

1. Romans 3:10 agrees with our scripture today by telling us, "There is no one righteous, not even one." Do you agree with this? Why or why not?

2. Read Genesis 7:2–3. Why do you think God instructed Noah to bring seven pairs of clean animals and only one pair of unclean animals? (Hint: Read Genesis 8:20.)

3. Read Genesis 8:21–22. Why do you think God said he would never flood the earth again? (Also see Genesis 9:8–11.)

4. Put yourself in Noah's sandals. Do you think you would have had the faith to build the ark?

5. The Story of the Garden can be titled, "Paradise Lost." Our longing should be to get back to this garden with God. What do you look forward to the most when we get back to this place of Paradise God had in mind for us in the very beginning?

SHARE THE STORY

Below is the first movement of the story—**The Story of the Garden**. To get you started in memorizing, fill in the blanks below. See page 11 for help.

In the Upper Story, God creates the world of the Lower Story. His vision is to come down and be with us in a beautiful _____. The first two people reject God's vision and are escorted from Paradise. Their decision to disobey God introduces _____ into the human race and keeps us from community with God. At this moment, God gives a promise and launches a plan to get us back. The rest of the Bible is God's story of how he kept that promise and made it possible for us to enter a loving relationship with him.

WEEK
5

Broken Praise

The Story of the Garden

JOB

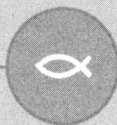

GENESIS 1–11

CREATION FALL FLOOD BABEL

🌿 **READ THE STORY** | Follow this reading guide if you want to pace yourself this week:

○ Day 1: Job 1–2

○ Day 2: Job 3

○ Day 3: Job 22–26

○ Day 4: Job 38–41

○ Day 5: Job 42

A VIEW FROM THE LOWER STORY

Job's life at the opening of the book that bears his name is a perfect picture of human flourishing. Job's spiritual, financial, relational, physical, emotional, and vocational life was fully intact.

Then, in a single day he lost everything. Two separate groups of people, the Sabeans and the Chaldeans, attacked and killed all the workers and ran off with five hundred oxen, five hundred donkeys, and three thousand camels. Fire killed all seven thousand sheep and the shepherds who oversaw them. If that weren't enough, on the same day a mighty wind came and collapsed his house on all ten of his children, and they died.

Then, a few days later, Job was afflicted "with painful sores from the soles of his feet to the crown of his head. Then Job took a piece of broken pottery and scraped himself with it as he sat among the ashes" (Job 2:7–8).

What are we to make of all this from the Lower Story?

Well, Job's wife felt this all came *from the hand of God*. God was responsible for all this calamity. She offered up this advice to her husband:

> "Are you still maintaining your integrity?
> Curse God and die!"
>
> Job 2:9

Job's three friends paid him a visit. With the initial goal to sympathize and comfort Job, they sat with him in the ashes, and no one said a word. At the end of the seven days Job spoke and poured out his heart to his friends. Out of his extreme pain, he wished he had never been born.

Then Job's friends spoke up one at a time. They felt all this calamity came *from the hand of God*. He had sinned, and God was punishing him. The four of them went through three cycles of speeches always with the same conclusion: "It's your fault, Job."

When everyone was done talking, Job maintained his devotion to God. He questioned God but never cursed him. Here is what he said:

> "The LORD gave and the LORD has taken away;
> may the name of the LORD be praised."
>
> Job 1:21

Job offered his broken praise to God.

A VIEW FROM THE UPPER STORY

Very few books in the Bible give us a clearer view from the Upper Story. While Job never knew what happened to cause all this, we do.

One day Satan visited God and suggested that Job only followed him because he surrounded Job with protection. If God were to remove the protection, Job would curse God. God disagreed and allowed Satan to do anything he wanted short of touching Job himself. This led to the complete loss of his business and his ten children. We are given this summary: "In all this, Job did not sin by charging God with wrongdoing" (Job 1:22).

Satan came for a second visit and sought permission to afflict Job physically. God allowed it and hence the painful boils all over his body. In all this Job maintained his devotion to God, even though he had no idea why this was all happening to him. Again:

He questioned God but did not curse God.

When we come to chapter 38, God speaks. God questioned Job and invited him to answer back. For four chapters, God put Job in his place by giving him a glimpse of God's eternal power and purpose. Sort of with tongue in cheek God said:

> "What is the way to the abode of light?
>   And where does darkness reside?
> Can you take them to their places?
>   Do you know the paths to their dwellings?
> Surely you know, for you were already born!
>   You have lived so many years!"
>
> Job 38:19–21

When God finished speaking, it was time for Job to answer. Recognizing that God can do all things, and his plans cannot be thwarted, Job responded:

"You asked, 'Who is this that obscures my plans
   without knowledge?'
Surely I spoke of things I did not understand,
   things too wonderful for me to know."

Job 42:3

Job got it:

"There is a God, and I'm not him."

God has a bigger Upper Story plan that can't be stopped. His plan is good, and we must trust him even when we don't have all the answers.

Once the test was complete, and Job showed Satan a thing or two about following God during extreme adversity, God blessed the later years of his life and restored all that Job lost one hundred times over.

God knew one other thing that Job didn't know at the time. That you would be reading his story four thousand years later to gain perspective on living successfully in the Lower Story by offering God our broken praise even during times of trouble and suffering.

GOD'S STORY . . . MY STORY

1. Read Job 1:9–10. Have you or someone you know blamed God for a tragedy and decided to curse him? What do you think of Job's response?

2. Read Job 22–23. Have you ever thought that the troubles you are experiencing are a result of God punishing you? Do you think this is always the cause of adversity in our lives?

3. Read Job 38–41. What are your top three favorite responses of God to Job? How does this cause you to look at God differently?

4. Read Job 42:1–6. What do you learn from Job's response back to God?

5. Read Job 42:12–16 and James 5:11. How would you feel if God used you for such an assignment?

SHARE THE STORY

We are continuing this week on memorizing the first movement of the story—**The Story of the Garden**. Fill in the blanks below. See page 11 for help.

In the Upper Story, God creates the world of the Lower Story. His vision is to come down and be with us in a beautiful _____. The first two people reject God's vision and are escorted from Paradise. Their decision to disobey God introduces _____ into the human race and keeps us from community with God. At this moment, God gives a _____ and launches a plan to get us back. The rest of the Bible is God's story of how he kept that promise and made it possible for us to enter a loving _____ with him.

God Will Make a Way

The Story of Israel

ABRAM AND SARAI

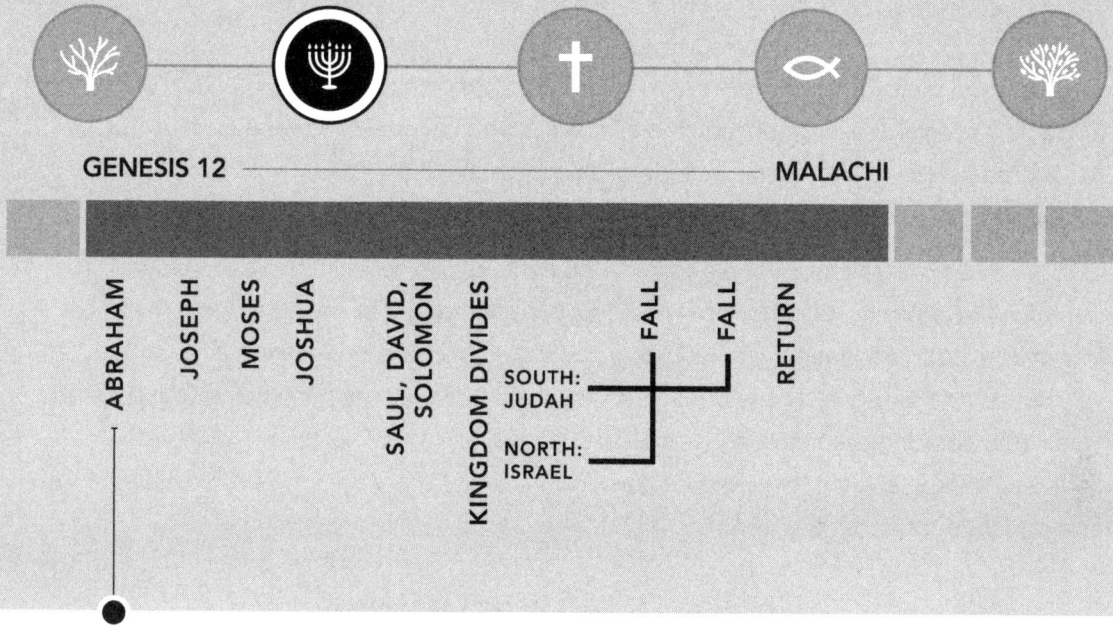

GENESIS 12 ——————————————— MALACHI

ABRAHAM JOSEPH MOSES JOSHUA SAUL, DAVID, SOLOMON KINGDOM DIVIDES SOUTH: JUDAH NORTH: ISRAEL FALL FALL RETURN

READ THE STORY | Follow this reading guide if you want to pace yourself this week:

○ Day 1: Genesis 12:1–9

○ Day 2: Genesis 12:10–20

○ Day 3: Genesis 13

○ Day 4: Genesis 14

○ Day 5: Hebrews 11:8–16

A VIEW FROM THE LOWER STORY

After the great flood, sin raised its ugly head again, beginning with Noah's son and culminating in the Tower of Babel (Genesis 11). The Tower of Babel was a united attempt of humanity, taking the ingenuity God gave us to build a life without him. This would not end well for humanity, so out of an act of grace, God scattered them and confused their languages. Left alone, humanity will move to greater expressions of evil.

Time for a new plan—one that would actually work this time.

God decided the best way to restore his grand vision of community with us was to establish a nation, a special group of related, like-minded people intent on knowing God as much as he wanted to know them. Through this specially chosen nation, God would reveal himself to everyone and offer a plan that would try to draw people back into a relationship with him.

God chose an old, childless couple to be the parents of this new nation he envisioned. You or I might have picked a young, newlywed couple brimming with health and energy to have lots of kids, but God made a dramatic point by picking Abram, age seventy-five, and his wife, Sarai, age sixty-five. The real kicker is that not only were they past their prime parenting years; they couldn't even have children due to Sarai's infertility. The lineage of Abram and Sarai was at its end when they died, at least from a Lower Story perspective. We will see this as a pattern throughout the story:

*God picks the least likely candidates
to accomplish his Upper Story plan.*

God invited Abram to leave the comforts of his homeland and go to a place that he would later show him. *Start walking guys, I'll let you know later where you are going.* He also promised Abram and Sarai children to make them into a great nation. Not only this, but this new nation would also one day be a blessing to all peoples on earth.

That's a lot.

The Bible simply says, "So Abram went . . . " (Genesis 12:4).

Now, there is one thing I know about most senior citizens, holding in my possession my own AARP card: They don't like change. (How many senior citizens does it take to change a light bulb? Change? Who said anything about change?) But this older couple—Abram and Sarai—dug down deep, went way beyond their comfort zone, and did what God asked them to do.

A VIEW FROM THE UPPER STORY

Keep in mind that Abram and Sarai didn't know Yahweh, as God is often called in the Old Testament. Abram's dad, Terah, worshipped false gods. Not only that but Terah was wealthy and provided great security for Abram and Sarai. So, what caused them to pick up and leave it all behind? From a Lower Story perspective, I think it was the promise of a child. Couples who experience infertility know what I am talking about. Or maybe they were just plain tired of living in his parents' basement and wanted more for their lives. Purpose. We are not told.

From the Upper Story, God is doing something bigger than just giving them their own digs and a couple of kids. From this new nation would come the solution, the way for all people to come back into the garden to be with God and live forever. It would take 2,086 more years to come to fruition, but "it," or rather "he," is coming from this new nation.

The New Testament book of Hebrews tells us that somewhere along the way, Abram did capture the Upper Story.

> *For he [Abram] was looking forward to the city with foundations, whose architect and builder is God.*
>
> *Hebrews 11:10*

This city is none other than a reference to the New Jerusalem mentioned in Revelation 21:2 where the garden from Genesis reappears in the center of the city. Abram saw it, and it drove his faith to keep moving forward.

GOD'S STORY . . . MY STORY

1. Read Genesis 12:1 and Hebrews 11:8. Have you ever had a time in your life when you felt God was inviting you to do something that represented a change and was somewhat scary? What did you do?

2. Read Genesis 12:10–13. How did Abram have enough faith to trust God to leave the comforts of his home, but not enough faith to tell the truth about his wife? How do you think Sarai felt? Do you think he was justified in doing this given the circumstances?

3. Read Genesis 13:8–9. Abram had seniority in the relationship with Lot. Why do you suppose he gave Lot the first pick of the land? Would you have done this?

4. Read Genesis 14:18–20 and Hebrews 7:1–4. King/Priest Melchizedek is seen as a prefiguration or type of Jesus himself. Have you ever had the sense that Jesus' presence showed up in your life when you needed him most?

5. Read Hebrews 11:8–9, 15–16. Have you ever been able to get a sense of the bigger thing God was doing in your life before it happened?

SHARE THE STORY

Fill in the blanks for the first movement—**The Story of the Garden**. See page 11 for help.

In the _____ Story, God creates the world of the Lower Story. His vision is to come down and be with us in a beautiful _____. The first two people reject God's vision and are escorted from _____. Their decision to disobey God introduces _____ into the human race and keeps us from community with God. At this moment, God gives a _____ and launches a plan to get us back. The rest of the Bible is God's story of how he kept that promise and made it possible for us to enter a loving _____ with him.

Do What?

The Story of Israel

ABRAHAM AND SARAH; ISHMAEL AND ISAAC

GENESIS 12 ——————————————————— MALACHI

ABRAHAM

JOSEPH

MOSES

JOSHUA

SAUL, DAVID, SOLOMON

KINGDOM DIVIDES

SOUTH: JUDAH

NORTH: ISRAEL

FALL

FALL

RETURN

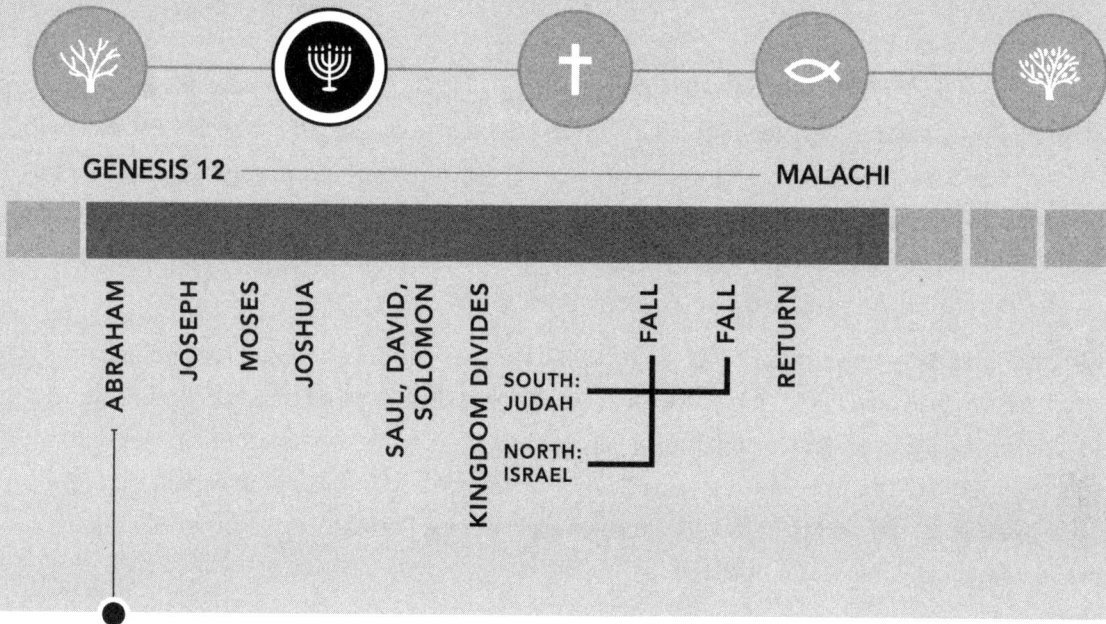

READ THE STORY | Follow this reading guide if you want to pace yourself this week:

○ Day 1: Genesis 15:1–21

○ Day 2: Genesis 16:1–16

○ Day 3: Genesis 17:1–8; 18:1–5

○ Day 4: Genesis 21:1–7

○ Day 5: Genesis 22:1–19; Hebrews 11:17–19

A VIEW FROM THE LOWER STORY

Abram and Sarai received a call from God to leave the comfort of life with their family and start walking to a place that God would show them. His plan was to build a new nation through them that would bless all nations. They moved out by faith. Abram was seventy-five years old; Sarai was sixty-five.

The first order of business was to have those long-awaited kids, right? To start a nation, you've got to have people. Using our Lower Story logic, you have to have at least one! Yet ten years went by . . . and still no children. Abram was now eighty-five and Sarai seventy-five.

So, Sarai got to thinking, *Maybe God needs our help.* (Have you noticed how this phrase almost always leads to disaster?) To "help" God along, she concocted a plan whereby Abram would sleep with her servant, Hagar—sort of her surrogate, as it were. Abram offered no objections, and Hagar delivered a baby boy named Ishmael. God came to them and said, "Uh, folks, thanks for your help, but no thanks. I will make Ishmael's offspring into a great nation, but this is not my plan for you, Abram and Sarai."

Ok, so if God didn't need their help, what gives? Thirteen more years went by, and still no child. Abram was now ninety-nine and Sarai eighty-nine. At this point, God up and decided to change their names. Abram's name, which ironically means "exalted father" in Hebrew, was changed to Abraham, which means "father of many," and Sarai's name, which meant "princess," was changed to Sarah, which essentially means "queen" or "mother of nations" in Hebrew. Ouch! This was a bold move.

God then told them they would have a child exactly one year from that point. Sarah burst out laughing. A year later Isaac was born, which means "he laughs." When situations look impossible to us, God always gets the last laugh.

Now listen to this. When Isaac was around fifteen years old, just about to get his camel's license, God came to Abraham and asked him to do an unthinkable, completely crazy thing. Here's how the story reads:

> *"God said, 'Take your son, your only son, whom you love—Isaac— and go to the region of Moriah. Sacrifice him there as a burnt offering on a mountain I will show you.'"*
>
> **Genesis 22:2**

Abraham obeyed. Maybe his previous experiences gave him the confidence that God would keep his promise to him no matter the circumstances. We are told in Hebrews 11 that Abraham figured God would raise Isaac from the dead (Hebrews 11:19). Now, that's faith!

But as Abraham was bringing the knife down to take the life of his son, an angel told Abraham to stop, that God was providing a ram that was caught by its horns in a nearby thicket. Abraham sacrificed the ram and took his son home. Talk about a cliffhanger—whew, that was close! So, what's the point? God needed to know that Abraham trusted him completely.

A VIEW FROM THE UPPER STORY

There is a huge Upper Story clue here—a foreshadowing of what is to come. Read Genesis 22:2 again. By the way, this is the first time the word "love" appears in the Bible. Now compare it to John 3:16:

> *For God so loved the world that he gave his one and only Son, that whoever believes in him shall not perish but have eternal life.*

God the Father would be in this same position two thousand years later, but in this case, there would be no ram nearby to take the hit. God's only Son, whom he loves, would be sacrificed for our sins.

I always wondered why God made Abraham travel three days to perform this sacrifice. Seems a bit cruel at first glance, but we know God isn't cruel. In 2 Chronicles 3:1 we are told that Mount Moriah is none other than Jerusalem. It would be on that same location two thousand years later that Jesus would be sacrificed. Every story of Israel points to Jesus!

GOD'S STORY . . . MY STORY

1. Read Genesis 17:17. Abraham and Sarah felt they were too old to accomplish God's plan. What would you say is your limitation that causes you to doubt that God can use you?

2. Read Genesis 16:11–12,15; 17:20; 25:16. Abraham and Sarah took matters into their own hands with Hagar. While God blessed Ishmael and fulfilled his promise to him, his offspring would be a constant source of hostility toward Isaac's offspring. Ishmael is considered a patriarch of Islam, and we know the tension exists to this day. Have you ever tried to "help God out" only to make things worse?

3. Read Genesis 22:2. This is the first time the word "love" appears in the Bible. What does this tell us about the character of love versus the way many people think about it today?

4. Read Genesis 17:1–6. God changed Abram's and Sarai's names. Based on your encounters with God to date, what would be your new name?

5. Read Genesis 22:15–18. Why did God put Abraham through all this? Do you think he wants the same thing with you?

SHARE THE STORY

One of the goals of this study is for you to be able to *share* the story with others. Below is the first of five movements to the story. Review it here, filling in the blanks as you go, and practice sharing it from memory with at least three people in the next three days.

In the _____ Story, God creates the world of the _____ Story. His _____ is to come down and be with us in a beautiful _____. The first two people reject God's vision and are escorted from _____. Their decision to disobey God introduces _____ into the human race and keeps us from community with God. At this moment, God gives a _____ and launches a _____ to get us back. The rest of the Bible is God's story of how he kept that _____ and made it possible for us to enter a loving _____ with him.

Sibling Rivalry Saves Israel

The Story of Israel

JOSEPH

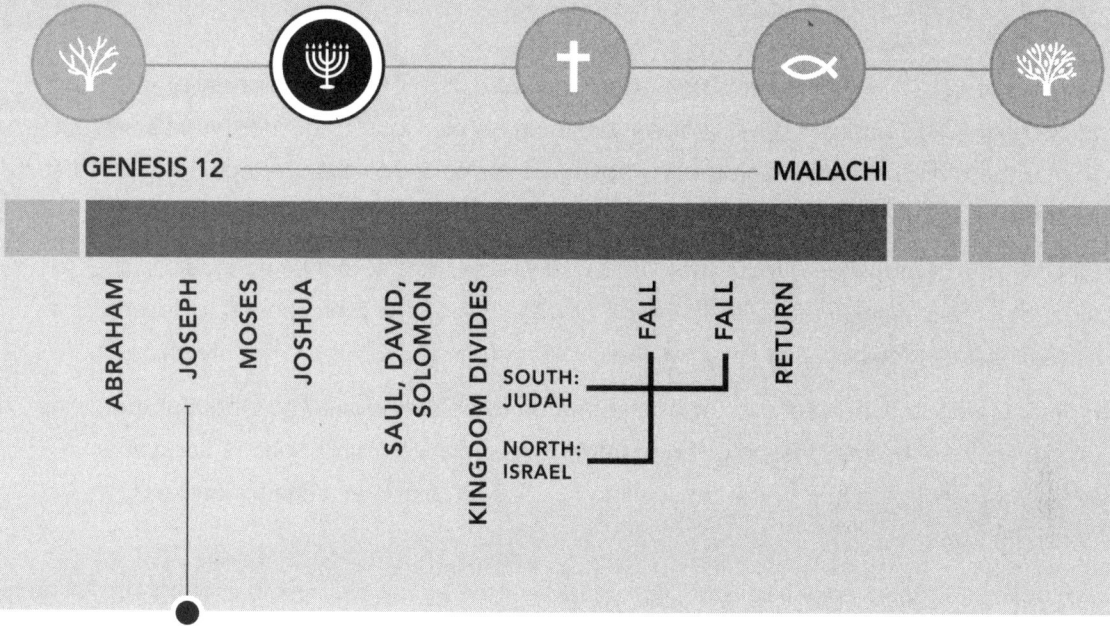

GENESIS 12 ———————————————— MALACHI

ABRAHAM
JOSEPH
MOSES
JOSHUA
SAUL, DAVID, SOLOMON
KINGDOM DIVIDES
SOUTH: JUDAH
NORTH: ISRAEL
FALL
FALL
RETURN

🎵 **READ THE STORY** | Follow this reading guide if you want to pace yourself this week:

○ Day 1: Genesis 37; 39

○ Day 2: Genesis 40–41

○ Day 3: Genesis 42–44

○ Day 4: Genesis 45–47

○ Day 5: Genesis 48–50

A VIEW FROM THE LOWER STORY

We are introduced to Joseph when he was around seventeen years old—the son of Jacob (renamed Israel), the grandson of Isaac, and the great-grandson of Abraham. We are finally getting some momentum in this nation-building agenda.

Joseph's family certainly didn't function like a divine dynasty out of which God was building his nation. They could barely get along with each other—and we're not talking about just the normal rivalry that often happens among brothers! Joseph's brothers literally left him to die.

Why? Joseph had several dreams that he sensed were from God. Each special dream ended with all his brothers bowing down to him. In his oblivious innocence, young Joe shared these dreams with his brothers, who in turn soon tried to change them into his worst nightmares.

One day out in the fields without their dad's knowledge, they sold their younger brother to a band of merchants on their way to Egypt. Once in Egypt, the merchants sold Joseph as a slave to serve in the house of Potiphar, the captain of the guard for the mighty Pharaoh.

From a Lower Story perspective, Joseph appeared to be abandoned by God. But there was quickly a turn of events. Joseph got promoted to lead Potiphar's household. Soon after, Potiphar's wife lied to her husband by telling him Joseph made an advance on her. Off to prison he went.

Up, down, up, down—like a seesaw! Two years later the young Hebrew in a foreign Egyptian land found himself on the rise again. Pharaoh called him out of prison to interpret a dream he kept having. Using a gift given to him by God, Joseph explained to Pharaoh that their land was about to experience seven years of bumper crops, followed by seven years of drought. If they were to survive the famine, they would need to set aside a surplus.

Pharaoh believed him and put him second-in-command over all of Egypt. Under Joseph's leadership, the Egyptians stored tons of food over the next seven years. When the famine struck, people from other countries began pouring into Egypt to beg and barter for food, including Joseph's brothers living in Canaan. When they arrived in Egypt, they bowed down before their punk brother, although they did not recognize him.

After several emotional encounters, Joseph revealed his identity to his brothers, assured them that he was not angry with them, and made plans to resettle them in Egypt. Out of his position of power, he gave them the fertile land of Goshen.

Israel is saved by what began as a bad case of sibling rivalry.

A VIEW FROM THE UPPER STORY

How did Joseph do it? How did he have such an amazing attitude through it all? How did he forgive his brothers after what they did to him? The answer is clear. Somewhere in the journey, Joseph caught a glimpse of God's Upper Story plan and his role in it. Read what he says to his brothers:

> *"I am your brother Joseph, the one you sold into Egypt! And now, do not be distressed and do not be angry with yourselves for selling me here, because it was to save lives that God sent me ahead of you. For two years now there has been a famine in the land, and for the next five years there will be no plowing and reaping. But God sent me ahead of you to preserve for you a remnant on earth and to save your lives by a great deliverance. So then, it was not you who sent me here, but God."*
>
> **Genesis 45:4-8**

Later he said it as succinctly as can be said:

> **What you meant for evil, God meant for good.**
>
> **Genesis 50:20 (paraphrased)**

Joseph lived to be 110 years old. Yes, he went through a period of twenty-two tough years from the age of seventeen on, but we must not forget that he ended up with seventy-one really great years after that. How rich it must have been to know he was used by God to save Israel and move the Upper Story plan forward to completion.

GOD'S STORY . . . MY STORY

1. Read Genesis 37:2; 41:46; 42:6. Why did God put Joseph through twenty-two years of hardship? Does this help you rethink how you feel about seasons of hardship in your own life?

2. Read Genesis 39:2, 21. Twice when Joseph was in a downward turn the story inserts that "the LORD was with [him]." Why do you think the author felt a need to insert this phrase in these particular spots? Do you think this is true of your life?

3. Read Genesis 45:3–8; 50:15–21. What enabled Joseph to forgive his brothers? How might this help you move on from a feeling of bitterness toward someone and feel the freedom that comes through the act of forgiveness?

4. Read Genesis 41:50–52. Joseph named his first son Manasseh, which means "to forget," and his second son Ephraim, which means "twice fruitful." What does this tell us about where Joseph was at in the healing process? What has enabled you to forgive someone who has deeply hurt you?

5. Read Romans 8:28. What are the conditions for God to write a good story with and through our lives? Do you feel your life is aligned to the purposes of God?

SHARE THE STORY

See if you can recite the first movement—**The Story of the Garden**—from memory by writing it out below. See page 11 for help.

_____

_____

_____

_____

_____

_____

_____

_____

_____

_____

_____

_____

_____

_____

The Basket Case

The Story of Israel

MOSES

GENESIS 12 ———————————————— MALACHI

ABRAHAM | JOSEPH | MOSES | JOSHUA | SAUL, DAVID, SOLOMON | KINGDOM DIVIDES | SOUTH: JUDAH | NORTH: ISRAEL | FALL | FALL | RETURN

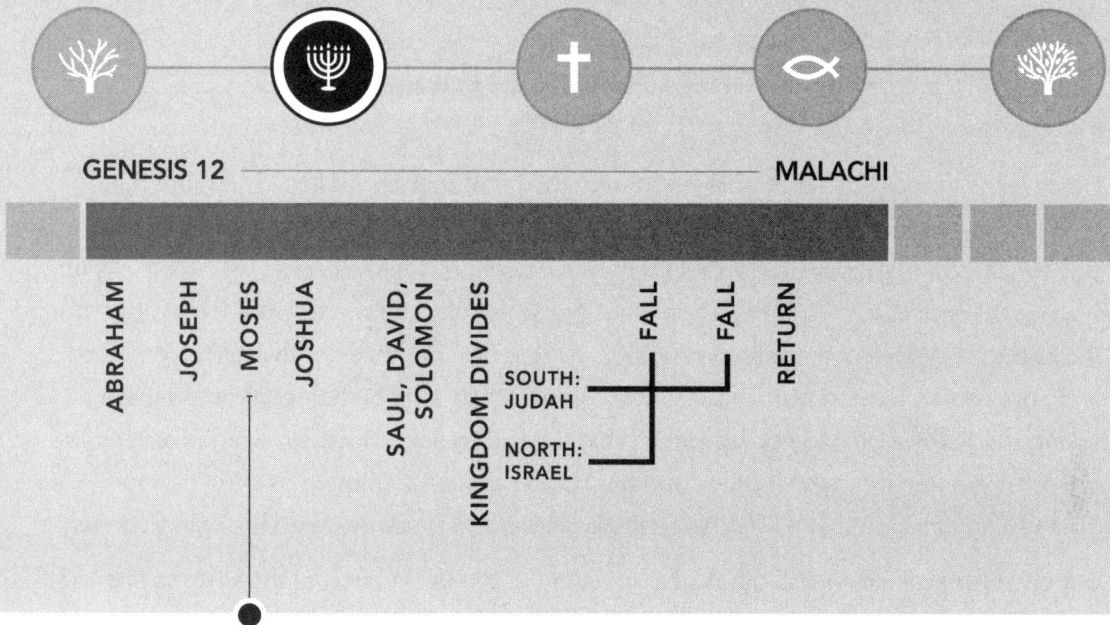

🌿 **READ THE STORY** | Follow this reading guide if you want to pace yourself this week:

○ Day 1: Genesis 15:12–16

○ Day 2: Exodus 1:6–10

○ Day 3: Exodus 1:10–21

○ Day 4: Exodus 1:22–2:10

○ Day 5: Genesis 6:1–18

A VIEW FROM THE LOWER STORY

Thanks to Joseph the Israelites lived in a lush part of Egypt called Goshen, and they truly became the size of a great nation. However, Joseph eventually died and years passed. We are told in the Scriptures, "Then a new king, to whom Joseph meant nothing, came to power in Egypt" (Exodus 1:8). He did not remember Joseph, the hero who saved Egypt from the seven years of famine. But as their numbers grew, the new pharaoh became fearful they would partner with Egypt's enemies to overthrow his rule. So, he made the Jews his slaves. Slavery continued for four hundred years. It appeared God had forgotten his people and the covenant and promises he had made to them, and Pharaoh was calling all the shots now.

However, the more Pharaoh oppressed them, the more they multiplied. The more they multiplied, the more fearful Pharaoh became of a coup d'état. What did the fearful king do? He called the midwives and told them that when the Hebrew babies were born, "If [it] is a boy, kill him; but if it is a girl, let her live" (verse 16). The midwives were to covertly kill the babies and present them to the mothers as stillborn. But these midwives feared God and could not follow through on the king's command. When Pharaoh confronted them asking them why they had not killed the baby boys, they said, "Hebrew women are not like Egyptian women; they are vigorous and give birth before the midwives arrive" (verse 19). So, the king declared that all Hebrew baby boys were to be thrown into the Nile to drown.

But one Hebrew mother could not bear to carry out the declaration of the king, so she hid her baby for three months until she could conceal him no longer. Rather than watch him die in the Nile, she placed him in a papyrus basket lined with pitch to waterproof it and launched him into the Nile.

Soon after she left her baby in the river, Pharaoh's daughter came to bathe there and discovered the basket. Her maternal instincts kicked in, and she adopted him and raised him as her own, a prince in her father's palace. She named him Moses, which means to "draw out" because she drew him out of the water.

A VIEW FROM THE UPPER STORY

While from the Lower Story it appears Pharaoh has taken control, we see so much in this story that gives us confidence that God is still in charge.

For example, God blessed the midwives for their faith in refusing to take the lives of innocent babies. They lived their lives defying Pharaoh, but God intervened and gave them families of their own.

Did the slavery catch God by surprise and thwart his plan? Absolutely not! As a matter of fact, when God made his covenant with Abraham to bring his people to the promised land, he also revealed to Abraham this enslavement in Egypt for four hundred years as well. The land of Goshen was also where God kept the lineage of his people pure. Hebrews were shepherds, which were considered an abomination to the Egyptians (Genesis 46:34), so they did not intermarry with them. Goshen would be the perfect place for them to hang out until the promised land was ready for them.

Oh, one more thing! The Hebrew word for "basket" is the same word used for the "ark" in Noah's story. It is the only other time the word is used in all the Bible.

> *As Noah's ark delivered his family from the flood,*
> *so Moses's little ark will deliver the future*
> *deliverer of Isael.*

God's Upper Story reigns!

GOD'S STORY . . . MY STORY

1. Read Exodus 1:11–14. With four hundred years passing without God intervening, how do you think the Hebrew people must have felt? Have you ever experienced a time in your life when you felt you waited a long time for God to intervene?

2. Read Exodus 1:8–10, 15–19. Where in these passages do you see clearly that God is still in control and not Pharaoh?

3. Read Numbers 26:59. If your government declared you needed to do something that went against God, would you have the faith of Jochebed, Moses' mother, and the midwives to stand in defiance and trust God?

4. Read Exodus 2:10. It is clear God saved Moses because he had a plan for his life— to deliver God's people out of slavery and into the promised land. Do you live with a sense that God has a special plan for your life?

SHARE THE STORY

Share the first movement—**The Story of the Garden**—from memory with at least three people. Practice below. See page 11 for help.

In the Upper Story, God _____ the _____ ____ _____
_____. His vision is to _____ _____ and _____ _____
_____ in a beautiful garden. The first two people _____ God's vision
and are _____ _____ Paradise. Their _____ to
_____ _____ introduces _____ into the human race and
keeps us from _____ with God. At this moment, God gives a
_____ and launches a _____ to get us back. The rest of the
_____ is God's _____ of how _____ _____ _____
_____ and made it _____ for us to enter a _____
_____ with him.

Parting Ways

The Story of Israel

MOSES

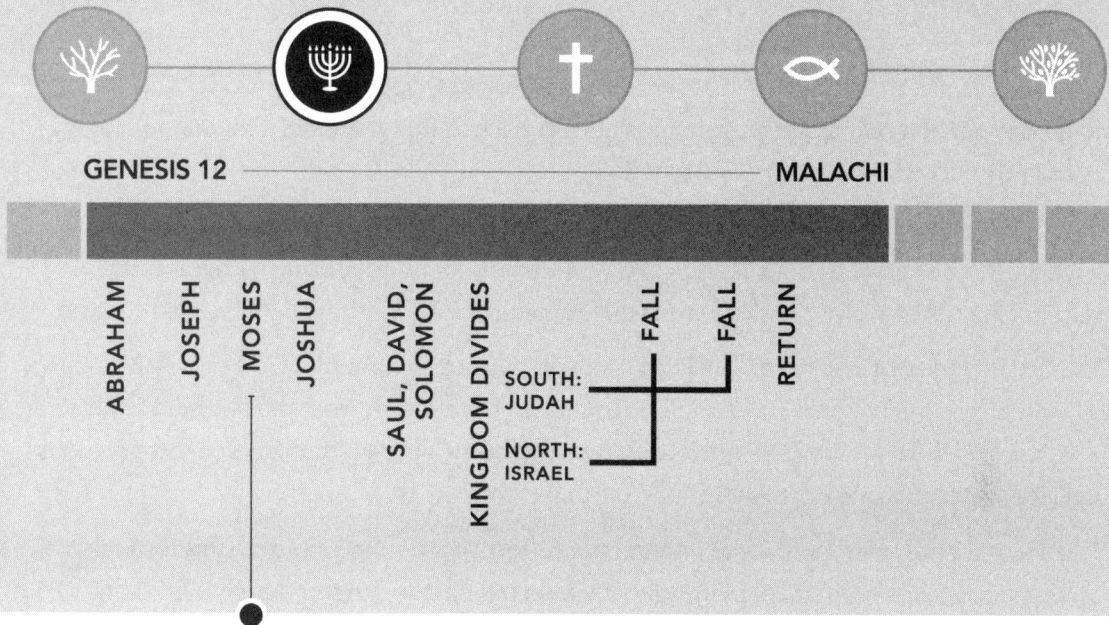

GENESIS 12 ———————————————— MALACHI

ABRAHAM
JOSEPH
MOSES
JOSHUA
SAUL, DAVID, SOLOMON
KINGDOM DIVIDES
SOUTH: JUDAH
NORTH: ISRAEL
FALL
FALL
RETURN

READ THE STORY | Follow this reading guide if you want to pace yourself this week:

○ Day 1: Exodus 3–4

○ Day 2: Exodus 5; 6:1–12; 7:1–7

○ Day 3: Exodus 8–10

○ Day 4: Exodus 11–12

○ Day 5: Exodus 13–14

A VIEW FROM THE LOWER STORY

Moses' mom put him in a little ark to deliver him from death. God would now use Moses to deliver the Hebrews from slavery. Time for God's people to part ways, or should we say "part waves," with the Egyptians.

Moses grew up in the palace of Pharaoh with all the privileges that came with it, and yet Moses knew he was different—a Hebrew. One day he saw an Egyptian beating a Hebrew and decided to kill the Egyptian. When Pharaoh found out, he attempted to kill his adopted grandson. Moses fled to the Midian desert where he got married and took on the life of a shepherd. It is here that Moses, minding his own business, got a visit from God who spoke to Moses out of a burning bush. The mission: Go back to Egypt and tell Pharaoh to "let my people go" (Exodus 5:1).

In the Lower Story Moses didn't see himself as a good candidate. He stammered in his speech, was a shepherd, not a leader, and was wanted for murder back in Egypt. But God said to him, not to worry, "I will be with you" (Exodus 3:12). That's all any of us need to win.

The first assignment was to reveal God's name to the Hebrew people. God said to Moses, "'I AM has sent me to you'"(Exodus 3:14). This is the first time we hear the name Yahweh, which simply means "The One who is and who will be," declaring that God's existence does not depend on anyone or anything.

The second assignment for Moses was to reveal God's power. He would do this through the unleashing of ten supernatural plagues that would ultimately cause Pharaoh to let God's people leave and move to the next chapter in their story.

The tenth plague is both devastating and revealing. God told Moses that at midnight, his angel would sweep through the entire kingdom of Egypt and take the life of every firstborn male. However, this angel of death would "pass over" any home that had the blood of the unblemished lamb brushed across the doorframe.

So, on that fateful night, all the firstborn sons of Egypt, including Pharaoh's son, died as the appointed angel made his rounds. However, the Hebrew sons were saved because Moses had instructed God's people to apply the blood of a lamb to their doorposts. Jews today still celebrate Passover.

Upon this tenth and final plague, Pharaoh let the people go, somewhere between one to three million Hebrews. God miraculously parted the Red Sea, and they crossed over into freedom.

A VIEW FROM THE UPPER STORY

There are two very significant things going on in the Upper Story that give us clues to God's plan and his intense love for us.

First, we notice on several occasions in the unleashing of the plagues, Pharaoh gave in and invited the Hebrews to leave. Then we learn God hardened his heart so that he changed his mind. What is going on here? God was using the disobedience in Pharaoh's heart to reveal God's power and his plan. God needed to get to the tenth plague, which is one of the biggest Upper Story clues of all. Pharaoh just didn't have the stomach for letting them go, so God helped him along.

The New Testament book of Romans gives us insight from the Upper Story: "For Scripture says to Pharaoh: 'I raised you up for this very purpose, that I might display my power in you and that my name might be proclaimed in all the earth.' Therefore God has mercy on whom he wants to have mercy, and he hardens whom he wants to harden" (9:17–18). God uses all of us to accomplish his grander story, whether we chose to play the part of a protagonist (aligned with God's plan) or an antagonist (against God's plan).

The second big aha is found in the Passover. As followers of Jesus Christ, we get a sneak peek at the way in which God will fulfill the need for a perfect, unblemished Lamb to provide the blood of salvation over the doorposts of our lives.

For Christ, our Passover lamb, has been sacrificed.

1 Corinthians 5:7

GOD'S STORY . . . MY STORY

1. Read Exodus 4:1–17. Do you feel like you are not qualified for any significant assignment from God? How does what God told Moses help you rethink this attitude?

2. Read Exodus 5:1–21. Do you have a "pharaoh" in your life right now? It could be a person, a circumstance, or a conflicted situation. What have you learned from Moses' story today to help you overcome your Pharaoh?

3. Read Exodus 4:21, 7:3, 9:12, 10:1, 10:20, and 11:10. Six times we are told that God hardened Pharaoh's heart. What do you think about this? Do you think God is still doing this today?

4. Read John 19:6–14. We find Jesus 1,476 years later crucified at the Passover celebration. What makes you believe that this was intentional on God's part versus coincidental? Why do you think he orchestrated it to happen then?

5. Read Exodus 14:10–18. Do you ever feel so scared or overwhelmed you want to give in to the enemy? What can we learn from God's and Moses' advice to the Hebrew people?

SHARE THE STORY

Recite **The Story of the Garden** from memory. Next, read the second movement—**The Story of Israel**.

God builds a brand-new nation called Israel. Through this nation, he will reveal his presence, power, and plan to get us back. Every story of Israel points to the first coming of Jesus—the One who will provide the way back to God.

God Lays Down the Law

The Story of Israel

THE TEN COMMANDMENTS

GENESIS 12 ——————————————————————— MALACHI

ABRAHAM

JOSEPH

MOSES

JOSHUA

SAUL, DAVID, SOLOMON

KINGDOM DIVIDES

SOUTH: JUDAH

NORTH: ISRAEL

FALL

FALL

RETURN

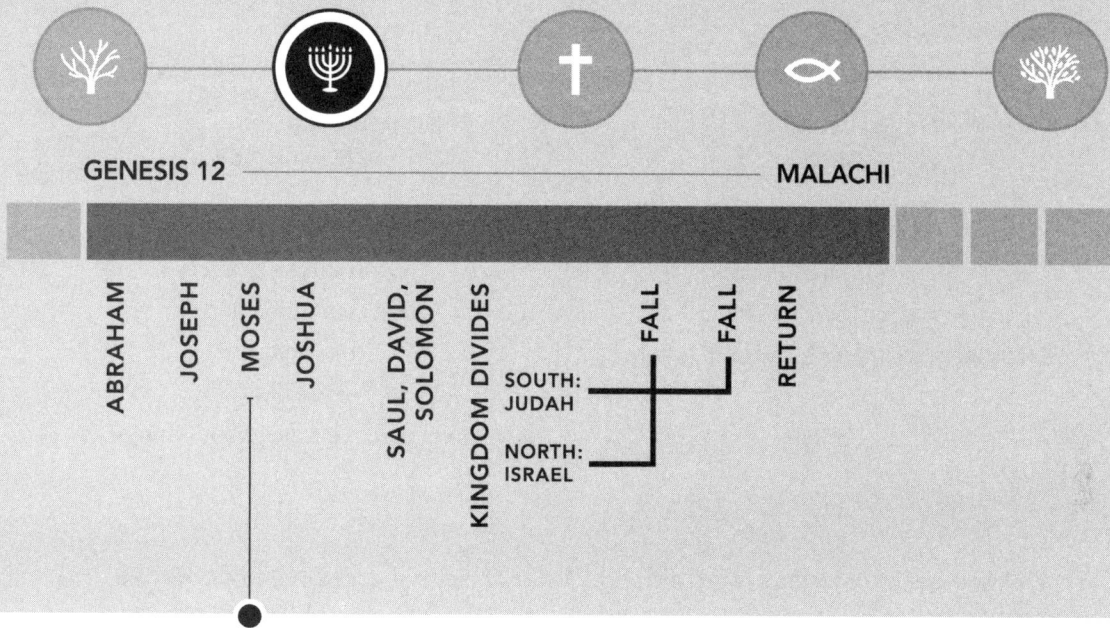

READ THE STORY | Follow this reading guide if you want to pace yourself this week:

○ Day 1: Exodus 20:1–24

○ Day 2: Exodus 32:1–14

○ Day 3: Exodus 32:19–35

○ Day 4: Matthew 5:17–20

○ Day 5: Matthew 22:34–40

A VIEW FROM THE LOWER STORY

God delivered his people out of their bondage and intended to lead them to the promised land. A land flowing with milk and honey—a new garden, really. In this new garden God envisioned a community where everyone gets along with one another and with God. Before he allowed them to enter this new garden, God wanted to make sure they knew how to behave. God called Moses to meet him up on Mount Sinai and gave him what we now call the Ten Commandments. It is interesting to note that the first four commandments deal with how we relate to God, or our vertical relationship, and the other six consider how we relate to each other, or our horizontal relationships.

GOD	EACH OTHER
No other Gods before me	Honor your father and mother
Make no graven images	Don't kill each other
Do not misuse God's name	Don't commit adultery
Remember the Sabbath and keep it holy	Don't steal
	Don't lie
	Don't covet your neighbor's things

In actuality, there are 613 laws listed among Exodus, Leviticus, and Deuteronomy (the second telling of the law). Pretty hard to remember, let alone keep, don't you think?

Before Moses even came down off the mountain, God's people had broken the first two commandments. The people believed Moses had died on the mountain since it had been a long time since they had heard from him. So, they approached Aaron, Moses' brother, and asked him to make them a physical god they could worship. Aaron collected gold jewelry from all the people and created a golden calf. Not good! God and Moses were furious. God wanted to destroy the people of Israel and begin again, making a new nation starting with Moses (Exodus 32:10), but Moses implored God to spare his people lest the Egyptians hear about it and say God failed to keep his promise to them. Apparently, he was trying to save God's reputation. (Not sure God needs any help in this department.)

A VIEW FROM THE UPPER STORY

God knows the presence of sin will destroy and keep us from a relationship with him. That message is clear from Adam and Eve, Noah, and now from the children of Israel, his chosen people.

> *From the Upper Story, the laws God*
> *put in place were to set boundaries*
> *for the only kind of community God desires.*

The truth of the matter is God knew the people would never be able to keep the law. Certainly, they would never be able to keep it perfectly. This was the point of the law. It highlighted their inability to keep the commandments and the need for some other way to get this perfect community. Going forward, God implemented a sacrificial plan. They were to sacrifice perfect, unblemished, innocent lambs to make restitution. The answer to forgiveness for breaking God's law was the shedding of blood, the same thing required in the first garden with Adam and Eve when God made the coverings for them from animal skins. But the animal sacrifices were temporary fixes. The people kept sinning, so they had to keep sacrificing.

What humanity really needed was a blood sacrifice that would give us a once-for-all kind of forgiveness. The sacrificial lambs were a hint to the future perfect sacrificial Lamb, Jesus, the Son of God, who would defeat not only sin but death as well.

For you know that it was not with perishable things such as silver or gold that you were redeemed from the empty way of life handed down to you from your ancestors, but with the precious blood of Christ, a lamb without blemish or defect. He was chosen before the creation of the world, but was revealed in these last times for your sake.

1 Peter 1:18–20

GOD'S STORY . . . MY STORY

1. Read Exodus 19:1–8. After being reminded of all God had done for them and just a short while before God gave Moses the Ten Commandments, the children of Israel agreed to do everything that the Lord said, but they disobeyed the first two commandments immediately. What human characteristics make it difficult for them and us to follow rules?

2. Read Hebrews 10:1–10 and Galatians 2:21. Describe in your own words why the animal sacrifices were insufficient to please God. What is a sufficient sacrifice in God's eyes?

3. Read Matthew 5:17–18. What does Jesus mean when he says he didn't come "to abolish the Law . . . but to fulfill [it]"?

4. Read Romans 7:12. What was the original purpose of the law? Although grace through Jesus Christ's sacrifice on the cross has replaced the animal sacrifices and reconciles us to a relationship with God, is there a role for the law even today?

5. Matthew 22:34–40. How did Jesus sum up the law for the Pharisees? How does this help us avoid legalism or imposing restrictions on ourselves and others?

SHARE THE STORY

Review the first movement of the story from memory. Then fill in the blanks for the second movement—**The Story of Israel**. See page 11 for help.

God builds a brand-new nation called Israel. Through this nation, he will reveal his
_____, power, and plan to get us back. Every story of Israel points to the
first coming of Jesus—the One who will provide the way _____ to God.

I Need a Place to Stay

The Story of Israel
THE TABERNACLE

GENESIS 12 ———————————————— MALACHI

ABRAHAM
JOSEPH
MOSES
JOSHUA
SAUL, DAVID, SOLOMON
KINGDOM DIVIDES
FALL
FALL
RETURN

SOUTH: JUDAH
NORTH: ISRAEL

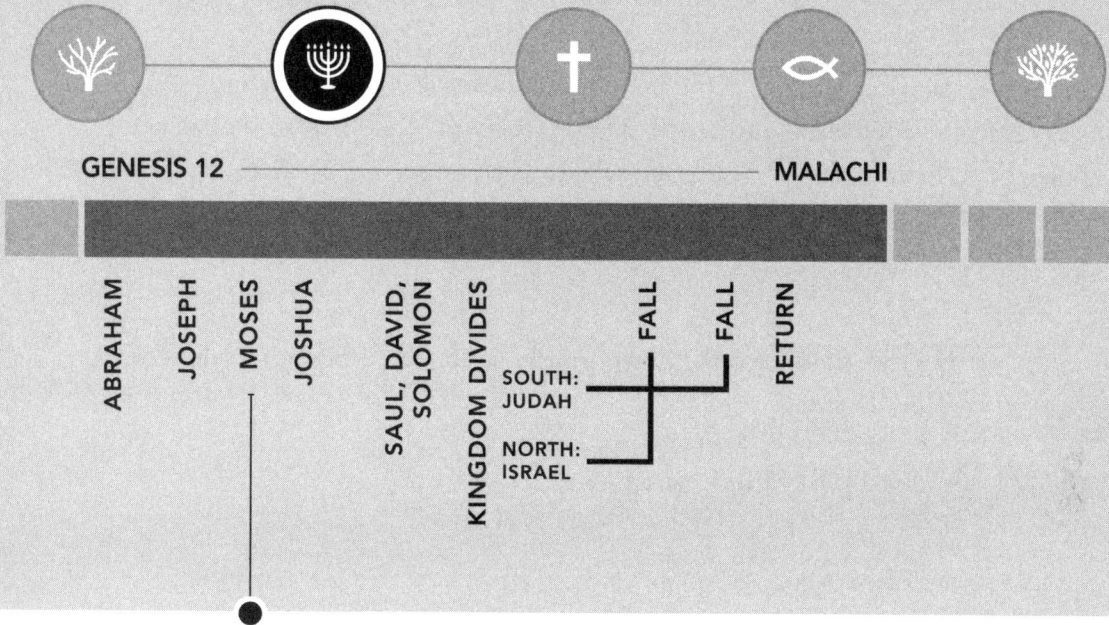

READ THE STORY | Follow this reading guide if you want to pace yourself this week:

○ Day 1: Exodus 25–27

○ Day 2: Exodus 35–37

○ Day 3: Exodus 38–39

○ Day 4: Exodus 40

○ Day 5: 1 Corinthians 3:16–17; 6:18–20; 2 Corinthians 6:14–18; Hebrews 10:19–25

A VIEW FROM THE LOWER STORY

God's people had been freed from four hundred years of slavery in Egypt. They were following God's plan down to the day as laid out to Abraham 646 years earlier (Genesis 15:13–14). There is no doubt God was running this show from the Upper Story. They were now in the wilderness on their way to a new garden to live; a garden God promised to give to Abraham's descendants. The time had come. Canaan was described as a "land flowing with milk and honey" (Exodus 3:8, 17). If there is milk, there is grass; if there is honey, there are bees; if there are bees, there are flowers. Hence, a garden.

God was working out a plan to come down and be with his people. That hadn't happened since God was with them in the garden of Eden. This was huge! Although God had continued to interact with his people after he expelled Adam and Eve from the garden, it was always from a distance.

God came to Moses and said,

> *"If I am going to come down and be with you, I am going to need a place to stay."*
>
> *Exodus 25:8 (paraphrased)*

Not just any ole place. A special place called the tabernacle. The Hebrew word for *tabernacle* means "tent" or "place of dwelling," and it is the place where God would meet his people. For six chapters in Exodus God laid out in extreme detail the layout of the tent, the exact materials to be used, and how it was to be constructed. Of particular note is the blueprint of a room in the back of the tabernacle called the Holy of Holies or Most Holy Place. This would be God's private room. His presence is represented by the ark of the covenant with the mercy seat lying on top of it.

The room was sectioned off by a curtain to prevent anyone from entering. It was forty-two feet wide and sixty feet tall. Keep in mind the average ceiling in a house today is between eight to ten feet high. Only the high priests could enter once a year, on the Day of Atonement, to offer a sacrifice for the sins of the people. The blood of an innocent lamb was sprinkled on top of the mercy seat for atonement of the people's sins. As we learned in our last study, these animal sacrifices could not actually atone for their sins once and for all, so the people could not have direct access to God.

When the tabernacle was erected at the end of the book of Exodus, the glory of the Lord descended upon it. God moved into the neighborhood. By day, a cloud hung over the Holy of Holies; at night it was a pillar of fire. As long as the cloud hovered over the tabernacle they would stay put. Whenever the cloud moved, it signaled that it was time to tear down the tent and follow God.

A VIEW FROM THE UPPER STORY

If you read all the chapters that lay out the details for the materials and building of the tabernacle your head is probably spinning. Why did God give us so much detail? Well, embedded in every detail is an Upper Story clue that points us to Jesus. For example, the curtain represents Jesus (Hebrews 10:19–20). At the exact moment of Jesus' death, the curtain in the temple was torn from top to bottom (Matthew 27:51). The tearing of the curtain symbolizes Jesus' death, which paid for our sins once and for all, removing the barrier between God and humans.

Now that God's presence no longer needs to be quarantined in a small room, where does it go? In the New Testament we are told:

> *Don't you know that you yourselves are God's temple and that*
> *God's Spirit dwells in your midst?*
>
> *1 Corinthians 3:16*

Because our sins have been permanently atoned, we who believe are made right with God. There is no barrier between us anymore. Christ tore that down through his sacrifice.

God is now "tabernacling" in us.

GOD'S STORY . . . MY STORY

1. Read Exodus 40:36–38. When the cloud hovered over the tabernacle the people stayed put. Whenever it moved, they moved. How does this inform our lives today with God's presence dwelling in us?

2. Read 1 Corinthians 6:18–20. Today we hear the phrase, "My body, my choice." How does God's indwelling presence in us change that mindset?

3. Read Exodus 31:1–11. We often think it is only the priest or the pastor who work in the church who are filled with God's presence. What does God teach us about our work through Bezalel and Oholiab?

4. Read Exodus 37:1–9, Leviticus 16:11–17, and 1 John 2:1–2. Are you able to connect the dots between the atonement cover (mercy seat), the Day of Atonement, and Jesus? How does this stir you?

SHARE THE STORY

Review the first movement of the story from memory. Then fill in the blanks for the second movement—**The Story of Israel**. See page 11 for help.

God builds a brand-new nation called _____. Through this nation, he will reveal his presence, _____, and plan to get us back. Every story of Israel points to the first _____ of Jesus—the One who will provide the way _____ to God.

Take Another Lap
Around Mt. Sinai

The Story of Israel

THE WILDERNESS

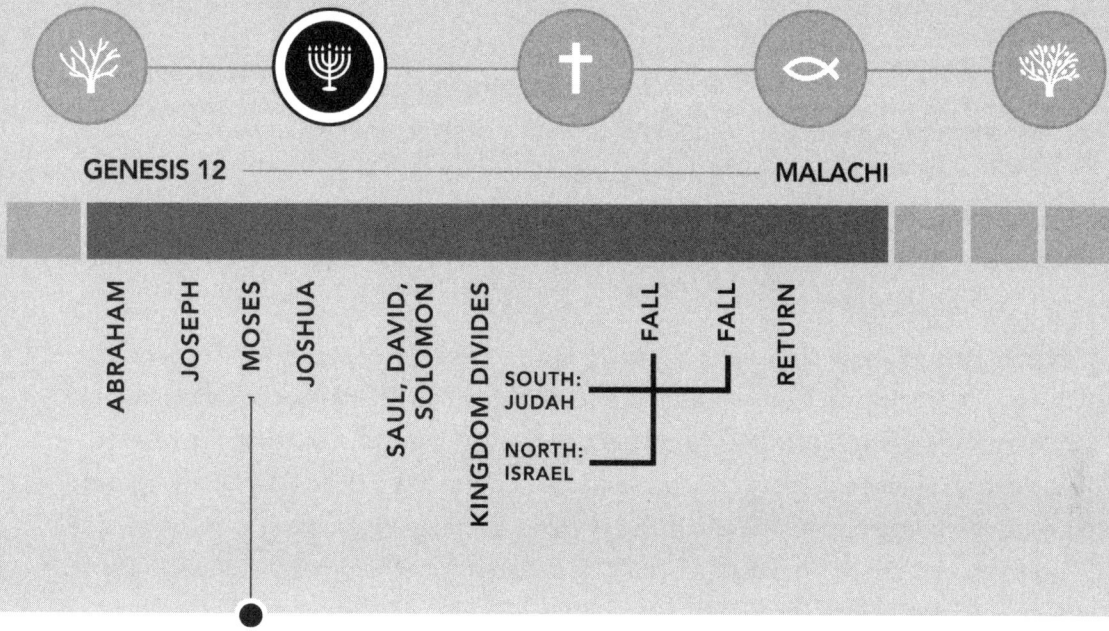

GENESIS 12 ——————————— MALACHI

ABRAHAM | JOSEPH | MOSES | JOSHUA | SAUL, DAVID, SOLOMON | KINGDOM DIVIDES | SOUTH: JUDAH | NORTH: ISRAEL | FALL | FALL | RETURN

🎵 **READ THE STORY** | Follow this reading guide if you want to pace yourself this week:

- ⬭ Day 1: Numbers 10:11–13; 11
- ⬭ Day 2: Numbers 13
- ⬭ Day 3: Numbers 14
- ⬭ Day 4: Deuteronomy 29
- ⬭ Day 5: Deuteronomy 30:11–31:8

A VIEW FROM THE LOWER STORY

The children of Israel were on a road trip from Egypt, where they had been enslaved for four hundred years, to the promised land—a land flowing with milk and honey. The distance? Around 275 miles. Let me give you some context. We live in San Antonio, Texas. The distance from San Antonio to Dallas is roughly 275 miles. Now, put yourself in Moses' sandals. He was charged with leading upwards of one to three million people through the wilderness with the entire population of San Antonio (which is roughly 1.5 million people) on foot. What could possibly go wrong?

When they got to Mount Sinai, where God gave Moses the Ten Commandments, they only had eleven more days of travel to go. Well, it was actually going to take them forty years to arrive at their final destination. What went wrong? We are told in the story, "Now the people complained about their hardships" (Numbers 11:1). They fell back into the tunnel vision of the Lower Story. It's hot. It's dusty. We're tired. It's taking a lot longer than we thought it would. Are we there yet?

They complained about not having any food. God provided a heavenly food to drop out of the sky, called manna. Not long after they complained about the lack of variety in their diet, they started longing for the "good old days" when they were slaves in Egypt. God gave them an unlimited supply of quail, which turned out to be quite tasty, in my opinion (particularly when wrapped in bacon!). But you know you are in trouble when God says he's going to give you so much meat that you'll be eating it "until it comes out of your nostrils and you loathe it" (Numbers 11:20).

But the fatal mistake they made is when they came to a place called Kadesh Barnea. They were so, so close. From there Moses sent in twelve spies, one from each of the tribes of Israel, to scope out the land and bring back a report.

Forty days later, they returned to give their report: "Yep, this land is flowing with milk and honey alright, just as God said." But the spies also reported the people were huge—giants really. And there were a bazillion of them! Ten of the twelve spies recommended Israel not enter the land. The people concurred, and the decision was made: They would not enter the land God promised to give them.

From the Lower Story perspective,
the giants were bigger than God.

A VIEW FROM THE UPPER STORY

In the Upper Story, the timing was right to take the land, and that is all that matters. God told Abraham he could not give Israel the land until "the sin of the Amorites [had] reached its full measure" (Genesis 15:16). This had now happened. And, just like God delivered them from slavery through ten powerful plagues, led them through the Red Sea on dry ground, crushed Pharaoh and his army, provided food and water in the desert, and guided them with a cloud during the day and a pillar of fire by night, so he would accomplish this for them. God had established a great track record that should have given them the confidence that he would do it again against all odds. Here is the main lesson they should have learned by now:

From the Upper Story perspective,
God is bigger than the giants.

For their lack of faith in God, he had to discipline them. They couldn't bring this attitude into the promised land. There is an old song from the 1970's by Alfred Poirier called "Walkin' Sinai." It aptly describes God's word back to them: "Go on and take another lap around Mt. Sinai till you learn your lesson."

And that is exactly what happened. They would hang out in the desert for forty more years until the generation of adults who made this decision died. In just a few short weeks or months their children could have been playing on green grass in their backyards, dreaming of getting their camel licenses and graduating from Jerusalem High. Instead they had to face the hardship of the desert. Yet, out of God's love for them, he provided what they needed. We are told that during that entire time the clothes on their backs and the sandals on their feet did not wear out (Deuteronomy 29:5).

At the end of the forty years, Moses gathered the new generation of adults together to issue them this challenge as they faced the choice to enter the land or not:

This day I call the heavens and the earth as witnesses against
you that I have set before you life and death, blessings and curses.
Now choose life, so that you and your children may live and that
you may love the LORD your God, listen to his voice, and hold
fast to him. For the LORD is your life, and he will give you many
years in the land he swore to give to your fathers, Abraham,
Isaac and Jacob.

Deuteronomy 30:19-20

God wanted the best for them because he loved them so much. What did they decide? Hold on to your seats as you dive into the next chapter.

GOD'S STORY . . . MY STORY

1. The Israelites wanted to go back to Egypt. It wasn't because they enjoyed slavery but because they were familiar with it. Does your familiarity with your current situation keep you from moving forward on what God has for you?

2. Have you ever felt as if you were "wandering in the wilderness"—spiritually or emotionally? Explain.

3. What are the giants you are facing in your life right now? Do you see them as bigger than God or smaller?

4. Take an inventory of God's track record in your life to provide, protect, and prosper you. Should this give you cause to trust him in what is yet to come?

5. The decision not to enter the land not only affected the adults but their children. Who are the people God has placed in your life who are affected by your decisions?

SHARE THE STORY

Review the first movement of the story from memory. Then fill in the blanks for the second movement—**The Story of Israel**. See page 11 for help.

God builds a brand-new nation called _____. Through this nation, he will reveal his presence, _____, and plan to get us back. Every story of Israel points to the first _____ Jesus—the One who will provide the way _____ to God.

The Battle Begins

The Story of Israel

JOSHUA

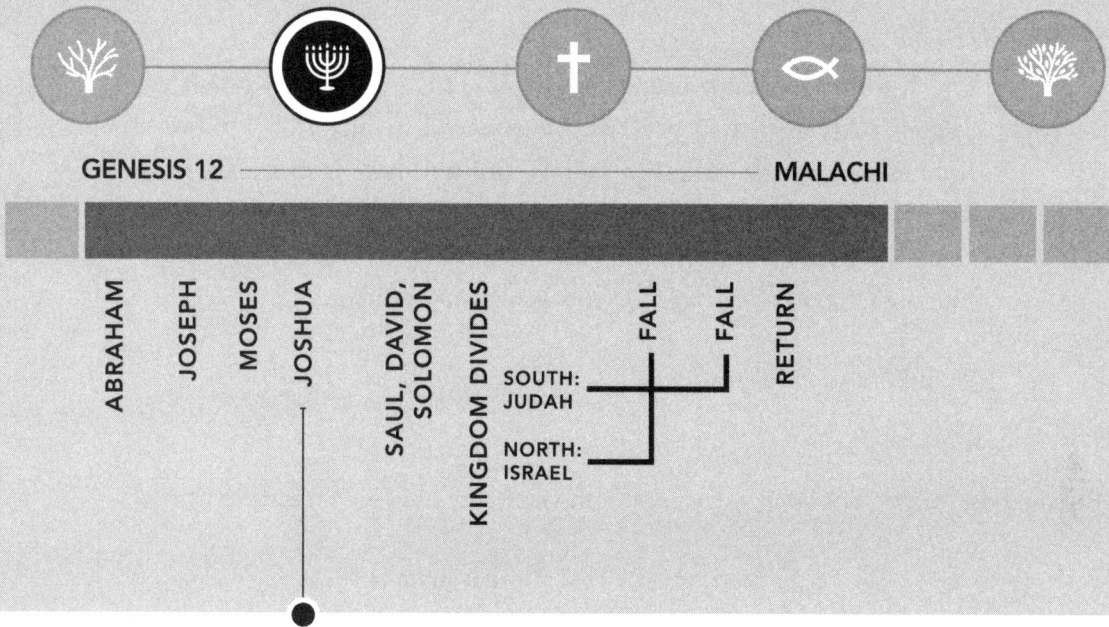

GENESIS 12 ——————————————— MALACHI

ABRAHAM · JOSEPH · MOSES · JOSHUA · SAUL, DAVID, SOLOMON · KINGDOM DIVIDES · SOUTH: JUDAH · NORTH: ISRAEL · FALL · FALL · RETURN

READ THE STORY | Follow this reading guide if you want to pace yourself this week:

○ Day 1: Joshua 1

○ Day 2: Joshua 2

○ Day 3: Joshua 3–4

○ Day 4: Joshua 5:1–12

○ Day 5: Joshua 5:13–6:27

A VIEW FROM THE LOWER STORY

Just before Moses died, he appointed a man named Joshua to succeed him as the leader of the nation God was building. Some forty years earlier, Joshua was one of the twelve spies whom Moses selected to sneak into Canaan (the promised land), check it out, and report back.

Only Joshua and his buddy Caleb thought they should go in and take the land. Read Joshua's plea:

The land we passed through and explored is exceedingly good.
If the LORD is pleased with us, he will lead us into that land, a
land flowing with milk and honey, and will give it to us. Only do
not rebel against the LORD. And do not be afraid of the people of
the land, because we will devour them. Their protection is gone,
but the LORD is with us. Do not be afraid of them.

Numbers 14:7–9

But the people didn't listen, and they spent the rest of their lives in the desert.

Sometimes the best punishment is to
give someone exactly what they want.

Forty years later God told Captain Joshua, "Get ready. It's time to go in." Before they crossed over the Jordan River and faced their first opponent, God instructed Joshua to circumcise all the men, something that should have happened when they were eight days old. Circumcision was an outward sign of God's covenant with his people. You got to bear the mark that you belong to Yahweh.

God's battle plan for their first conquest—at the walled city of Jericho—had to give Joshua pause, but he went with it. He shared God's plan with the people: "Folks, we're going to cross that raging river on the edge of town without any boats or bridges. Once we get to the other side, I want all the guys to meet me in this big tent. Bring your knives and a Band-Aid. When we're finished there, we're all going to form a big column and parade around that huge walled fortress where soldiers will be waiting to ambush us. No need to bring any weapons, except for seven of you. Bring your trumpets. When I say the word, make some noise—and I think that'll do it. Are you with me?"

When we read this with our Lower Story eyes, it would be funny if there weren't so much at stake. This was exactly what they did, and the walls came a-tumblin' down. Just as God had promised.

The rest of the story of Joshua is all about conquest. Seven years later, he conquered all the land, defeating thirty-one kings, and dividing the land according to the twelve tribes of Israel. Astounding!

A VIEW FROM THE UPPER STORY

Another piece of the vision God gave to Abraham over seven hundred years ago had come about. God's Upper Story and his love for Israel cannot be thwarted. It wasn't because Israel earned it. They resisted God almost every step of the way. Moses gave us the Upper Story scoop before he died:

> *It is not because of your righteousness or your integrity that you are going in to take possession of their land; but on account of the wickedness of these nations, the LORD your God will drive them out before you, to accomplish what he swore to your fathers, to Abraham, Isaac and Jacob.*
>
> *Deuteronomy 9:5*

It wasn't in their own strength that they took the land.

Success was already declared before the first foot was placed into the Jordan River. Why? Because this battle belonged to the Lord. When we are careful to choose battles that fall within the word and will of God, we too will be successful. If we choose battles that fall outside the word and will of God, we are on our own, and the outcome is unpredictable. Choose the Lord's battles and then charge!

GOD'S STORY . . . MY STORY

1. Read Joshua 1:7–9. What is the basis God gave Joshua for being strong and courageous in the face of his enemies? What implication does this have for your life?

2. Read Joshua 2:1–11 and Hebrews 11:31. How is it that Rahab, the Canaanite prostitute, saw God's Upper Story plan when the Israelites who experienced it couldn't? What can we learn from this for our own lives? In Hebrews 11:31, Rahab is commended for her actions. How do we reconcile the fact that she lied to the king of Jericho? Is there any situation today where we might be called to do the same thing?

3. Read Joshua 3–4. What is the significance of the ark of the covenant leading the procession across the Jordan River? What are the implications for our lives today? Why did they set up a memorial of twelve stones to commemorate this event? Is there an application in this act for us today?

4. Read Joshua 5:1–12. Why did Joshua have the men circumcised before they entered the battle? Do you think baptism is the equivalent for us today? Have you been baptized?

5. Read Joshua 5:13–6:27. Why do you believe God didn't let the Israelites fight in the battle of Jericho? Is there an application in this for our lives today?

SHARE THE STORY

Review the first movement of the story from memory. Then fill in the blanks for the second movement—**The Story of Israel**. See page 11 for help.

_____ builds a brand-new nation called _____. Through this nation, he will reveal his presence, _____, and plan to get us back. Every story of _____ points to the first _____ of Jesus—the One who will provide the way _____ to God.

Cracked Pots

The Story of Israel

GIDEON

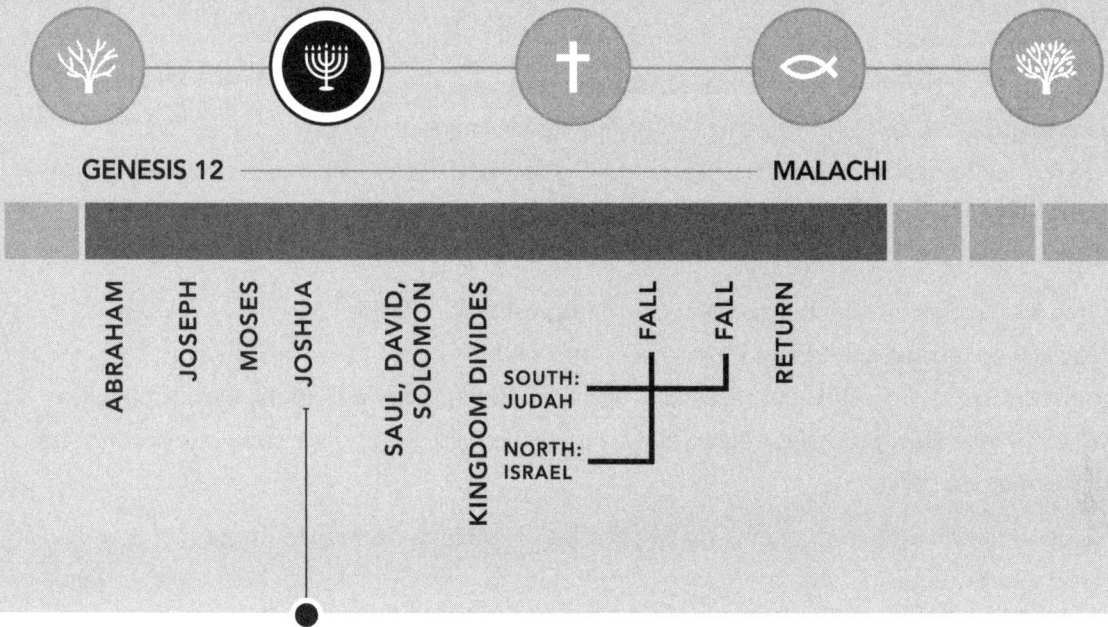

GENESIS 12 ———————————————— MALACHI

ABRAHAM JOSEPH MOSES JOSHUA SAUL, DAVID, SOLOMON KINGDOM DIVIDES SOUTH: JUDAH NORTH: ISRAEL FALL FALL RETURN

READ THE STORY | Follow this reading guide if you want to pace yourself this week:

- ○ Day 1: Judges 6:1–16
- ○ Day 2: Judges 6:17–40
- ○ Day 3: Judges 7:1–8
- ○ Day 4: Judges 7:9–25
- ○ Day 5: Matthew 22:34–40

A VIEW FROM THE LOWER STORY

If you've ever felt outnumbered, unqualified, or disadvantaged, you will be encouraged by Gideon's story. It began at a time when Israel had been living in the land of Canaan for nearly three hundred years. God had given them everything they needed to be a great nation: a set of guidelines on how to live, his presence in the tabernacle, a way to atone for their sins, land he had promised their ancestors, and God as their King to lead and guide them. But it wasn't enough. The children of Israel could not stay focused on the Upper Story. Specifically, they were addicted to worshiping other gods, a blatant violation of the very instructions God gave them.

God severely punished this behavior by allowing other rulers to oppress them, often scattering the Israelites into the mountains to hide in caves. Eventually they reached a point of utter desperation and called out to God to rescue them, and God responded by sending judges to free them from their enemies. We see this pattern twelve times in the book of Judges.

One such judge is Gideon. Israel was being oppressed by the Midianites for seven long years. God tapped Gideon on the shoulder and said, "You're my guy." Gideon couldn't believe God had chosen him. He proclaimed to God that he was from the weakest family within the weakest tribe of Israel, which was true. God did this for a reason—to demonstrate his power and glory.

Gideon assembled his army of thirty-two thousand soldiers. God said, "That's too many." God then helped him whittle it down to ten thousand men by allowing the men who were scared to go home. God said, "Still too many." Finally, the army got trimmed to three hundred men. God said, "That will do." Some suggest the Midianites had two hundred thousand soldiers. That is a 666:1 ratio. What could possibly go wrong? Unless God is involved from the Upper Story.

The Midianites knew there was no way Israel could defeat them. Gideon laid out God's military strategy to his ragamuffin band of soldiers. He told his tiny army to light torches and then hide them inside jars of clay. Each soldier carried the clay pitcher in his left hand; in the other hand, following Gideon's instruction, each carried a trumpet. They snuck up on the Midianite army at night, and at Gideon's signal, they smashed the clay pots and blew on their trumpets. Gideon had the soldiers shout in unison, "A sword for [Yahweh] and for Gideon" (Judges 7:20). The flashing fires and sounding horns confused and frightened the Midianites so greatly that they ran around like chickens with their heads cut off! They must have been thinking, *If Israel has that many torchbearers and troubadours, just think how many soldiers they have.* They tried to flee, but in the darkness, they turned on each other with their swords. The battle was over before it started.

> **When the Midianites said, "No way,"**
> **Israel shouted, "Yahweh."**

A VIEW FROM THE UPPER STORY

In Paul's second letter to the Corinthians he wrote these words, no doubt drawing on the story of Gideon:

> **But we have this treasure in jars of clay to show that this all-surpassing power is from God and not from us. We are hard pressed on every side, but not crushed; perplexed, but not in despair; persecuted, but not abandoned; struck down, but not destroyed. We always carry around in our body the death of Jesus, so that the life of Jesus may also be revealed in our body.**
>
> **2 Corinthians 4:7-10**

We are the clay jar, and the treasure inside of us is the light of Jesus. One of the best ways for that light to shine out of us is through our brokenness.

**In and through our human weakness
God displays his power, making us who believe
a bunch of "cracked pots."**

The Enemy thinks there is no way we can win. But when others shout "No way!", we shout, "YAHWEH!"

GOD'S STORY . . . MY STORY

1. Read Judges 6:13–16. In what ways do you feel weak and unqualified, and it keeps you from pursuing what God has for you? What was God's counsel to Gideon? Might this work for you?

2. Read Judges 6:36–40. Based on how you saw Gideon use a fleece, how might you use fleeces in your own life when faced with challenging decisions?

3. Read Judges 7:1–7. Why did God stack the odds against Gideon? Have you ever had a time when you felt God stacked the odds against you? If not, what do you think you would do if he did?

4. Read Judges 7:16–17. What do you think of Gideon's weapons of warfare? Why was Gideon confident that such a ridiculous strategy would work?

5. Read 2 Corinthians 4:7–10. Do you find it discouraging or freeing to know that we are called "jars of clay" in the Bible? Why or why not?

SHARE THE STORY

Review the first movement of the story from memory. Then fill in the blanks for the second movement—**The Story of Israel**. See page 11 for help.

_____ builds a brand-new _____ called Israel. Through this nation, he will reveal his presence, _____, and _____ to get us back. Every story of _____ points to the first _____ of Jesus—the One who will provide the way _____ to God.

Redeeming Love

The Story of Israel
RUTH

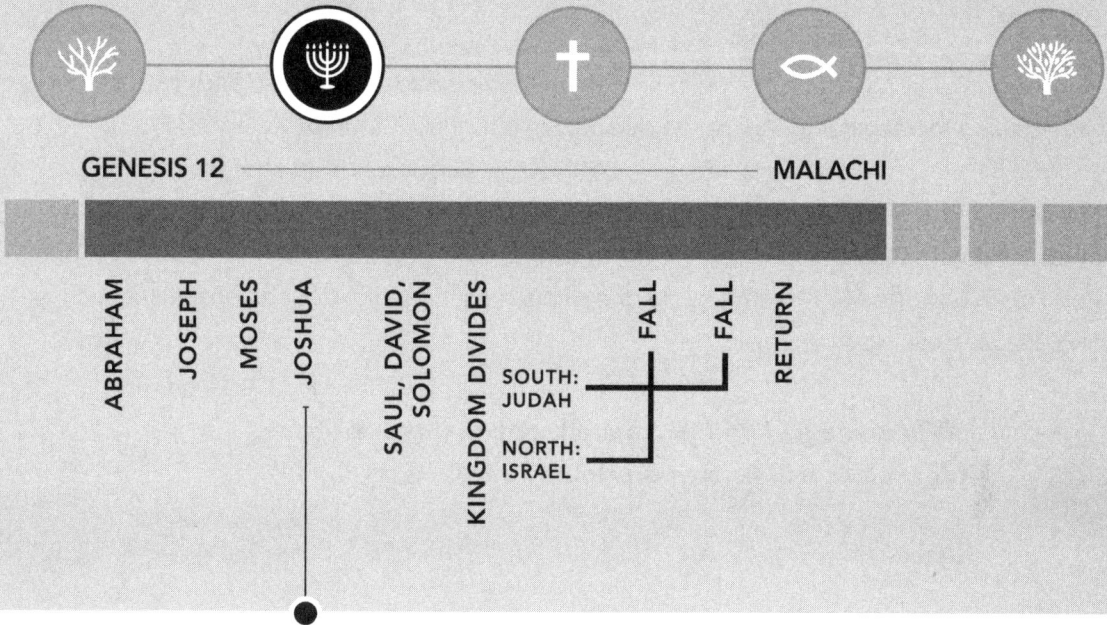

GENESIS 12 ———————————————— MALACHI

ABRAHAM | JOSEPH | MOSES | JOSHUA | SAUL, DAVID, SOLOMON | KINGDOM DIVIDES | SOUTH: JUDAH | FALL | NORTH: ISRAEL | FALL | RETURN

READ THE STORY | Follow this reading guide if you want to pace yourself this week:

○ Day 1: Ruth 1

○ Day 2: Ruth 2:1–3:18

○ Day 3: Ruth 4

○ Day 4: Joshua 2:1–21; 6:20–25

○ Day 5: Matthew 1:1–6

A VIEW FROM THE LOWER STORY

During the period of the Judges, God highlights the story of a family from Bethlehem. Although the name Bethlehem means "house of bread," the city in Judah had become plagued with severe famine. To feed their two sons, Mahlon and Kilion, Elimelek and his wife, Naomi, decided to head to Moab. The Moabites, enemies of Israel, worshiped other gods. Because of this, moving there may have been a bad decision. However, during this season the two nations were at peace. Before long Elimelek died. After that, Mahlon and Kilion married Moabite women, but the two sons also died, leaving Naomi and her daughters-in-law, Ruth and Orpah, widows.

Naomi eventually heard the famine in Bethlehem had passed. Devastated and despondent, with nothing to keep her in Moab, she decided to return home. Unexpectedly her daughters-in-law decided to go with her. But Naomi feared she could offer these girls nothing in the way of a future, not to mention the difficulty they might face in a land with so much tension toward their people. Orpah reluctantly said goodbye and returned home. But Ruth, resolved to go with Naomi, made one of the most beautiful declarations of affection and devotion ever spoken:

> *"Where you go I will go, and where you stay I will stay. Your people will be my people and your God my God."*
>
> **Ruth 1:16**

What tremendous faith! Together, they embarked on their long journey.

Harvest season was in full swing when our widows arrived in Bethlehem, and Ruth convinced Naomi to let her glean in nearby fields. God's instructions required wealthy farmers to allow the poor to follow behind harvesters and gather scraps of grain they had missed. Naomi reluctantly agreed, knowing that a foreigner from an enemy land showing up in a field in a small town where everyone knows everyone could be dangerous. Can you say, "homeland security"?

Ruth unknowingly chose a field owned by a relative of her deceased father-in-law. His name was Boaz. Boaz saw Ruth and found out she was Naomi's daughter-in-law. He had heard about Ruth's loyalty and love for Naomi and asked her to continue to glean only in his field.

Ruth arrived home and shared her day with Naomi. Naomi asked her where she worked. When Ruth told her it was Boaz's field, a glimmer of hope began to flicker in Naomi's previously numb heart. Naomi explained that Boaz, as a relative, could become their guardian-redeemer. Boaz could save them by buying her sons' and husband's land and marrying Ruth if he chose. This could be at great risk to his own estate. The land would not be his own but would remain Elimelek's family estate.

What happened next can be described as nothing less than a fairy tale. Naomi told Ruth to take a shower, splash on a little Chanel No. 5, put on her Sabbath best, and go to Boaz's threshing floor after he finished eating—never approach a man on an empty stomach—and went to sleep. She was to sneak in, uncover his feet, and lie down at the foot of his bed. Boaz would understand exactly what Ruth was doing.

Ruth followed Naomi's instructions perfectly. Her behavior conveyed to Boaz she was available and interested in marriage. Apparently, she was bold and beautiful!

Boaz awakened in the middle of the night startled and asked, "Who's there?" Ruth answered, "I am your servant Ruth . . . . Spread the corner of your garment over me, since you are a guardian-redeemer" (3:9). With charm and integrity, Boaz became Ruth's prince . . . I mean guardian-redeemer.

A VIEW FROM THE UPPER STORY

What would possess Boaz to do this? The Bible doesn't explicitly tell us, but perhaps it is because Boaz, the strong, wealthy, respected man, knew what it was like to be an outsider. We learn in Matthew 1 of the New Testament that Boaz's mother was Rahab, the Canaanite harlot, who hid the spies as they were scoping out the promised land. Because she risked her life, she was adopted into the family of Israel. The same thing happened to Ruth because of Boaz's compassion, integrity, and grace.

In the Lower Story, Naomi thought her life was over. However, at the end of the book we are given the genealogy of Boaz's family. Through this redeeming act, Naomi's life was restored. We learn that Boaz and Ruth had a son named Obed who grew up and had a son named Jesse. Jesse grew up to have a son named David.

> *Twenty-eight generations later, a little baby named Jesus was born in a stable in the town of Bethlehem, our Guardian-Redeemer.*

Jesus risked everything, even his own life, by dying on the cross to redeem us. God went out of his way to include Rahab and Ruth in the lineage of our Guardian-Redeemer, signaling to us that salvation is not only for the Jews but for all people.

GOD'S STORY . . . MY STORY

1. What does Ruth's story teach us about poor decisions we make?

2. Explain how Jesus becoming our Guardian-Redeemer makes you feel.

3. Naomi evoked such wonderful love and loyalty from her daughters-in-law. If you are a mother-in-law or a daughter-in-law, does this speak to you in a special way?

4. What characteristics enabled Ruth to make her declaration to Naomi, or choose to take refuge under the wings of the one true God? Do we need to demonstrate a similar attitude to have a relationship with God?

5. The lineage of Jesus includes four women. What significance can you see in these women being mentioned (Matthew 1:1–16)?

SHARE THE STORY

Review both the first and second movements of the story—**The Story of the Garden** and **The Story of Israel**—from memory. See page 11 for help.

WEEK 17

Peer Pressure

The Story of Israel

SAMUEL AND SAUL

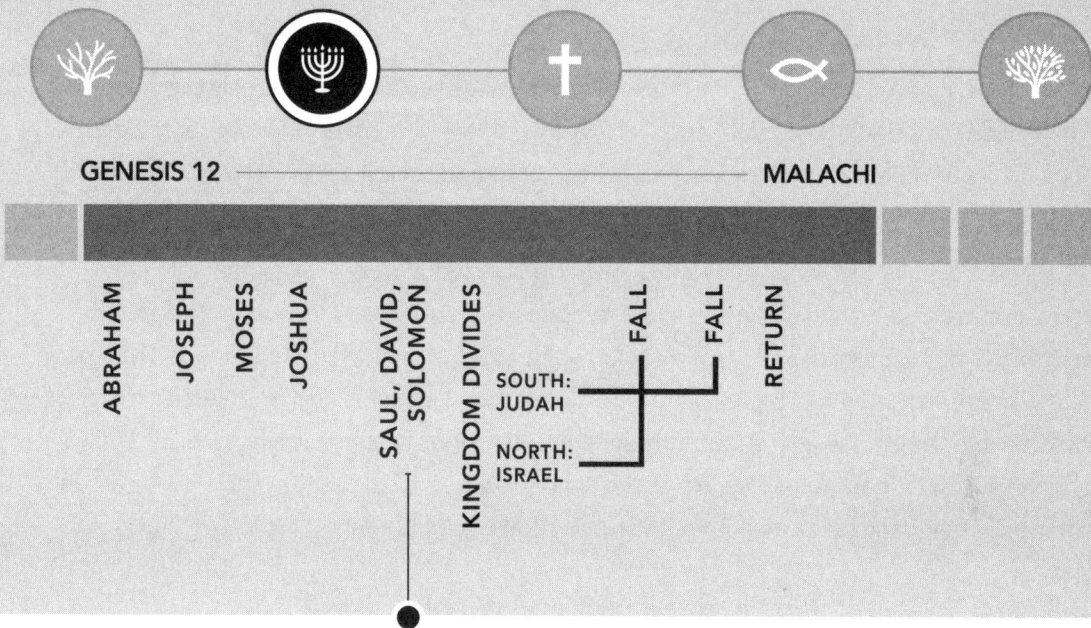

GENESIS 12 ———————————————————————— MALACHI

ABRAHAM | JOSEPH | MOSES | JOSHUA | SAUL, DAVID, SOLOMON | KINGDOM DIVIDES | SOUTH: JUDAH | NORTH: ISRAEL | FALL | FALL | RETURN

🌿 **READ THE STORY** | Follow this reading guide if you want to pace yourself this week:

- ◯ Day 1: 1 Samuel 1:1–27; 2:1–11
- ◯ Day 2: 1 Samuel 3:1–4:21
- ◯ Day 3: 1 Samuel 8
- ◯ Day 4: 1 Samuel 11–12
- ◯ Day 5: 1 Samuel 15

A VIEW FROM THE LOWER STORY

This next chapter in God's saga of the construction of a nation begins with a happy ending. God opened the womb of a barren woman named Hannah and provided her with the child she so longed to have. She had promised God that if he gave her a child, she would in turn give the child back to him. And she did. At the age the child was weaned, she took him to the temple and gave him to Eli, the priest, to serve there. Hannah saw him only once a year, but God kept her womb open, and she had five other children.

Samuel grew up, had two sons, and took over for his mentor, Eli. Eli suddenly died because the Philistines had attacked Israel and won, taking captive the ark of the covenant. God allowed his new nation to be defeated because of their disobedience and corrupt leaders.

Samuel had appointed his two sons to lead the people, but they were a huge disappointment to Samuel as they were anything but godly. Samuel's spiritual advisers knew that the two brothers needed to be removed from power, so they went to Samuel and told him, "Your sons do not follow your ways; now appoint a king to lead us" (1 Samuel 8:5). Samuel warned the people a king would limit their freedoms and put them and their children into the king's service, but they still wanted a king. Their reasoning was confirmed in 1 Samuel 8:20, "Then we will be like all the other nations." God granted their wish. Samuel anointed a tall, handsome man named Saul to be king over Judah.

> *They achieved their goal of being like all other nations! Be careful what you ask for. . . .*

Saul started out well, following God and experiencing some great victories in battle. Samuel resigned as the leader since they now had a king. During his swan song as leader, Samuel reminded the people that if they sought God and served him with all their hearts they would be just fine.

Saul and the children of Israel were at war for most of his reign, first with the Philistines and then with the Amalekites. When God instructed him to completely obliterate the Amalekites, Saul disobeyed and allowed Agag, the king, to stay alive along with the livestock. When Samuel confronted Saul, Saul lied and said he followed God's instructions. Samuel replied, "What then is this bleating of sheep in my ears? What is this lowing of cattle that I hear?" (15:14). Saul justified this by saying, "We kept the best to sacrifice to the Lord." Samuel replied, "To obey is better than sacrifice" (verse 22).

A VIEW FROM THE UPPER STORY

What's so bad about being like everyone else? Simply put, God has a better plan for his people, and for us as well. In the Upper Story, God wanted to be Israel's only king. With no human layer between God and his people, he could best govern and guide them.

God still longs to be with us and be our only focus and leader. But he will honor our free will sometimes and alter the Lower Story plan. Like any good father, God will allow us to live out the consequences of our own choices if we insist. However, this usually turns disastrous for his people.

Sticking with God's plan is always
the best way to overcome peer pressure
and to feel God's love for us.

When God set the children of Israel apart, he was wanting them to stand out. God's people are called to be different so that we may reflect his character. Saul failed in the mission to represent God and created long-term consequences for Israel. God intervened and removed Saul from the throne.

Time to find a new king.

GOD'S STORY . . . MY STORY

1. Apparently, peer pressure is not just for junior high and high school students. Adults fall prey to this as well. Can you remember a time in your life when you asked God for something, and he granted your request, only to find out it wasn't what you really wanted or needed at all?

2. Are you bothered by God's mandate that the whole Amalekite nation be destroyed—men, women, children, and livestock? What important characteristics of God do we need to remember?

3. Read 1 Samuel 10:20–24 and 1 Samuel 15:7–23. How did Saul's demeanor change between his anointing as king and the war with the Amalekites?

4. What can you learn from Saul when you look at our national/world leaders today?

SHARE THE STORY

Share the first two movements of the story with five people this week. See page 11 for help.

WEK 18

The Heart of the Matter

The Story of Israel

DAVID

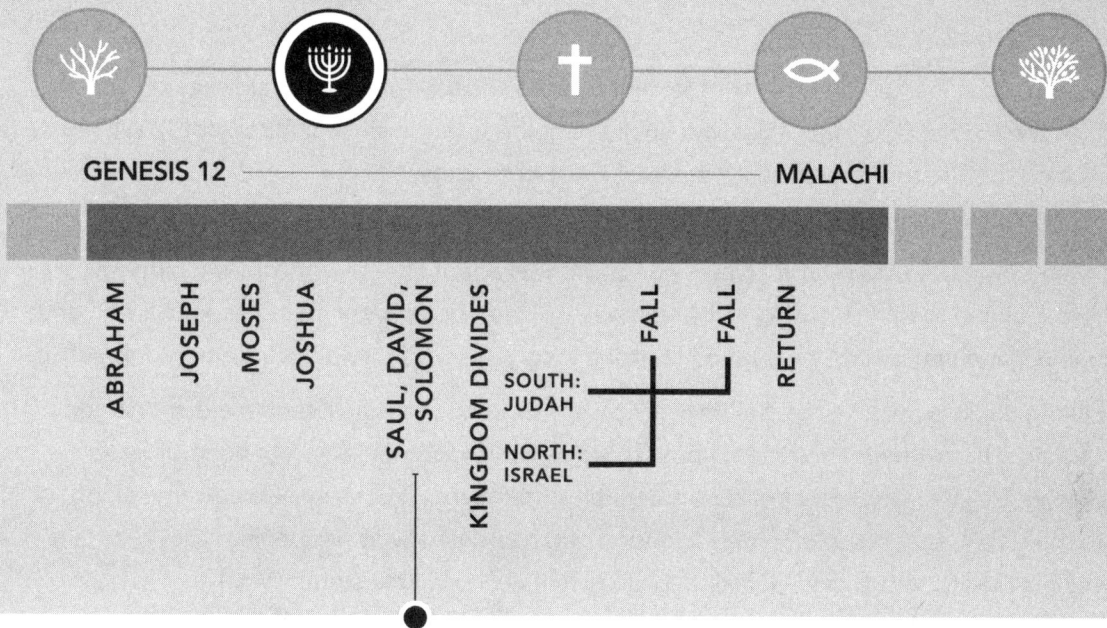

GENESIS 12 ——————————————— MALACHI

ABRAHAM | JOSEPH | MOSES | JOSHUA | SAUL, DAVID, SOLOMON | KINGDOM DIVIDES | FALL | FALL | RETURN

SOUTH: JUDAH

NORTH: ISRAEL

READ THE STORY | Follow this reading guide if you want to pace yourself this week:

- ○ Day 1: 1 Samuel 16:1–13
- ○ Day 2: 1 Samuel 17:1–38
- ○ Day 3: 1 Samuel 18:1–15
- ○ Day 4: 1 Samuel 20
- ○ Day 5: 1 Samuel 24; 26

A VIEW FROM THE LOWER STORY

God was going to replace King Saul. Samuel the prophet was sent to the house of a man named Jesse and told him to call all his sons together. As Samuel met each of the sons, the Lord rejected every one even though Samuel and Jesse believed it would be one of them. Perplexed by the Lord's rejection of all the sons, Samuel asked Jesse if he had any other sons. Jesse admitted he did have one more son who was the youngest and was out in the field tending the sheep. Jesse saw him as a little "runt." This is the Hebrew word he actually used to describe his son. They sent for him, and no sooner had Samuel laid eyes on him than the Lord told Samuel, "Rise and anoint him; this is the one" (1 Samuel 16:12). Who would have thought the "runt" of the family would be chosen?

As soon as David was anointed to become king, the Bible tells us, "The Spirit of the LORD came powerfully upon David" (verse 13). David was about fifteen years old when he was first anointed to be the next king, but there is a difference between being anointed king and being inaugurated king. It would be fourteen long years until David became king of Israel.

During the in-between time, the Philistines were taunting the Israelites with a giant named Goliath. They wanted a soldier to come face this Goliath one-on-one, but none of Saul's men would dare go up against such a daunting opponent. That is until David came along to bring his brothers some homemade food and heard what was happening. David volunteered to stand up to Goliath and killed him with one little stone. Wow!

David entered Saul's service, and Saul made him a leader in his army. He also struck up a strong friendship with Saul's son, Jonathan, who would naturally be in line to become king after Saul. Jonathan loved David and understood somehow that God had chosen David to be the next king of Israel, and he accepted that he would not rule in his dad's place. Like God, Jonathan saw a king in David.

 After several victorious battles, Saul overheard the women singing about their military successes. They sang, "Saul has slain his thousands, and David his tens of thousands" (1 Samuel 18:7). As you can imagine, this sparked terrible jealousy in the heart of Saul, and he began to threaten David's life. Jonathan warned David that he should flee because his dad was on a rampage against David.

David fled and was on the run from Saul for thirteen years. During that time, he had at least two opportunities to kill Saul but refused. When David and Abishai, one of David's trusted warriors, entered Saul's camp unnoticed at night, "Abishai said to David, 'Today God has delivered your enemy into your hands. Now let me pin him to the ground with one thrust of the spear; I won't strike him twice'" (26:8). To which David replied, "Don't destroy him! Who can lay a hand on the LORD's anointed and be guiltless?" (verse 9). David chose to remain under the pressure and life-threatening pursuit of Saul. Rather than take him out, David waited patiently for God's timing to elevate him to king.

A VIEW FROM THE UPPER STORY

God's choice for Israel's next leader wasn't based on what men think. He went beyond the outward appearance and looked at the heart (1 Samuel 16:7). People saw a simple shepherd boy, but God saw a king. He saw David's integrity, leadership skills, and dependence on God and enabled him to do the impossible.

The sinful pattern of Israel and their persistent violations of the law he gave through Moses had not gone unnoticed by God. Their evil continued to grow, and God would be justified in removing his blessing from them, but he had made an unconditional promise to Abraham to bring the way for everyone to come back into a relationship with God from this nation. So, God narrowed his scope to the tribe of Judah with a new unconditional promise made to David—that the promised Messiah would come from his tribe.

GOD'S STORY . . . MY STORY

1. Read 1 Samuel 17:34–36. Where did David's power to slay bears, lions, and giants come from?

2. Have you ever met someone new and made a judgment about their character, either good or bad, only to discover later that you can't judge a book by its cover?

3. Does David's respect for Saul's position as God's anointed influence you on how you should behave toward government leaders even if you disagree with them (Daniel 2:21)?

4. Have you ever felt overlooked or underestimated by someone significant in your life?

5. Jonathan is not a character to be ignored in David's story. His awareness of God's calling on David's life and submission to it is inspiring. He saw what God saw in David even when David couldn't. Do you have a Jonathan in your life who sees what God sees in you? Are you a Jonathan to anyone else in your life?

SHARE THE STORY

Review the first two movements of the story from memory. Next, read the third movement—
The Story of Jesus. See page 11 for help.

Jesus left the Upper Story to come down into our Lower Story to be with us and provide the way for us to be made right with God. Through faith in Christ's work on the cross, we can now overturn Adam's choice and have a personal relationship with God.

But God

———————————

The Story of Israel

PSALMS

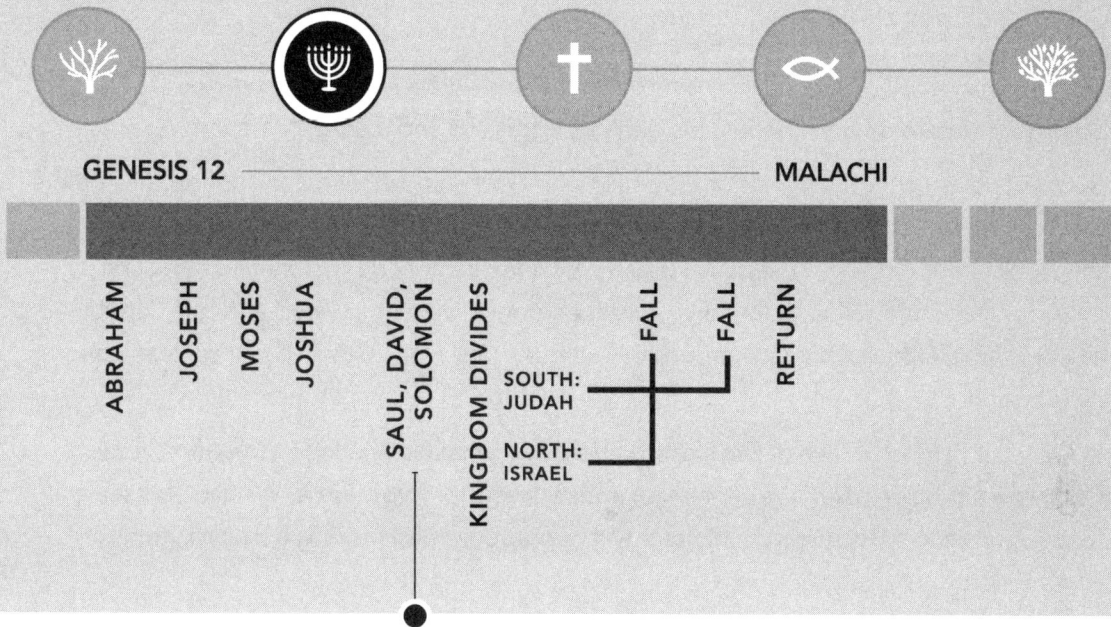

GENESIS 12 ———————————————— MALACHI

ABRAHAM | JOSEPH | MOSES | JOSHUA | SAUL, DAVID, SOLOMON | KINGDOM DIVIDES | SOUTH: JUDAH | NORTH: ISRAEL | FALL | FALL | RETURN

🌿 **READ THE STORY** | Follow this reading guide if you want to pace yourself this week:

○ Day 1: Psalm 8; 19 (Praise)

○ Day 2: Psalm 27; 34 (Trust)

○ Day 3: Psalm 23; 91 (Comfort)

○ Day 4: Psalm 22; 69; 110 (Prophetic)

○ Day 5: Psalm 73; 136 (But God . . .)

A VIEW FROM THE LOWER STORY

Our shepherd boy transformed to king was not only a great leader and a man after God's own heart but a prolific poet/songwriter as well. The book of Psalms gives testimony to this fact. Of the one hundred fifty poems or songs recorded in this book, the primary writer is none other than David. When David was still young, King Saul was perplexed by an evil spirit, and he called David to play the lyre for him. When David played, the evil spirit left Saul alone (1 Samuel 16:23). David wrote eighty-nine of the one hundred fifty psalms while the remaining sixty-one are spread over several other writers—one of whom was David's son Solomon. Apparently, he inherited his dad's love for God and music.

Some of these songs are hymns of praise for who God is and what he has done, while others are laments, or expressions of deep sorrow, suffering, or sadness. We can learn much from this book about God from the praise psalms, besides garnering the benefits of trusting God during human suffering that brings peace from a God who created and is in control of everything. Other psalms are prophetic in nature, describing Jesus' coming, death, and resurrection.

While we find much praise of God for who he is and what he has done in creation in the Psalms, we also see psalms of confession and requests for forgiveness. We can also see God responding to the hymns of lament with a gracious hand moving to guard, guide, and comfort.

> *This book is a great book of instruction on how our Lower Story, imperfect lives can be taught to align with God's perfect Upper Story.*

Many times, as we read the stories in the Bible, we see the plot heading toward insurmountable circumstances that will overwhelmingly destroy God's people. Just when the plot thickens and the future looks grim, we see a "But God" moment, a moment when God steps in and brings the outcome he wants and/or has promised from the Upper Story far beyond what human strength and determination could have afforded. These "But God" moments abound in the Psalms.

A VIEW FROM THE UPPER STORY

Through the Psalms we see a God who loved his creation, man and woman, so much he created a lavish world for them to live in. Psalm 8 asks the question, "What is mankind that you are mindful of them?" (verse 4). How could such a creative, great, and powerful God be interested in creatures who mess up and choose another plan than he has in mind? But God . . . does. He continues throughout his grand story to show us that love.

So many of the psalms of lament end in "But God . . . "

- But God...you hear the plea of my heart.
- But God...you are still in control.
- But God...you get the victory.
- But God...you keep your promises.

Even in the prophetic psalms we see "But God" moments. For example, it appears God has turned his face away from Jesus on the cross (Matthew 27:46). But Psalm 22, which is a prophetic psalm regarding the crucifixion of Jesus, tells us otherwise. In verse 24, David explicitly declares, "[But God] has not hidden his face from him but has listened to his cry for help."

From the Upper Story, God the Father walked with his Son every step of the way through this horrific but necessary event. A good father would never turn his face from his son in his hour of need. He will never turn his face from us when we need him.

Spending time in the Psalms teaches us to have bold faith, to trust in God, to find peace in our aching souls. They also show us a merciful and loving God who allows us to approach him with our praise, thanksgiving, sorrow, regrets, and fears.

> *In our Lower Story in the here and now,*
> *God is still intervening with,*
> *"But God" moments.*

His love endures forever! (Psalm 136)

GOD'S STORY . . . MY STORY

1. After reading several of the psalms this week, is there a new freedom you find to go before God with your petitions and prayers?

2. A prevailing concept in the Psalms is that God is the ruling and reigning king forever. How does this shape your concept of creation, history, and your future?

3. Why do you think the evil spirit left Saul when David played the lyre for him? Does worship music play a part in lifting your spirit?

4. Do you have a "But God" story in your life?

5. Do you have a favorite psalm that brings peace to your heart or joy to your soul?

SHARE THE STORY

Review the first two movements of the story from memory. Then fill in the blanks for the third movement—**The Story of Jesus**. See page 11 for help.

Jesus left the _____ Story to come down into our Lower Story to be with us and provide the way for us to be made right with God. Through faith in Christ's work on the cross, we can now overturn Adam's choice and have a personal _____ with God.

The Good, the Bad, and the Ugly

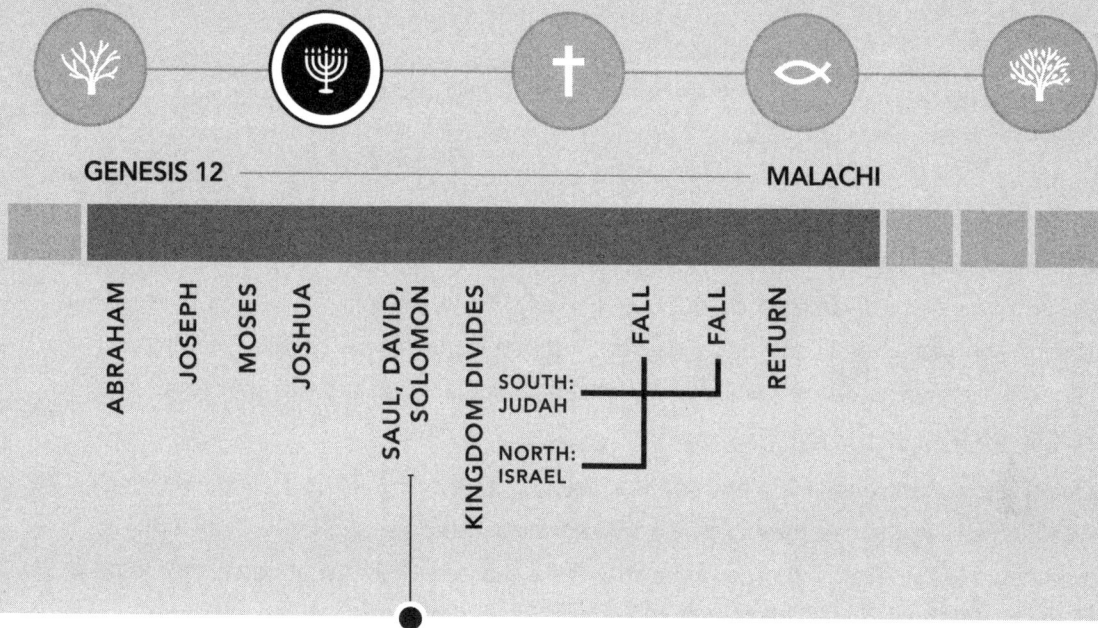

GENESIS 12 ——————————————— MALACHI

ABRAHAM • JOSEPH • MOSES • JOSHUA • SAUL, DAVID, SOLOMON • KINGDOM DIVIDES • SOUTH: JUDAH • NORTH: ISRAEL • FALL • FALL • RETURN

READ THE STORY | Follow this reading guide if you want to pace yourself this week:

○ Day 1: 2 Samuel 5

○ Day 2: 2 Samuel 6:1–12; 7:1–8:15; 13:1–38

○ Day 3: Psalm 51

○ Day 4: 2 Samuel 11:1–12:24

○ Day 5: 2 Samuel 15:1–18; 17:24–29

A VIEW FROM THE LOWER STORY

After fourteen years of boot camp for kings, David was finally inaugurated king of Israel. David seemed to have the Midas touch, or the Mighty-God touch. Everything his hand found to do turned to gold. Success on every front. Israel had a string of attacks from enemies, yet they racked up an impressive string of victories. The ark of the covenant was returned to Jerusalem, and the people were following God because their king was leading the way. Above all, David loved and served God with great passion. The dusty shepherd boy became Israel's Renaissance man. Life was good for David.

Until one night when sweet sleep eluded him. He tossed and turned until he got up and walked on his rooftop to get some fresh air. There he observed a woman bathing at her home below the palace. She was beautiful—David couldn't help but notice her. But he not only noticed her, he had to have her. He sent his servant to find out who she was. She was the wife of Uriah, one of David's loyal soldiers who was off fighting a war for his king. Next this situation became an episode out of a reality TV show. He sent the servant to bring her to him—he was, after all, the king—he slept with her (consider the power dynamic) and sent her back home. A short while later, she sent word to David she was pregnant. What's a king to do?

David decided to send Uriah, Bathsheba's husband, to the front line where the fighting was the fiercest, then secretly told his commander to withdraw and leave Uriah alone and vulnerable to the enemy. As you might suspect, Uriah was killed. What's a king to do now but to marry the widow? The cover-up seemed to be complete.

God sent Nathan, a prophet, to David to confront him with his sin. Nathan reminded him that his sin was not just against Uriah and Bathsheba, but also against God. David responded with six simple words: "I have sinned against the LORD" (2 Samuel 12:13).

We see a huge shift in David's life at this point. In fact, God told David that he was going to bring calamity on David's household. Bathsheba's baby died; David's daughter was raped by her half-brother; his son Absalom mounted a revolt against him and tried to take the throne. Then Absalom died in another attempted rebellion against David. Everything was headed downhill for David.

God is always willing to forgive us, but it seldom removes the consequences of our actions. "If we confess our sins, he is faithful and just and will forgive us our sins and purify us from all unrighteousness."

1 John 1:9

But instead of becoming angry at God, David accepted responsibility for what had come upon him and wrote a most beautiful psalm confessing his sin and asking God to forgive him (Psalm 51).

A VIEW FROM THE UPPER STORY

Even though David made a huge mistake that brought a string of negative consequences, God deposited a sweet drop of grace in David's life from the Upper Story. When it came time to select one of David's sons to be his successor, no one could have ever guessed it would be a child with Bathsheba . . . but it was. His name was Solomon.

> *When we approach God with a contrite heart,*
> *God can take the brokenness from our Lower Story*
> *and redeem it for his Upper Story purposes.*

God did not hide this act of grace. In the genealogy of Jesus found in Matthew he calls out Bathsheba, but not by name. Here is how God instructed Matthew to write it down: "David was the father of Solomon, whose mother had been Uriah's wife" (1:6). What God did for David and Bathsheba, he is still doing today—even for you.

GOD'S STORY . . . MY STORY

1. Saul and David both sinned against God. The Lord removed his Spirit from Saul, but David is called "a man after [God's] own heart" (Acts 13:22) even after his sin against Bathsheba. What do you suppose is the difference?

2. If you were God, wouldn't you try to cover up what David did? Why did God choose to include this in his story?

3. If God forgave David for assault and murder, do you believe God can forgive you for what you have done?

4. Is there a mistake you have made in your past that may still carry negative consequences, but you have seen God use it for his good purpose?

5. Do you have someone in your life who is trusted enough to be a "Nathan"? Are you a "Nathan" for someone else?

SHARE THE STORY

Review the first two movements of the story from memory. Then fill in the blanks for the third movement—**The Story of Jesus**. See page 11 for help.

Jesus left the _____ Story to come down into our Lower Story to be with us and provide the way for us to be made _____ with God. Through faith in Christ's work on the _____, we can now overturn Adam's choice and have a personal _____ with God.

Be Careful What You Ask For

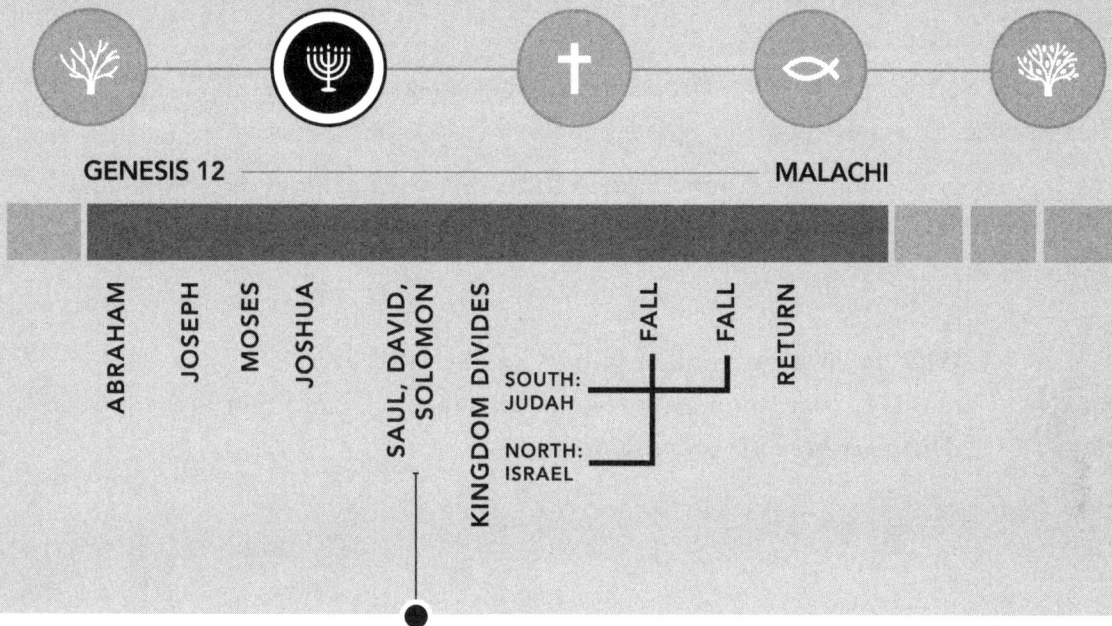

GENESIS 12 ———————————— MALACHI

ABRAHAM
JOSEPH
MOSES
JOSHUA
SAUL, DAVID, SOLOMON
KINGDOM DIVIDES
SOUTH: JUDAH
NORTH: ISRAEL
FALL
FALL
RETURN

READ THE STORY | Follow this reading guide if you want to pace yourself this week:

- ◯ Day 1: 1 Kings 1:1–52
- ◯ Day 2: 1 Kings 3
- ◯ Day 3: 1 Chronicles 29:1–20
- ◯ Day 4: 1 Kings 5–6
- ◯ Day 5: 1 Kings 11:1–13

A VIEW FROM THE LOWER STORY

You've probably heard about the phenomenon of putting a frog in a pot of boiling water. What happens? Of course, he immediately jumps out. But if you put him in a pot of lukewarm water, he becomes quite comfortable and enjoys his cozy setting. Then if you turn the heat up slowly, the frog doesn't even notice until it is too late, and he gets boiled to death. This is what happened to our next character in God's story. Here's how the story goes.

David was becoming more and more feeble, and his son Adonijah knew it, so he tried to usurp the throne from his father before he died. When David heard about Adonijah's plot, he kicked into one last hoorah, because God had already told David who the next king should be. So Solomon, the son of David and Bathsheba, was crowned the new king of Israel before his brother could say, "Kiss my ring!"

As the leadership baton passed from David to Solomon, Israel was strong and prosperous. They were not at war. What a great time to be king in Israel! David charged his son with these words:

> *"Walk in obedience to him [God], and keep his decrees . . . .*
> *Do this so that you may prosper in all you do . . . and that the*
> *LORD may keep his promise to me."*
>
> 1 Kings 2:3-4

Early in Solomon's reign, God approached Solomon and told him to ask for anything. A divine genie in the bottle of sorts. No boundaries, no rules; just ask and God will give it. Wow! Imagine all the things you could ask for!

Solomon asked for wisdom. Seems he already had a bunch at his young age! God honored Solomon's request. It didn't take long for him to put his new gift to the test. Shortly after Solomon took the reins of the kingdom, two women came to him with a baby. They both claimed to be the mother, and it was Solomon's job to decide what to do. You or I might have flipped a coin, but not Solomon! He asked one of his attendants to cut the baby in two and give each mother half of the baby, knowing that the real mother would not allow the baby to be killed. Sure enough, the true mom said, "No, no! Let her have the baby." Solomon knew this was the rightful mother.

As if being given exceptional wisdom were not enough, in 1 Kings 6:11–13, Solomon received explicit instruction from the Lord about how to live his life and the direct results and consequences:

> *The word of the LORD came to Solomon: "As for this temple you*
> *are building, if you follow my decrees, observe my laws and keep*
> *all my commands and obey them, I will fulfill through you the*
> *promise I gave to David your father. And I will live among the*
> *Israelites and will not abandon my people Israel."*

Solomon was shaping up to be the perfect king! Right? That is until he let his love for beautiful foreign women interrupt his better judgment. These wives (a mere one thousand of them) brought their "other" gods to the palace. Solomon's heart was turned to these gods. As Solomon found out:

It's easy to start out strong, but much more difficult to finish well.

The Bible tells us in 1 Kings 11:9, "The LORD became angry with Solomon because his heart had turned away from the LORD." Then in verses 11–12 he continued, "Since this is your attitude . . . I will most certainly tear the kingdom away from you . . . . Nevertheless, for the sake of David your father, I will not do it during your lifetime. I will tear it out of the hand of your son."

A VIEW FROM THE UPPER STORY

God's Upper Story never changes. From the time he established this new nation, he told the Israelites to obey his commandments so other nations might see him as the one true God. However, again and again they strayed from God's ways. Now Solomon, who had more wisdom than anyone ever, made the same terrible misstep. He violated God's commands—especially the one about having "no other God's before me"—and put his kingdom in jeopardy by diluting Israel's witness to other nations. A lesson we can all learn from.

When we ignore God's requirements for living, we compromise our witness to those around us.

Solomon started out strong and probably thought, "I have the willpower to withstand the pull of these women to worship their gods." He did not. But God still preserved David's lineage because Jesus would come from the house of David (Luke 1:27). Solomon's poor finish caused the kingdom to be torn in two—literally—as you will see in a later chapter.

GOD'S STORY . . . MY STORY

1. Be honest, if you could ask for anything from God, what would it be?

2. Have you ever been in a situation where you thought you would have the willpower to abstain from doing something wrong, but succumbed to the temptation after all?

3. Have you ever been in a place where you wished you had Solomon's wisdom?

4. What are some things you can do to make sure your heart stays in tune with God's best will for you?

5. Notice Solomon's declaration that the children of Israel are "too numerous to count" (1 Kings 3:8). Does this take you back to a declaration God made to Abraham 895 years prior (Genesis 15:5)? What does this tell you about the character of God? How does God keeping his promises to Abraham and to David make you feel?

SHARE THE STORY

Review the first two movements of the story from memory. Then fill in the blanks for the third movement—**The Story of Jesus**. See page 11 for help.

Jesus left the _____ Story to come down into our _____ Story to be with us and provide the way for us to be made _____ with God. Through faith in Christ's work on the _____, we can now overturn _____ choice and have a personal _____ with God.

WEEK 22

Lower Story Wisdom

The Story of Israel

PROVERBS AND ECCLESIASTES

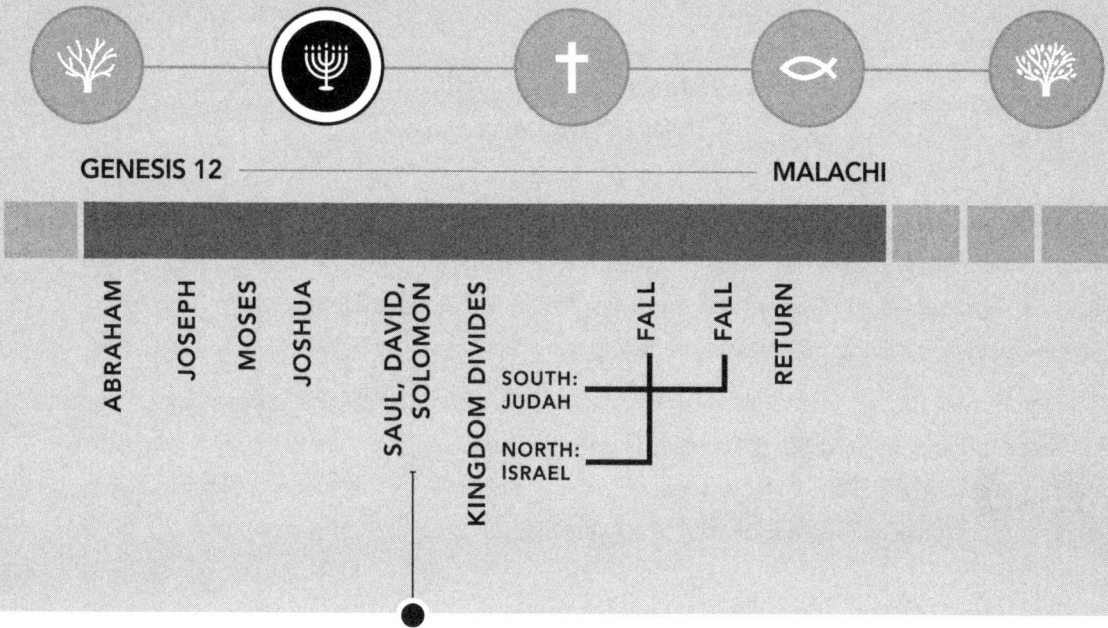

GENESIS 12 ——————————————— MALACHI

ABRAHAM JOSEPH MOSES JOSHUA SAUL, DAVID, SOLOMON KINGDOM DIVIDES

SOUTH: JUDAH

NORTH: ISRAEL

FALL FALL RETURN

❧ **READ THE STORY** | Follow this reading guide if you want to pace yourself this week:

○ Day 1: Proverbs 1–6

○ Day 2: Proverbs 7–13

○ Day 3: Proverbs 14–20

○ Day 4: Proverbs 21–27

○ Day 5: Proverbs 28–31

A VIEW FROM THE LOWER STORY

God gave Solomon the chance to ask for anything he wanted. He chose to ask for wisdom, and God granted it to him as well as throwing in all the other things to boot—wealth, honor, and long life. Wisdom can be defined as "a skill for living." It is something to be put into action in our lives, versus just a nice discussion around a cup of coffee or a glass of wine filled with good intentions.

Wisdom's goal is to give us the opportunity to live our best life in the Lower Story. When we activate from a position of wisdom, we put ourselves in the optimal place to thrive.

The secret to success is to string together
a series of good decisions.

 The wisdom that Solomon dishes out in the book of Proverbs and Ecclesiastes is not mere human wisdom, but axioms inspired by God. There is a difference. As the prophet Isaiah told us, God's ways are higher than our ways (Isaiah 55:9). He is looking down from the Upper Story and giving us insights that are pure gold (Proverbs 3:13–18).

The late Derek Kidner, former warden of Tyndale House in Cambridge, categorized Proverbs under six practical Lower Story topics—The Fool, The Sluggard, The Friend, Words, The Family, and Life and Death. As you read the book of Proverbs this week keep your eye out for these categories. Take a look at a few examples:

Friend —————— "Faithful are the wounds of a friend,
But deceitful are the kisses of an enemy."
(Proverbs 27:6 NASB)

Words —————— "Hard work always pays off;
mere talk puts no bread on the table."
(Proverbs 14:23 MSG)

The Sluggard ——— "The sluggard will not plow by reason of the winter;
Therefore he shall beg in harvest, and have nothing."
(Proverbs 20:4 ASV)

The Fool ————— "Like the useless legs of one who is lame is a proverb
in the mouth of a fool."
(Proverbs 26:7)

Family —————— "Start children off on the way they should go,
and even when they are old they will not turn from it."
(Proverbs 22:6)

Life and Death —— "A heart at peace gives life to the body, but envy rots the bones."
(Proverbs 14:30)

Wisdom is not far away. It is found in God's Word and in the lives of godly people who have gone before you. Be wise and seek it out. Be even wiser and put wisdom into action and see if you don't experience a fruitful life.

A VIEW FROM THE UPPER STORY

Proverbs are not promises. You can apply wisdom to the best of your ability and still experience difficulties. There are external circumstances beyond our control. Solomon wrote about this in Ecclesiastes:

> *The race is not to the swift*
>   *or the battle to the strong,*
> *nor does food come to the wise*
>   *or wealth to the brilliant*
>   *or favor to the learned;*
> *but time and chance happen to them all.*
>
> *Ecclesiastes 9:11*

Life happens to us without our permission. It is harsher to those who don't apply wisdom on a daily basis, but even the wise do not escape the vulnerability and fragility of life in a fallen world. Here the wise person emerges the victor by how they respond to what life throws at them.

Then there is God working from the Upper Story interceding in our lives. God honors those who align their lives to the bigger story he is writing. That is why Proverbs tells us:

> *The fear of the LORD is the beginning of wisdom.*
>
> *Proverbs 9:10*

The journey to our best life begins with taking God seriously. Solomon made a lot of great Lower Story decisions but ultimately failed at the bigger Upper Story decisions—he let his many wives lead him to worship other gods. At the end of Solomon's life, he reflected and came to this conclusion:

> *Now all has been heard;*
> *here is the conclusion of the matter:*
> *Fear God and keep his commandments,*
> *for this is the duty of all mankind.*
> *For God will bring every deed into judgment,*
> *including every hidden thing,*
> *whether it is good or evil.*
>
> *Ecclesiastes 12:13–14*

We would be wise to heed his advice!

GOD'S STORY . . . MY STORY

1. As you read through the entire book of Proverbs this week, identify at least one proverb a day that speaks the loudest to you.

2. Who in your life embodies wisdom? Tell them.

3. How good are you at receiving counsel and constructive criticism from others? Do you think you could improve in this area?

4. Identify a time in your life where you made a wise decision. What was the outcome?

5. Identify a time in your life where you made an unwise decision. What was the outcome?

SHARE THE STORY

Review the first two movements of the story from memory. Then fill in the blanks for the third movement—**The Story of Jesus**. See page 11 for help.

Jesus left the _____ Story to come down into our _____ Story to be with us and provide the _____ for us to be made _____ with God. Through _____ in Christ's work on the _____, we can now overturn _____ choice and have a personal _____ with God.

A Tale of Two Kings

The Story of Israel

REHOBOAM AND JEROBOAM

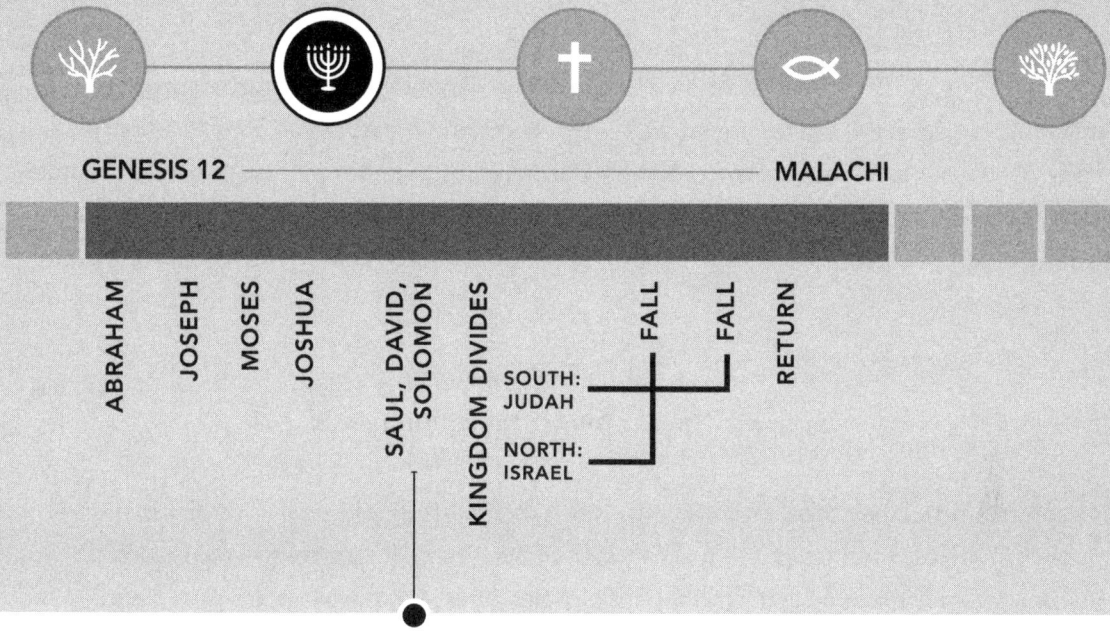

GENESIS 12 ——————————————— MALACHI

ABRAHAM
JOSEPH
MOSES
JOSHUA
SAUL, DAVID, SOLOMON
KINGDOM DIVIDES
SOUTH: JUDAH
NORTH: ISRAEL
FALL
FALL
RETURN

🎵 **READ THE STORY** | Follow this reading guide if you want to pace yourself this week:

◯ Day 1: 1 Kings 11:1–13

◯ Day 2: 1 Kings 12

◯ Day 3: 1 Kings 13

◯ Day 4: 1 Kings 14:1–20

◯ Day 5: 1 Kings 14:21–31

A VIEW FROM THE LOWER STORY

As Solomon approached the end of his reign over Jerusalem, two new characters entered the scene, whose names couldn't be much more confusing or fun to say out loud— Jeroboam and Rehoboam.

During this season of Israel's story, God's reflection was becoming distorted, which meant Israel was about to be disciplined, and it started with Jeroboam, one of Solomon's officials.

After Solomon died, his son Rehoboam became king. Apparently, Solomon accumulated much of his wealth the old-fashioned way—high taxes and forced labor. Thus, the first Tea Party. Jeroboam and a huge crowd of angry citizens went to Rehoboam and asked for a little relief. King Rehoboam, ignoring the council of elderly men and embracing the counsel of younger men, replied, "You ain't seen nothing yet." Jeroboam and his many followers then said, "We're outta here."

As a general rule—
experience speaks louder than enthusiasm.

They retreated to their tribal regions in the north and made Jeroboam king over all of Israel since they represented ten of the twelve tribes of the nation. Rehoboam remained king, but only over his tribe of Judah and the tribe of Benjamin. What was once a proud and prosperous nation was now a divided kingdom—Israel to the north and Judah to the south.

From a Lower Story point of view, it appeared the nation of Israel was divided because of the immature response of Solomon's son Rehoboam.

A VIEW FROM THE UPPER STORY

From the Upper Story point of view, we learn that the division came as a part of God's plan. Lower Story logic tells us that Rehoboam should have launched a massive battle against the northern rebel kingdom. He was just about to do that when God stepped in and offered a glimpse into his Upper Story plan with these four simple words, "This is my doing" (1 Kings 12:24). It was as if he was saying, "I was behind this from the beginning. I knew you would heed the advice of your yes-men instead of that of your father's wise elders. I knew Jeroboam would rebel against you. And I knew you would do everything in your power to bring your divided kingdom back together. But it's in my control, not yours. So go home. Your role in this story is just about over."

If God indeed did this—if he orchestrated it all along—the question remains, Why? We need to go back to the story of Solomon. Due to Solomon's repeated disobedience, God said to him:

"Since this is your attitude and you have not kept my covenant and my decrees, which I commanded you, I will most certainly tear the kingdom away from you and give it to one of your subordinates. Nevertheless, for the sake of David your father, I will not do it during your lifetime. I will tear it out of the hand of your son. Yet I will not tear the whole kingdom from him, but will give him one tribe for the sake of David my servant and for the sake of Jerusalem, which I have chosen."

1 Kings 11:11–13

If you want to sum up God's message in a short phrase, it is this: I keep my word.

Solomon's disobedience would have given God just cause to scrap the whole plan. But God promised David that his tribe—the tribe of Judah—would be established forever. Why? Because in God's plan to invite us back to him out of his insatiable love for us, Jesus the Messiah would come from the line of David, and he will reign forever as the King of kings. Because of David's great love for God, the perfect community God is building will be traced backed to David's tribe. None of the twelve tribes deserved to be used by God, but to keep his promise, God zeroed in on just the tribe of Judah as we move forward.

God always keeps his promises.

GOD'S STORY . . . MY STORY

1. Read 1 Kings 11:1–13 and Deuteronomy 5:8–10. Poor decisions don't just affect us but can affect up to four generations after us. In what way does this motivate you to monitor your decisions?

2. Deuteronomy 5:10 tells us that our devotion to God unleashes his love to a thousand generations. In what way does this motivate you to monitor your decisions?

3. Read 1 Kings 12:1–15. Who do you listen to for advice on making critical decisions in your life?

4. Read 1 Kings 12:15, 24. Even though people acted on their own free will, God knew this and used it to advance his Upper Story plan. Do you think God is still doing this today? Can you think of any examples?

5. Read 1 Kings 14:21–24. Rehoboam ended up not being any better than Jeroboam and yet God continued to advance his Upper Story plan through the tribe of Judah from his unconditional promise to David. This feels like the promises of God on our lives through Jesus. Even though we continue to fall short, he doesn't abandon us. Write out a word of gratitude for his great love for us.

SHARE THE STORY

Review the first three movements of the story from memory. See page 11 for help.

Mulligans

The Story of Israel

JONAH

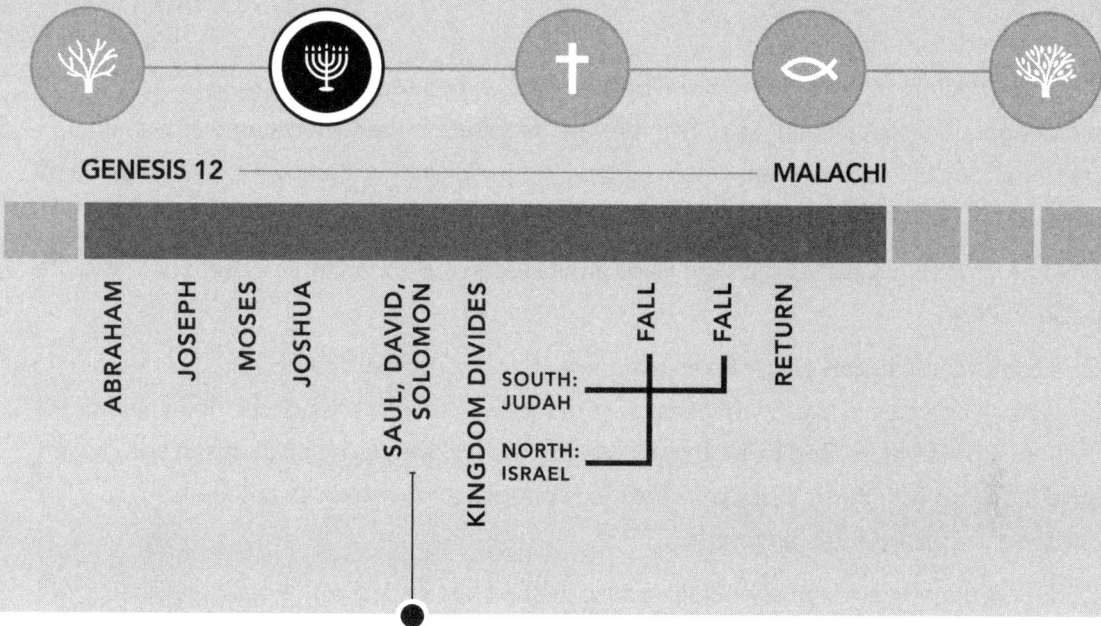

GENESIS 12 ———————————————— MALACHI

ABRAHAM | JOSEPH | MOSES | JOSHUA | SAUL, DAVID, SOLOMON | KINGDOM DIVIDES | SOUTH: JUDAH | NORTH: ISRAEL | FALL | FALL | RETURN

READ THE STORY | Follow this reading guide if you want to pace yourself this week:

○ Day 1: Jonah 1

○ Day 2: Jonah 2

○ Day 3: Jonah 3

○ Day 4: Jonah 4

○ Day 5: Matthew 12:38–41

A VIEW FROM THE LOWER STORY

In the game of golf, a mulligan is an informal term for a do-over or a second shot after a poor first shot, without the first shot counting against the score. It's not a part of the official rules of golf, but it is sure a welcome offer.

This is exactly what is happening in our story today. The nation of Israel was divided due to their repeated disobedience, particularly by King Solomon—the ten tribes of Israel to the north and the two tribes of Judah to the south.

God passionately wanted them to turn back to him, so he raised up prophets to be his messengers. Someone counted sixty-three total prophets in the Old Testament. Sixteen stand out. Jonah is one of them whom God called to deliver his message to the kingdom of Israel to the north.

Most prophets were not liked by the kings and leaders, but Jonah, to the contrary, was quite popular. Why?

God came to Jonah and gave him an assignment he did not want to do. God wanted him to head north and east to the city of Nineveh, the capital of the evil Assyrian Empire, and urge them to repent before God brought massive judgment down upon them. Jonah didn't want anything to do with these despicably nefarious people, and he didn't want them to have any chance of avoiding God's judgment.

Of course, Jonah decided he wouldn't go, so instead he headed in the opposite direction. He jumped on a ship on his way to a place called Tarshish. It was believed in that day that Tarshish was a place outside of the presence of God. On his way there, God caused a turbulent storm to break out, and the other men on the boat didn't want to participate in God's discipline of Jonah, so they threw him overboard.

From here, Jonah was swallowed by a great fish where he would spend three days and three nights, which modern science has determined is completely possible. You might call it his "come to Jesus" meeting. Jonah was vomited back on the shore facing Nineveh. God offered Jonah a mulligan—a do-over—to reconsider his answer. This time, he went.

When he got to Nineveh he preached a sermon with just seven words: "Forty more days and Nineveh will be overthrown" (Jonah 3:4). Without hesitation, the king and everyone in Nineveh believed. So, God changed his mind. God also offered the people of Nineveh a mulligan, a second chance.

> **Out of God's love for us, he often presents us with a mulligan.**

But this ticked Jonah off. Here is his reply to God:

> *"Isn't this what I said, LORD, when I was still at home? That is what I tried to forestall by fleeing to Tarshish. I knew that you are a gracious and compassionate God, slow to anger and abounding in love . . . . Now LORD, take away my life, for it is better for me to die than to live."*
>
> *Jonah 4:2-3*

Jonah did not want to go home as the guy who prevented Nineveh from getting what was rightfully coming to them. On this day, however, he got a massive lesson on the extent of God's love for all people.

A VIEW FROM THE UPPER STORY

From the Upper Story perch God is moving the plot along. We are getting closer and closer to the arrival of the promised Messiah. A gift of intense love for his people.

But as we look in the gospel of Matthew, we see that this story is providing an Upper Story clue of what is to come. When the people of Jesus' day asked for a sign that he was the promised Messiah, he replied,

> *"A wicked and adulterous generation asks for a sign! But none will be given it except the sign of the prophet Jonah. For as Jonah was three days and three nights in the belly of a huge fish, so the Son of Man will be three days and three nights in the heart of the earth."*
>
> *Matthew 12:39-40*

Jonah's story is the first hint Jesus gives of his coming death and resurrection.

Jonah's "death and resurrection" led to the turning of evil people to the Lord. Jonah was a sign of a greater one coming who would provide the way for the entire world, regardless of what they had done, to return to God forever. Oh, what love!

GOD'S STORY . . . MY STORY

1. Read Jonah 1 and Psalm 139:7–12. Jonah thought there was a place that was outside of the presence of God. Do you sometimes believe there is such a place?

2. Read Jonah 2. Sometimes God can't get our attention until he puts us on our back, takes us out of the game, or has us swallowed by a great fish. Have you ever been in a place where God finally got your attention? What did you do?

3. Read Jonah 3. Do you think there are people today who are beyond receiving God's love and forgiveness? What if God called you to go talk to them? Which direction would you head? What do you think about God changing his mind?

4. Read Jonah 4. What do you think of the object lesson God provided for Jonah with the shade tree? Do you believe God's love extends even to you? God offers us all a mulligan. Will we take it?

5. Read Matthew 12:38–40. What do you think of Jesus as a modern-day Jonah who has brought us the message of salvation if we will just turn to him?

SHARE THE STORY

Share the first three movements of the story with five people this week. See page 11 for help.

Crazy Love

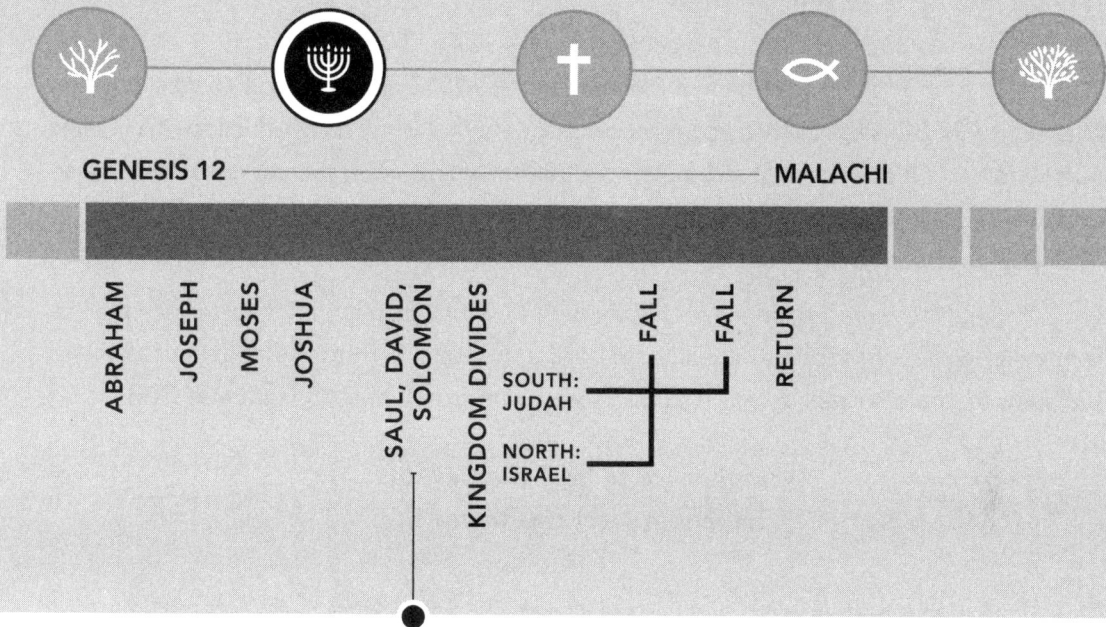

GENESIS 12 —————————————————————————— MALACHI

ABRAHAM JOSEPH MOSES JOSHUA SAUL, DAVID, SOLOMON KINGDOM DIVIDES SOUTH: JUDAH NORTH: ISRAEL FALL FALL RETURN

※ **READ THE STORY** | Follow this reading guide if you want to pace yourself this week:

○ Day 1: Hosea 1

○ Day 2: Hosea 3

○ Day 3: Hosea 4

○ Day 4: Hosea 11

○ Day 5: Hosea 14

A VIEW FROM THE LOWER STORY

On April 10, 1912, the British passenger liner called the *Titanic* took off on its maiden voyage from England to New York City. Four days later the ship hit an iceberg. At 2:20 a.m. on the fifth day it sank to the bottom of the Atlantic Ocean, claiming the lives of 1,519 of the 2,224 passengers.

Here's the tragedy: They received warnings of the iceberg on several occasions but decided to ignore them. The *Titanic*'s operator was focused on getting passengers' messages out. He sent this reply to the *Californian* operator: "Shut up. Shut up. I am busy."

What happened to the passengers of the *Titanic* in AD 1912 also happened to the kingdom of Israel in 722 BC. With all the success and prosperity that Israel enjoyed for so many years, no one thought it could sink. It did, but not without warning. Over the course of 208 years, God, out of his intense love for Israel, sent nine prophets to warn them of the upcoming "iceberg" that was going to destroy them if they continued in the direction they were going.

For 208 years, he waited patiently for his children to return, but he didn't wait passively. He sent messengers, or prophets, to call them back to his ways. These messengers used their bullhorns to implore Israel to return to God's ways and trust him as the one true God.

We, too, need to heed the warnings of impending icebergs in our life.

One of the nine prophets was a guy named Hosea. God asked him to do something in the Lower Story that didn't make much sense. He asked Hosea to marry a prostitute. And he did. Her name was Gomer. At first you might think this is a story of where Gomer, overwhelmed by the love of Hosea, turned her life around. That is not what happened. She continued her promiscuous evening escapades. Jewish law would give him the right to divorce her, but he didn't. Under the instruction of God, he continued to support Gomer.

One day God told Hosea to find his wife and show her that he still loved her. Hosea headed down to the dingy office building and handed over some money to the "office manager" just so he could talk to her. When Gomer heard a knock on her door and opened it, planning to give her next customer a seductive look, she must have been stunned to see her husband. Before she could say anything, he whispered, "Oh, Gomer, I love you more than you will ever know. Please come home with me."

Curiously, we never learn from the Bible if Hosea and Gomer lived happily ever after. That is not the point of the story.

A VIEW FROM THE UPPER STORY

What is going on in the Upper Story? I think God wanted to use Hosea's example to show us how far God himself is willing to go to reclaim those who have turned against him. Read what this prophet says to Israel, and see if you can catch the parallels:

> Hear the word of the LORD, you Israelites,
>   because the LORD has a charge to bring
>   against you who live in the land:
> "There is no faithfulness, no love,
>   no acknowledgment of God in the land.
> There is only cursing, lying and murder,
>   stealing and adultery."

Hosea 4:1-2

> "Their deeds do not permit them
>   to return to their God.
> A spirit of prostitution is in their heart;
>   they do not acknowledge the LORD."

Hosea 5:4

> "Return, Israel, to the LORD your God.
>   Your sins have been your downfall!"

Hosea 14:1

The relationship of Hosea and Gomer mirrors God's relationship with Israel and with us. Despite their covenant with God, Israel had been unfaithful. They had pledged their loyalty to God but snuck out at night to worship other gods. God not only knew this, but he caught them in the act. And what did he say? *Come home.*

No matter what we have done, God will always invite us to come home.

Will we say, like the *Titanic* operator did, "Shut up. Shut up. I am busy," or will we all listen and make the necessary turn to avoid disaster?

GOD'S STORY . . . MY STORY

1. Read Hosea 1:1–3. What do you think of God asking Hosea to marry Gomer, the prostitute? Can you think of any modern-day examples of this?

2. Read Hosea 3:1–3. What does Hosea's continued support and love tell us about unconditional love? Have you ever continued to love someone after they hurt you? Has someone ever continued to love you after you hurt them?

3. Read Hosea 4. Look at the language God used against Israel and compare it to Hosea's relationship with Gomer. What was Israel doing to be unfaithful to God? What do we do today to be unfaithful to God?

4. Read Hosea 11. Can you feel the pain in God's voice as he talks about his love for Israel? Do you sense God loves you this much?

5. Read Hosea 14. Hosea was telling the people it is not too late to return to God. Have you ever had a time in your life when you turned back to God? Describe that journey. Do you know of someone who needs to turn back to God? Pray for them.

SHARE THE STORY

Review the first three movements of the story from memory. Next, read the fourth movement—**The Story of Church**. See page 11 for help.

Everyone who comes into a relationship with God through faith in Christ belongs to the new community God is building called the church. The church is commissioned to be the presence of Christ in the Lower Story—telling his story by the way we live and the words we speak. Every story of the church points people to the second coming of Christ, when he will return to restore God's original vision.

When God's Patience Runs Out

The Story of Israel
FALL OF ISRAEL

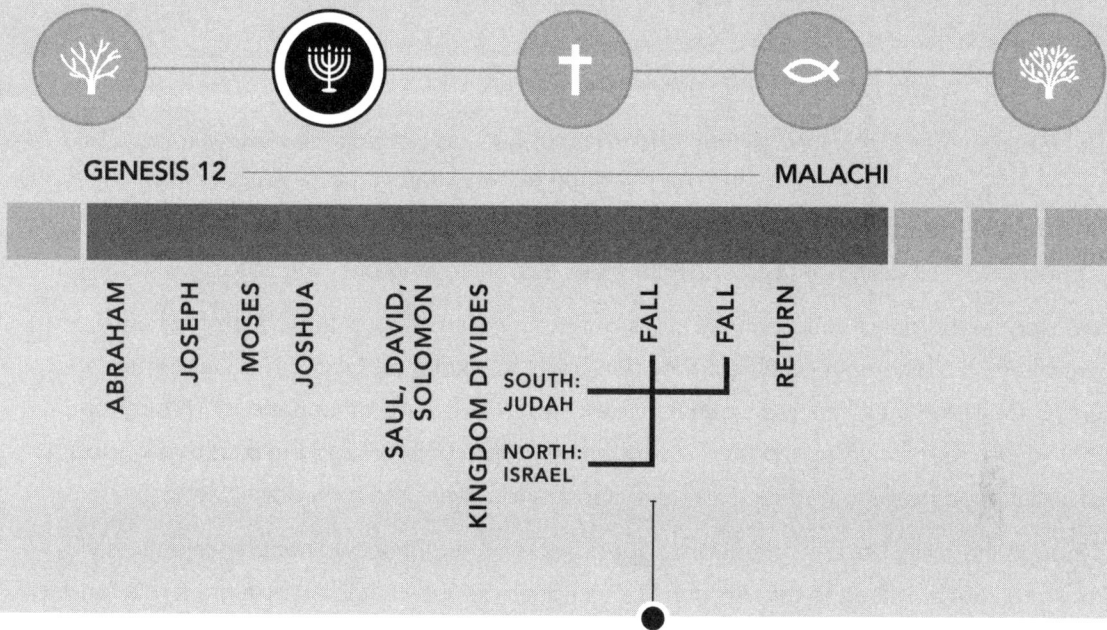

GENESIS 12 ———————————————————— MALACHI

ABRAHAM JOSEPH MOSES JOSHUA SAUL, DAVID, SOLOMON KINGDOM DIVIDES FALL FALL RETURN

SOUTH: JUDAH

NORTH: ISRAEL

❧ **READ THE STORY** | Follow this reading guide if you want to pace yourself this week:

○ Day 1: 2 Kings 17:1–23

○ Day 2: 2 Kings 17:24–41

○ Day 3: 2 Kings 18

○ Day 4: 2 Kings 19

○ Day 5: Isaiah 53

A VIEW FROM THE LOWER STORY

I discovered one morning watching *The Today Show* that George Washington turned down the opportunity to be king of America. But what if he had accepted? Who would be king today? I almost spilled coffee all over me when the face of a father and son I knew appeared on national television. They attended the church I pastored at the time. Their last name was . . . you guessed it . . . Washington, but I had never put the two together. The son spent the night at my house on many occasions and failed to mention he could have been my king.

This is how I would have led out in every conversation.

But George Washington refused the offer to become king because he wanted to avoid getting into the same situation that had brought the Pilgrims to the colonies in the first place. Perhaps it is best summed up by a motto set forth by the Committees of Correspondence just prior to the Revolutionary War: "No king but King Jesus."

We wonder if Israel, a nation whose kings got them into a heap of trouble, might have experienced a different outcome if they declared, "No king but God." This was certainly God's ideal plan they rejected when they demanded to be like other nations. Throughout 208 years under forty kings, both the northern kingdom of Israel and the southern kingdom of Judah repeatedly turned their backs on God, and it was time for a drastic action.

Through the prophets God warned, begged, and cajoled these two nations, relentlessly trying to convince then to turn from their wickedness so they could enjoy a great relationship with him. This is all God has ever wanted. In the Lower Story, both Israel and Judah couldn't resist worshiping all the gods of neighboring nations.

God dealt first with Israel to the north. He deployed the Assyrian Empire, one of the evilest and cruelest nations, to defeat and deport the ten tribes of Israel. This was the same group of people who around fifty years earlier repented and turned to God through the words of Jonah.

Let us be reminded that faith is only one generation away from extinction.

The Assyrians defeated Israel and deported them. Today the exiled ones are referred to as the lost tribes of Israel. They are essentially written out of the rest of the story.

So now all that was left of God's special nation was tiny Judah to the south. The king of Judah at the time of Israel's fall was Hezekiah. He was one of only five good kings of the forty. He removed all the idols left over from his evil predecessor and pointed his citizens to the one true God.

When Assyria came after them with an offer to surrender, Hezekiah refused. Instead, he fell to his knees and prayed these words: "Deliver us from [the king of Assyria's] hand, so that all the kingdoms of the earth may know that you alone, Lord, are God" (2 Kings 19:19).

As it turned out, there was no attack. The angel of the Lord entered the Assyrian camp just outside of Judah and killed 185,000 enemy soldiers.

You would think that after seeing what happened to Israel and the miraculous way in which God spared them from a similar fate, Judah would never have considered abandoning God and returning to idol worship. Well, when Hezekiah died and passed the throne to his son Manasseh, this is exactly what happened. Let us be reminded that faith is only one generation away from extinction.

A VIEW FROM THE UPPER STORY

The overarching theme of the Upper Story:

I love you and want you to be a
part of my perfect community, and all you
have to do is put me first in your life.

Judah just couldn't get there. So, God disciplined them with a tough love, as we will see in our next chapter. However, he doesn't eliminate them, because he promised, even in their disobedience, the Messiah would come from David, who was from the tribe of Judah.

Enter the prophet Isaiah. While Isaiah had many harsh things to say to Judah, he also told them they would not be held captive forever. He also revealed a glimpse into the Upper Story with these famous words of prophecy that spoke of the coming of Jesus. Read just one of the things he said from the Lord:

But he was pierced for our transgressions, he was crushed for our iniquities; the punishment that brought us peace was on him, and by his wounds we are healed.

Isaiah 53:5

GOD'S STORY . . . MY STORY

1. Read 2 Kings 17:1–23. List out all the things Israel did that caused God to exile them. All this took place over a 208-year period. What does this teach us about the love and patience of God?

2. Read 2 Kings 17:24–41. Do you sense God is still interacting with nations today as he did then? Be specific.

3. Read 2 Kings 18. Have you ever been bullied or threatened like King Hezekiah was by the King of Assyria, particularly for your faith or for doing the right thing? What would be your answer if someone challenged you by asking, "On what are you basing this confidence of yours" (18:19)?

4. Read 2 Kings 19. What inspires you about Hezekiah's response to this crisis? Can you imagine yourself doing the same thing? Why or why not?

5. Read Isaiah 53. Isaiah gave this prophecy seven hundred years before Jesus was born. He was signaling that there will be "no king but King Jesus." How many of these prophecies can you identify that were fulfilled by Jesus?

SHARE THE STORY

Review the first three movements of the story from memory. Then fill in the blanks for the fourth movement—**The Story of the Church**. See page 11 for help.

Everyone who comes into a relationship with God through faith in Christ belongs to the new community God is building called the _____. The church is commissioned to be the presence of Christ in the Lower Story—telling his story by the way we live and the words we speak. Every story of the church points people to the _____ coming of Christ, when he will return to restore God's original vision.

Humpty Dumpty Dilemma

The Story of Israel

FALL OF JUDAH

GENESIS 12 ———————————— MALACHI

ABRAHAM

JOSEPH

MOSES

JOSHUA

SAUL, DAVID, SOLOMON

KINGDOM DIVIDES

FALL

FALL

RETURN

SOUTH: JUDAH

NORTH: ISRAEL

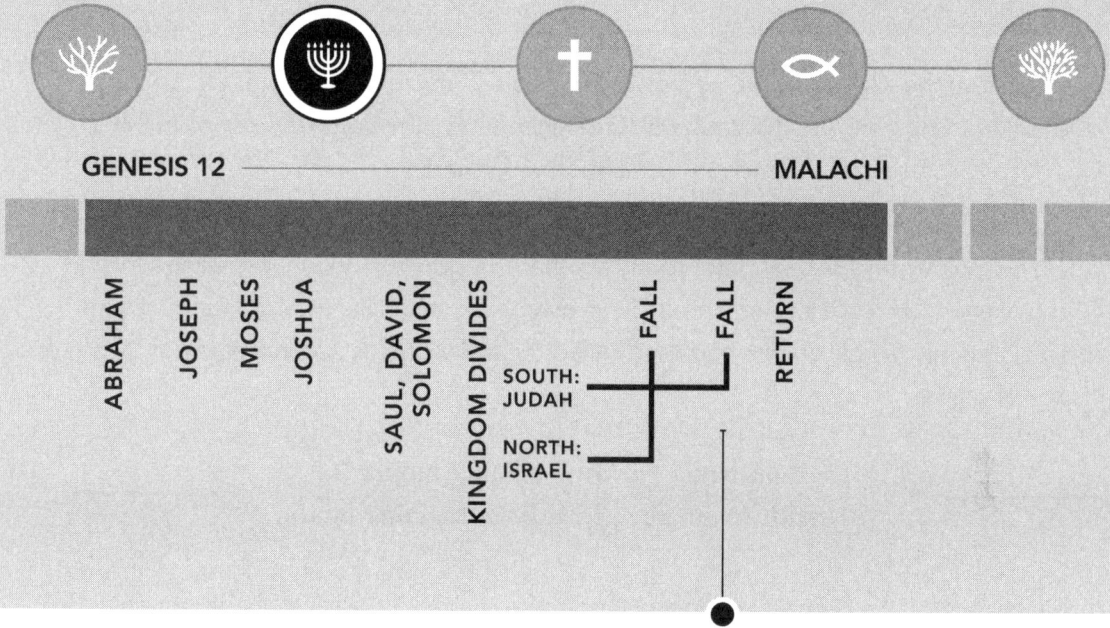

READ THE STORY | Follow this reading guide if you want to pace yourself this week:

◯ Day 1: 2 Kings 23:1–35

◯ Day 2: 2 Kings 23:36–24:20

◯ Day 3: 2 Kings 25

◯ Day 4: Habakkuk 1

◯ Day 5: Jeremiah 29:1–14

A VIEW FROM THE LOWER STORY

If you are familiar with the classic nursery rhyme, say it out loud with me:

Humpty Dumpty sat on a wall

Humpty Dumpty had a great fall

All the king's horses and all the king's men

Couldn't put Humpty Dumpty together again

Some believe the alleged fragile egg of a man who fell off the wall and was cracked and crushed was a reference to the defeat of King Richard III in the Battle of Boswell in 1485. This defeat represented the end of the Plantagenet Dynasty.

This is precisely what happened to the northern kingdom of Israel in our last chapter and would happen again 136 years later to the southern kingdom of Judah. Hezekiah's trust in God prevented the evil Assyrian Empire from overtaking them like they did the kingdom of Israel. But now a new empire had risen called the Babylonians. Judah would not be so "lucky" this time.

> ### Sometimes our disobedience makes it difficult to put the pieces back together again.

Nebuchadnezzar, the Babylonian king, waged three campaigns against Judah from 605 BC to 586 BC. In the final campaign, Nebuchadnezzar defeated King Zedekiah (aka Humpty Dumpty). Thousands were deported from Jerusalem to Babylon, the temple was destroyed, and the city was burnt to the ground. This would signal the end of the dynasty of the kings of Israel.

A VIEW FROM THE UPPER STORY

This is how things looked from the Lower Story, but there is much more going on from the Upper Story. The prophet Habakkuk asked God about Judah's evil behavior:

> *How long, LORD, must I call for help, but you do not listen? Or cry out to you, "Violence!" but you do not save? Why do you make me look at injustice? Why do you tolerate wrongdoing?*
>
> *Habakkuk 1:2-3*

God answered with a chilling response:

"Look at the nations and watch—and be utterly amazed. For I am going to do something in your days that you would not believe, even if you were told. I am raising up the Babylonians, that ruthless and impetuous people, who sweep across the whole earth to seize dwellings not their own."

Habakkuk 1:5-6

God orchestrated all this from the Upper Story. God used all the characters in the Lower Story to achieve his Upper Story plan—even evil people.

The question is why. Why would God do this to a people he loved?

The answer is really no more complicated than why parents discipline their children whom they love. Some parents must finally say about their child what God finally had to say about Judah: "There was no remedy" (2 Chronicles 36:16). They are forced to exile their children in the hope of restoring them to health and purpose. God was doing the same to Judah. He waited 444 years in hopes they would turn toward the good, but Judah left God with no remedy.

But God was going to bring them back home. He must. He made an unconditional promise to David that the Messiah would come from his family. God made this promise to the exiled children of Judah:

"When seventy years are completed for Babylon, I will come to you and fulfill my good promise to bring you back to this place. For I know the plans I have for you," declares the LORD, "plans to prosper you and not to harm you, plans to give you hope and a future. Then you will call on me and come and pray to me, and I will listen to you. You will seek me and find me when you seek me with all your heart."

Jeremiah 29:10-13

Just like parents disciplining their children, if they wait and don't give in, they might find their fortitude produces the good results they long for. The child's rebellious spirit most likely will break, much like Judah's. The light finally came on in the heads and hearts of Judah. They came to understand what we need to understand:

That tough love is just that—God's resilient love for us.

Judah's homecoming was an emotional event filled with the happiest tears one will ever see, like the tears and the joy that parents of a prodigal child will see when that child returns. This was God's plan for Judah. This is God's plan for us.

GOD'S STORY . . . MY STORY

1. Read 2 Kings 23:1–35. King Josiah turned Judah back to God during a dark season. In what ways does this inspire you with what is going on in the world today?

2. Read 2 Kings 21:1–16 and 24:1–4. What was the final straw that caused God to move forward on disciplining Judah? Do you see any parallels to what is happening today in our world?

3. Read 2 Kings 25. Can you think of a time when you were disciplined (by a parent, teacher, police officer) and it got you back on the right course?

4. Read Habakkuk 1. What do you think about God using evil people to accomplish his Upper Story plan? Do you sense that God is doing something like that today?

5. Read Jeremiah 1:1–10 and 29:1–4. Have you been able to discern the Upper Story plan and purpose that God has for your life?

SHARE THE STORY

Review the first three movements of the story from memory. Then fill in the blanks for the fourth movement—**The Story of the Church**. See page 11 for help.

Everyone who comes into a relationship with God through _____ in Christ belongs to the new community God is building called the _____. The church is commissioned to be the _____ of Christ in the Lower Story— telling his story by the way we live and the words we speak. Every story of the church points people to the _____ coming of Christ, when he will return to restore God's original vision.

Faith in a Foreign Land

The Story of Israel
DANIEL

GENESIS 12 ———————————————— MALACHI

ABRAHAM

JOSEPH

MOSES

JOSHUA

SAUL, DAVID, SOLOMON

KINGDOM DIVIDES

SOUTH: JUDAH

NORTH: ISRAEL

FALL

FALL

RETURN

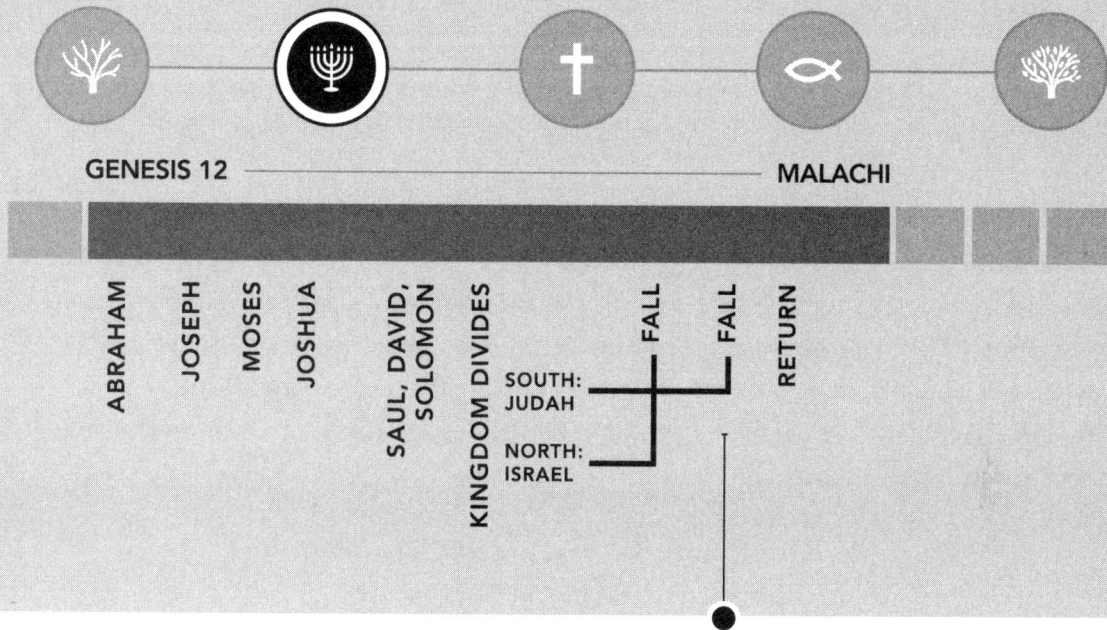

❧ **READ THE STORY** | Follow this reading guide if you want to pace yourself this week:

◯ Day 1: Daniel 1

◯ Day 2: Daniel 2:1–48

◯ Day 3: Daniel 3

◯ Day 4: Daniel 6

◯ Day 5: Daniel 12

A VIEW FROM THE LOWER STORY

Judah was enslaved by the pagan nation because of their obstinate disobedience to God. Their city, Jerusalem, and their temple were turned to rubble. Most of their citizens were deported to Babylon. What does any nation do when they capture thousands of people and bring them into their country as prisoners? Put them to work. The king recognized the talent of some of these new deportees and handpicked the best and brightest to serve him as special advisers. Enter Daniel and his three friends—Shadrach, Meshach, and Abednego. They were groomed for three years to serve by the king's side.

Brought into the king's house, they were to be fed the finest foods and wine, but Daniel and his friends, being sure a portion of the king's meat and wine had been offered to the gods of this strange land, refused to eat from the king's pantry. Instead, they requested to eat only vegetables and drink merely water. Mortified this would literally be the death of Daniel, the king's official begged him to eat the royal food and wine, but Daniel offered a compromise. They would eat their vegetarian diet for ten days and then see if Daniel and his friends were weaker than the other men. After the trial period the men who were on the "Daniel Diet" were healthier and more fit than any of the men who ate the royal cuisine. The new official diet for all the men in the king's court became vegetables and water, which I am sure made them all very happy . . . not!

> ### *Like Daniel, we, too, are called to live distinctively different lives in our modern-day Babylon.*

Daniel not only became stronger physically but also grew in favor with the king. One night King Nebuchadnezzar had a dream he wanted interpreted, but all the king's men could not interpret the dream for him because the king put forth an impossible test. He wanted the men not only to interpret the dream, but to tell the king what his dream was. God gave Daniel the ability to do exactly that! Unbelievable? For men, yes—but not for God!

When King Nebuchadnezzar built a ninety-foot statue of himself, he required everyone in the kingdom to bow down to it or risk being thrown into a fiery furnace. Shadrach, Meshach, and Abednego refused. Into the furnace they went! Not one hair was singed on their heads nor their clothes scorched. Nebuchadnezzar looked in and saw four men instead of the three he had thrown into the furnace walking around unscathed. When they came out of the fire there was not even the smell of smoke on them. Nebuchadnezzar exuberantly exclaimed that no one should speak ill of their God.

Daniel's life spanned the reigns of three different kings. No doubt you have heard of Daniel standing up to the great King Darius who also wished for his subjects to pray only to him. Daniel continued to pray to God openly and was found out and reported. The king had him thrown into the den of lions for such insubordination. But Darius liked Daniel. He could not sleep wondering if Daniel's God would save him. Darius woke and rushed to find out if Daniel's God had rescued him. He found him not only alive but without one scratch. A decree went out from Darius that all the kingdom should now fear and revere the God of Daniel.

A VIEW FROM THE UPPER STORY

The Upper Story reveals Israel is in a divine "time-out." Even during this time of exile, God spoke through Daniel as a prophet to the Israelites about their future—and to ours as well (Daniel 9:9–11). His prophecies brought hope and confidence to all God's people that, against all odds, he would keep his unconditional promises. Through lions' dens, fiery furnaces, and divine time-outs, God was always with them.

Remember how Nebuchadnezzar threw three men into the furnace, but when he looked, he saw a fourth? That fourth person was none other than Jesus himself.

> *No matter how hot the flames get in life,*
> *Jesus will show up and see you through it.*

As believers we, too, are in exile in a foreign land, but God is with us through the fiery trials we find ourselves in. Daniel's prophecies reinforce a very important transgenerational principle. God's love for us has compelled him to create an eternal home for us that is much better than the world we live in right now. He longs to come down and live with us forever. One of Daniel's prophecies enlightens us to the fact that those whose names are found written in the Book of Life will be delivered to live eternally with God (Daniel 12:1–4; Revelation 21:27).

GOD'S STORY . . . MY STORY

1. Do you find it hard to resist the temptation to fit in with the culture of today's world? Be specific.

2. Have you had an experience where someone asked you to do something against God's principles and you had to refuse (perhaps peer pressure, a boss, a coworker, a "friend")?

3. What are some things you can do to bolster your courage in following God?

4. How does knowing how God's story ends affect how you live today?

5. Does the prophecy at the end of Daniel bring you hope and faith that God has you no matter what? Do you believe your name is written in the Book of Life? Why or why not?

SHARE THE STORY

Review the first three movements of the story from memory. Then fill in the blanks for the fourth movement—**The Story of the Church**. See page 11 for help.

_____ who comes into a relationship with God through _____ in Christ belongs to the new community God is building called the _____. The church is commissioned to be the _____ of Christ in the Lower Story—telling his story by the way we live and the words we speak. Every story of the _____ points people to the _____ coming of Christ, when he will return to restore God's original vision.

Homecoming

The Story of Israel

JUDAH'S RETURN FROM EXILE

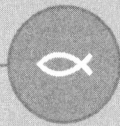

GENESIS 12 ——————————————————— MALACHI

ABRAHAM | JOSEPH | MOSES | JOSHUA | SAUL, DAVID, SOLOMON | KINGDOM DIVIDES | FALL | FALL | RETURN

SOUTH: JUDAH

NORTH: ISRAEL

🌿 **READ THE STORY** | Follow this reading guide if you want to pace yourself this week:

◯ Day 1: Ezra 1

◯ Day 2: Ezra 3

◯ Day 3: Ezra 4–5

◯ Day 4: Ezra 6

◯ Day 5: Haggai 1–2

A VIEW FROM THE LOWER STORY

C. S. Lewis once wrote,

> *"Put first things first and we get second things thrown in; put second things first and we lose both first and second things."*[4]

4   C. S. Lewis, *The Collected Letters of C.S. Lewis, Volume 3: Narnia, Cambridge and Joy, 1950–1963,* ed. Walter Hooper, (HarperOne, 2007), 111.

That is what our story is all about today.

The children of Israel passed through seventy winters in Babylonian exile. Their city was razed; their beloved temple was ransacked. Except for the courage of Daniel and his three friends, the era would have been a completely shameful one. But after seven decades of darkness, a tunnel of sunlight pierced the clouds and surprised the people.

In 538 BC, fifty thousand Jews, funded by King Cyrus of the Persian Empire, made the nine-hundred-mile trek from Babylon to Jerusalem and got to work. God's big thing became their big thing, and they rolled up the sleeves of their robes and began building the temple.

One thing we know for sure is that whenever you attempt something big for God, you can always count on opposition, and that is exactly what happened as they began to build the temple. Dissenters tried everything they could to block their efforts, but God's chosen people maintained their resolve—at least for a few years. Then it started to happen. Little by little, they lost their focus. They began to turn less attention to the house of God and more attention to their own personal projects.

*God's big thing had become
a small thing to his people.*

For sixteen years, the temple project sat untouched! It turned into an abandoned construction site—enough time for the weeds and the grass to grow up over the footers of the foundation. Enough time for all the surrounding nations to look at the temple and think, *Well, they sure don't take their God very seriously.* Enough time for a whole generation of children to grow up and look at the abandoned project and think, *Well, I guess our parents don't care much about the temple.*

A VIEW FROM THE UPPER STORY

From the Upper Story, we realize it was God behind it all. It was God's plan all along to prompt King Cyrus to facilitate and fund the temple project. Remember Isaiah? About one hundred years earlier, we are told that God would raise Cyrus up and make him a strong leader even though he did not believe in the one true God. Isaiah even called Cyrus "the [Lord's] anointed," which is the same as calling him a messiah (Isaiah 45:1).

The temple is a physical place that reminds us that God wants to enter into our Lower Story to be with us. Physical presence brings great comfort. Every time anyone walked past the temple, they were reminded that God wanted to be right there with them. He wants to be in the neighborhood. The temple reminded them that God wanted to be with his people.

So, God sent them a message through the prophet Haggai:

> *Now this is what the LORD Almighty says: "Give careful thought to your ways. You have planted much, but harvested little. You eat, but never have enough. You drink, but never have your fill. You put on clothes, but are not warm. You earn wages, only to put them in a purse with holes in it."*
>
> *Haggai 1:5-6*

> *God's message to Israel through Haggai, and his message to you, is, "I won't stay in anyone's closet. I want to be there with you, wherever you are, whatever you're doing."*

He loves us too much to leave us to our own devices. So, he pulls us aside for a heart-to-heart chat. He asks us to give careful thought to our ways and get his work accomplished. Amazingly, this is just what the Jews did. The Lord stirred up the leadership and the people got to work on the house of God. And they finished it. And God was once again living and dwelling among the people.

Back to C. S. Lewis's quote: "Put first things first and we get second things thrown in; put second things first and we lose both first and second things."[5] This is a paraphrase from the teaching of Jesus: "But seek first his kingdom and his righteousness, and all these things will be given to you as well" (Matthew 6:33). When we put God's Upper Story plan first, it is amazing how he adds in all the other things. When we don't, as we have seen through the story of Israel, we lose both.

What will it be for you?

---

5 Lewis, *Collected Letters of C.S. Lewis*, 3:111.

GOD'S STORY . . . MY STORY

1. Read Ezra 1. What do you think about God carrying out his Upper Story plan by using the hearts of people who don't believe in him? Have you ever witnessed this in your lifetime?

2. Read Ezra 3. The Israelites, after seventy years of being stuck, have positive momentum once again. Are you in a season right now where you feel you have good traction with God and the things he has called you to? Why or why not?

3. Read Ezra 4–5. Anything good or from God is going to experience opposition. Are you in a season where you are experiencing opposition right now? Where is it coming from and how is it keeping you down?

4. Read Ezra 6. There is nothing quite like crossing the finish line on a work that matters to God. What is something you hope to finish this year that will advance what God is calling you to do?

5. Read Haggai 1–2. How might you heed the message of Haggai right now by "[giving] careful thought to your ways" (1:5, 7)?

SHARE THE STORY

Review the first three movements of the story from memory. Then fill in the blanks for the fourth movement—**The Story of the Church**. See page 11 for help.

_____ who comes into a relationship with God through _____ in Christ belongs to the new community God is building called the _____. The church is commissioned to be the _____ of Christ in the Lower Story—telling his story by the way we live and the words we speak. Every story of the _____ points people to the _____ coming of Christ, when he will return to restore God's original _____.

The Hidden Star in the Scepter

The Story of Israel

ESTHER

GENESIS 12 ——————————— MALACHI

ABRAHAM

JOSEPH

MOSES

JOSHUA

SAUL, DAVID, SOLOMON

KINGDOM DIVIDES

SOUTH: JUDAH

NORTH: ISRAEL

FALL

FALL

RETURN

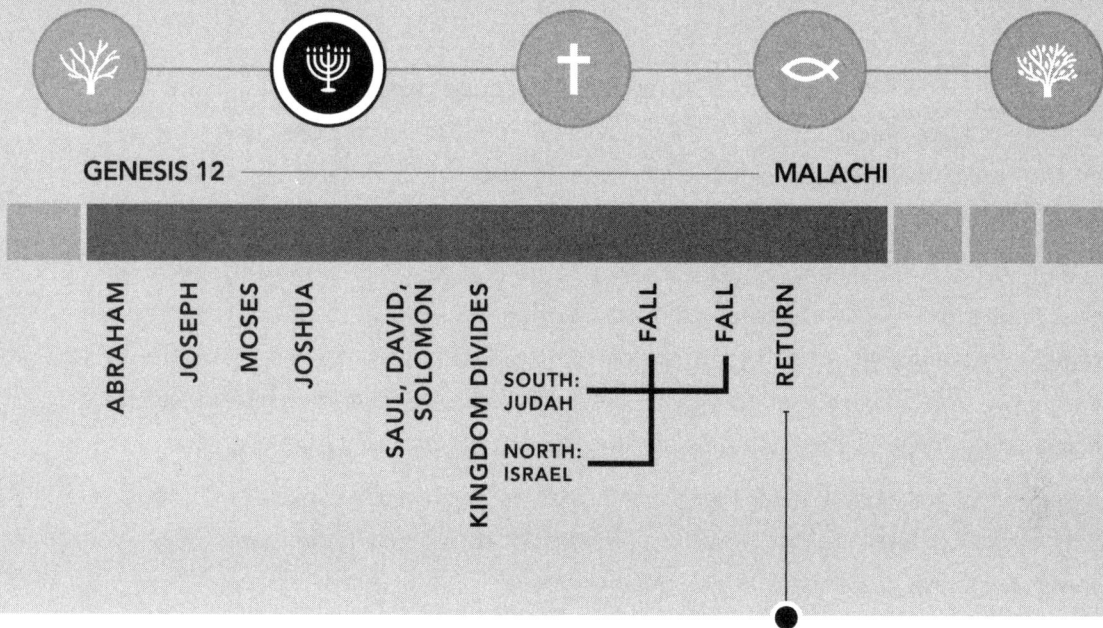

READ THE STORY | Follow this reading guide if you want to pace yourself this week:

○ Day 1: Esther 1–2

○ Day 2: Esther 3–4

○ Day 3: Esther 5–6

○ Day 4: Esther 7–8

○ Day 5: Esther 9–10

A VIEW FROM THE LOWER STORY

At first glance the story of Esther seems like a fairy tale, but a closer look reveals it is a story of faith and courage. Esther is our young heroine. Her Persian name means "star," or if you dig deeper to the root, satar, it means "hidden." This seems so fitting as Esther hid her nationality from King Xerxes and his court, along with the fact that God himself seems hidden in the book.

Disobedience to God led the Israelites into exile in Babylon under the rule of King Nebuchadnezzar. During the reign of Cyrus the Great, under Persian rule, the Jews were permitted to return to Jerusalem. Only about fifty thousand Jews returned. For whatever reason—old age, familiarity with the Babylonian lifestyle, or being born during the exile and not knowing Jerusalem as home—a portion remained. Esther's family is numbered among those.

Esther's faith kicked in early in life as she lost her parents at a young age and was raised by her cousin Mordecai. Mordecai was a good and righteous man. Esther was gathered up with the rest of the young girls to be added to King Xerxes' harem when his ex-wife, Queen Vashti, was exiled for not complying with the king's request to entertain his drunken male friends at his party. Mordecai told Esther to conceal her nationality from everyone.

It was love at first sight when the king met Esther (no joke!), and he made her his queen. Sounds like Cinderella to me! However, it is no coincidence that in the Lower Story a young Jewish girl found herself wearing the queen's crown.

With a literal roll of the dice, the tables turned, and Esther's good fortune seemed to end. A man named Haman was elevated to Xerxes' right hand. He was likely a descendant of Agag, king of the Amalekites, whose family God told King Saul to annihilate, but Saul did not (1 Samuel 15; Deuteronomy 25:17–19).

In his new position Haman decided everyone should bow down to him as he passed. Apparently, everyone did, except for Mordecai. Haman's anger burned against Mordecai, and Haman received permission from the king not just to kill Mordecai but all the Jews in the kingdom.

Neither Haman nor Xerxes knew Esther was a Jew. So, Haman literally rolled the dice to decide what month the massacre would happen. It was the month of Adar, eleven months from the time he rolled the dice. Every Jew would sit on death row for those eleven months. When Mordecai heard this, he approached Esther and told her she must save her people by going to the king. Immediately fear set in because no one approached the king who had not been summoned. But Mordecai reminded Esther that perhaps she was placed in the king's court "for such a time as this" (Esther 4:14).

Could it be that, like Esther, you are living right now because you were born for such a time as this?

To make matters worse, Xerxes had not called for Esther for thirty days. Remember Vashti? Esther did. It appeared her good luck may have run out!

A VIEW FROM THE UPPER STORY

"But God"—there is no other explanation for what happened next. While God's name is never mentioned in this book, his sovereignty and control show up on every page.

Esther did approach Xerxes after three days of fasting and prayer, and he held out his scepter to her, offering her up to half his kingdom. Whew! She asked to have dinner with the king and Haman, where she requested to have a second dinner with them. At the second dinner she exposed Haman's plot to destroy her and her people, revealing for the first time she was a Jew. The king was so upset he stormed out of the room. Haman stood up to plead for his life, but as luck would have it, he fell on top of Esther. When Xerxes returned, he assumed Haman was molesting the queen, so he declared Haman would die.

We may throw the dice, but the LORD determines how they fall.

Proverbs 16:33 NLT

Esther made one more request of the king: to overrule the decree of Haman to have the Jews annihilated. Xerxes, unable to reverse the decree, declared the Jews were allowed to defend themselves against the attack, and the Jews prevailed. Mordecai replaced Haman in the king's court. Again, God saved and protected his people and lineage that would provide our way back to God.

Remember Haman was a descendant of King Agag, whom King Saul kept alive against God's orders? Not only was Haman killed and hung on a pole originally meant for Mordecai, but Haman's ten sons were killed, ending the lineage of the Amalekites. Esther finished what Saul failed to do.

If we choose to ignore what God wants us to do in our Lower Story, he will bring someone to finish his Upper Story plan.

GOD'S STORY . . . MY STORY

1. Read Esther 2:1–4 and Esther 5:1–3. What do you think King Xerxes was feeling when it says his "fury had subsided, [and] he remembered Vashti"? Do you think it had anything to do with him later raising his scepter to Queen Esther when she approached him uninvited?

2. Read Esther 2:15–18. As a young girl, plucked from a life to which she would never return, Esther found a way to win "the favor of everyone." What feelings might Esther have had to overcome to pull this off? Would you have been able to do the same?

3. Read Esther 5:9–13. Have you discounted all the good things happening in your life because you were hung up on one negative situation as Haman was?

4. After reading the entire story, even though God's name is never mentioned, do you see God's hand in Esther's story? Do you see God still determining how the dice fall in your life?

SHARE THE STORY

Recite the first four movements of the story from memory. See page 11 for help.

On the Rebound

The Story of Israel

NEHEMIAH AND MALACHI

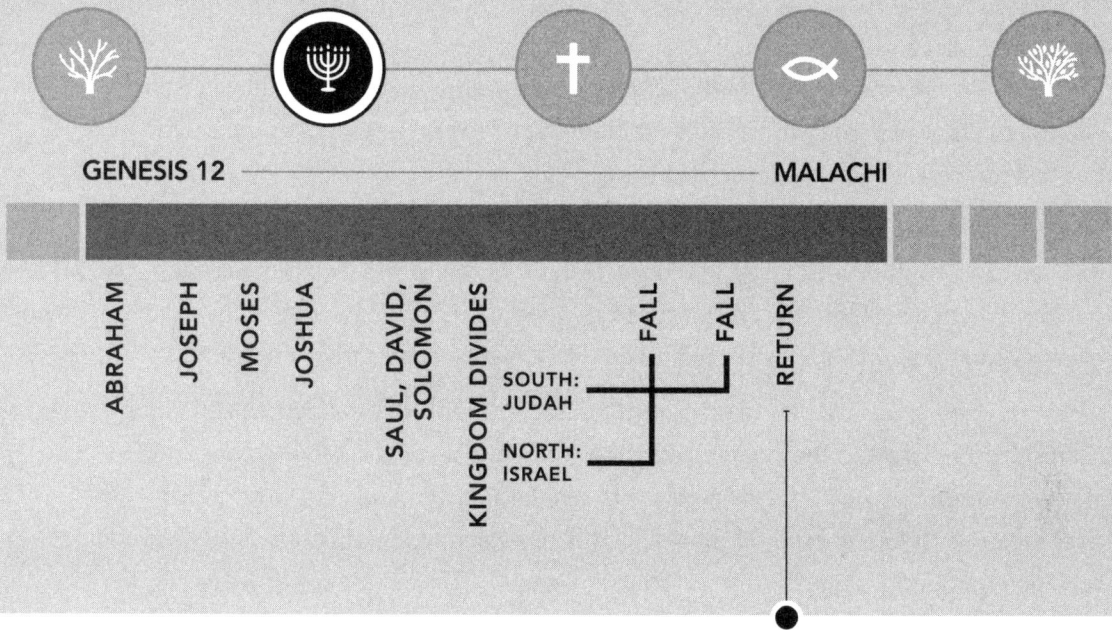

GENESIS 12 ——————————————— MALACHI

ABRAHAM
JOSEPH
MOSES
JOSHUA
SAUL, DAVID, SOLOMON
KINGDOM DIVIDES
SOUTH: JUDAH
NORTH: ISRAEL
FALL
FALL
RETURN

❧ **READ THE STORY** | Follow this reading guide if you want to pace yourself this week:

○ Day 1: Nehemiah 2

○ Day 2: Nehemiah 8–9

○ Day 3: Malachi 1–3

○ Day 4: Malachi 4

○ Day 5: Joel 2:28–32; Zephaniah 1:2–18

A VIEW FROM THE LOWER STORY

The Old Testament comes to an end with three building projects. There was the rebuilding of the temple under Zerubbabel—God again had a place to dwell among his people. Sacrifices were being made for their sins. Under much opposition and ridicule, the second rebuilding project was the wall around the city of Jerusalem under Nehemiah's leadership. The people now had protection from the bullies who taunted them on and off for years. But the third and most important rebuilding project was the reestablishment of their relationship with God. As evidence of the heart makeovers they were experiencing, they initiated an event that was not Zerubbabel's idea nor Nehemiah's idea. The people themselves initiated this restoration with God—as it should be.

The people realized it had been 140 years since they had heard anyone read God's word to them as God commanded through Moses (Deuteronomy 31:9–13). Spiritually famished and hungry to hear from God, they requested Ezra read the entire Book of the Law to them. This exercise served to refocus, recenter, and remind Israel of what is truly important.

When Ezra, the priest, began to read from the sacred book—from daybreak until noon—he shared God's story, and the people began to weep and mourn. As they listened to God's instructions for living well in community with him and each other, they were heartbroken over their past failure to obey. Nehemiah, who was standing near Ezra during the reading, saw their tremendous grief and shouted to the crowd, "Do not mourn or weep. . . . Go and enjoy choice food and sweet drinks. . . . Do not grieve, for the joy of the LORD is your strength" (Nehemiah 8:9–10).

> *We, too, when confronted with the mistakes of our past, need to grieve but not pitch a tent there so we can quickly move forward, for the joy of the Lord is our strength.*

As the people heard the law, they discovered important things they had put by the wayside. They no longer wanted to be those people. From this public reading of scripture, they realized the next major event on the Jewish calendar was the Festival of Tabernacles. Because it was coming quickly, they got after preparing for such an immense celebration. We are told, "From the days of Joshua . . . until that day, the Israelites had not celebrated [this festival] like this. And their joy was very great" (verse 17).

Their hearts were so transformed that they made no mention of reinstating a king. They had been there, done that! Now their desire was truly to have a relationship with God and to let him lead them. They wanted to align their Lower Story with God's Upper Story.

A VIEW FROM THE UPPER STORY

The last person to speak before the conclusion of the Old Testament was the prophet Malachi. Malachi foretold that God would be silent. It turned out he would be silent for four hundred years. This period is between the end of the Old Testament and the beginning of the New Testament. During this time there would be no prophetic word or revelation. This is known as the Intertestamental Period, or the Silent Years.

The next prophet to speak would be a "messenger, who will prepare the way" for the Promised One "whom you desire" (Malachi 3:1). He is referring to none other than John the Baptist. John would introduce us to the long-awaited Messiah—Jesus, the one who would love us back to God.

The primary role of Israel in telling God's Upper Story and pointing us to the first coming of Jesus has come to fruition.

While the Old Testament teaches us much about how God would have us live in our Lower Story world, these events are not unrelated stories with no connection, like the paintings in the Louvre. More like Michaelangelo's painting in the Sistine Chapel, these narratives come together as a beautiful mural to tell one grand story—the story of God's great love for us and the extent to which he will go to get us back. Although silent for four hundred years, he's not done yet!

GOD'S STORY . . . MY STORY

1. At the beginning of Malachi, the Israelites doubt God's love for them. What might have contributed to this feeling of rejection?

2. In the last few verses of Malachi, there is another prediction about Elijah, the prophet, returning before a great and dreadful day when the Lord comes. What do you think this is referring to? (Read Malachi 4:1–6 for a hint.)

3. Have you ever experienced a season in your life where you thought God was silent or felt far away, when you desperately wanted to hear from him?

4. Israel's best seasons were when they were aligning their Lower Story to God's Upper Story. What can you do to make sure your relationship with God stays strong and your life is aligning with his Upper Story?

5. Where is your heart in relationship to God right now? Are you more like the children of Israel before their captivity? Or more like their newfound desire to align their lives with God's Upper Story?

SHARE THE STORY

Share the first four movements of the story with five people this week. See page 11 for help.

The Birth of a Scandal

The Story of Jesus
JOSEPH

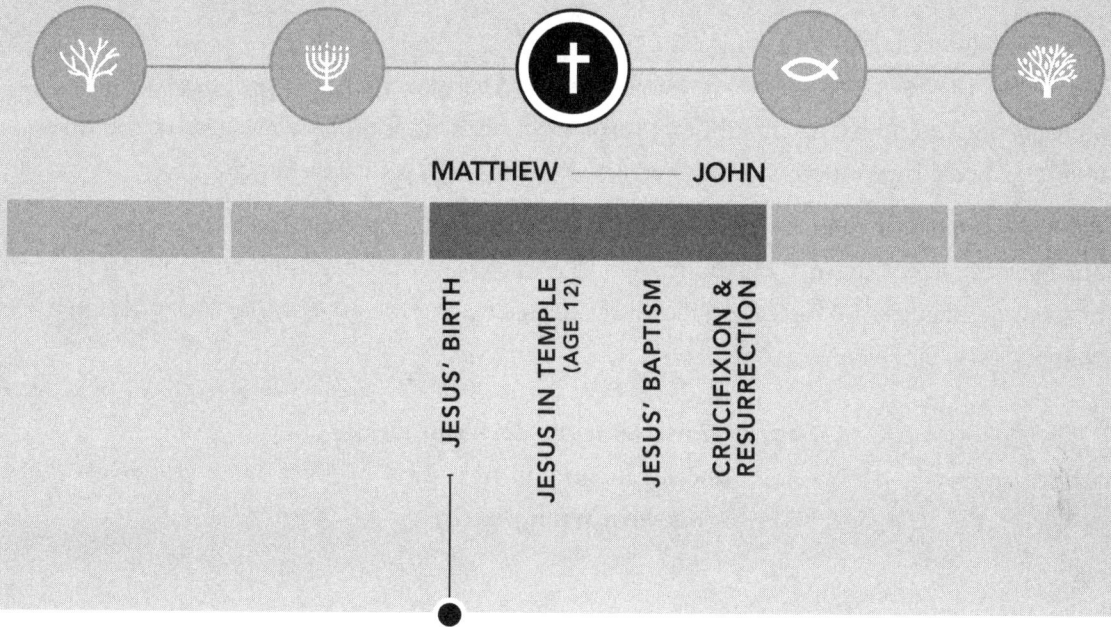

Timeline labels: JESUS' BIRTH · JESUS IN TEMPLE (AGE 12) · JESUS' BAPTISM · CRUCIFIXION & RESURRECTION

MATTHEW ——— JOHN

READ THE STORY | Follow this reading guide if you want to pace yourself this week:

○ Day 1: Matthew 1:1–17

○ Day 2: Matthew 1:18–25

○ Day 3: John 1:1–18

○ Day 4: Genesis 3:15; Isaiah 7:14

○ Day 5: Romans 5:15–21

A VIEW FROM THE LOWER STORY

Nine months is a long time to wait for a baby . . . but so is four hundred years.

That is how long God's people had to wait after the temple was built at the close of the Old Testament. Except they weren't waiting for a baby; they were looking for a king who would "reign on David's throne and over his kingdom" (Isaiah 9:7).

Instead, they got a scandal.

At least this was what it looked like in the Lower Story. A young couple—Joseph and Mary—were engaged to be married. Then Mary gave Joseph the news: "I'm pregnant." Put yourself in his shoes. You fall in love with a beautiful young woman. You propose to her, and she accepts. You have been taught that sex is a gift reserved for marriage, so you honor the love of your life by not sleeping with her. And then she tells you she is pregnant.

Most guys would be furious. They would accuse her of messing around with someone. But Joseph was decent about it. He didn't want to add to Mary's problems by getting mad at her, and he decided the best thing to do was to quietly end the relationship and move on with his life.

> *Just because someone does you wrong*
> *doesn't mean you have to*
> *do them wrong back.*

A VIEW FROM THE UPPER STORY

What he couldn't have known was that God sees things differently in the Upper Story.

> *What was a scandal to Joseph*
> *was a solution to God.*

Remember, God's Upper Story has one major theme: "I want to give you a way to come back to me so we can do life together." And Joseph has a major role to play in this plan. God could not let him get away, so he sent one of his angels to give him a glimpse of the Upper Story. In a dream, the angel told him,

> *"Joseph son of David, do not be afraid to take Mary home as your wife, because what is conceived in her is from the Holy Spirit. She will give birth to a son, and you are to give him the name Jesus, because he will save his people from their sins."*
>
> *Matthew 1:20–21*

And the part about the baby being conceived by the Holy Spirit—what's that all about? Remember we learned in the story of Cain and Abel that sin nature is transmitted to all Adam and Eve's offspring through the seed of the man—because of Adam and Eve's choice to disobey God, sin is in our DNA from conception.

That is why starting over with Noah's family didn't work. While Noah was truly a righteous man and really tried hard to do what was best, even he was a carrier of the virus. It is also why, no matter how hard you and I try to be good, we cannot succeed on our own. Sooner or later, sin wins out over our good intentions, separating us from God.

The promised Messiah, who would provide each of us a way back to God to live with him forever in perfect community, had to be free of this virus. Mary's child could not be given to her by any man—even a godly man like Joseph. The baby in Mary's womb had been placed there by the very Spirit of God.

> **What appears to be a scandal in the Lower Story was a solution to our scandal in the Upper Story.**

In what must be the first recorded sonogram, the angel told Joseph, "It's a boy!" and his name was to be Jesus—which means "the Lord saves." The Bible tells us:

> **All this took place to fulfill what the Lord had said through the prophet: "The virgin will conceive and give birth to a son, and they will call him Immanuel" (which means "God with us").**
>
> **Matthew 1:22-23**

What was happening to Mary was foretold by the prophet Isaiah seven hundred years earlier. Everything in the life and history of Israel had been pointing to Jesus' arrival—absolutely everything. Hope wrapped in God's love had finally arrived!

GOD'S STORY . . . MY STORY

1. Read Matthew 1:18–25. What would go through your mind when it dawned on you that you were to raise the Son of God?

2. In Matthew 1:25 we are told that Joseph didn't consummate his marriage to Mary until after Jesus was born. Why do you think God gave this instruction? How hard to you think this was for Joseph? How hard would it have been for you?

3. Read Ephesians 1:4–5. In New Testament times, it was the father's prerogative to name the child. When Joseph named Jesus, it signaled the adoption of Jesus as his legal son. Through Jesus we are now adopted as sons and daughters of God. How does this speak to your soul?

4. Read John 1:1–18. Why is what John told us here so important? The nature of Jesus' arrival made it hard for people to grasp who he was. What is the outcome for people who do grasp it?

5. Read Romans 5:15–21. Adam and Jesus are the only two men who entered our world without sin. What is the difference between them? What does this mean to you and me?

SHARE THE STORY

Review the first four movements of the story from memory. Next, read the fifth movement—**The Story of the New Garden**. See page 11 for help.

God will one day create a new earth and a new garden and once again come down to be with us. All who place their faith in Christ in this life will be eternal residents in the life to come.

Be Counted

The Story of Jesus

MARY

JESUS' BIRTH

JESUS IN TEMPLE
(AGE 12)

JESUS' BAPTISM

CRUCIFIXION &
RESURRECTION

MATTHEW ——————— JOHN

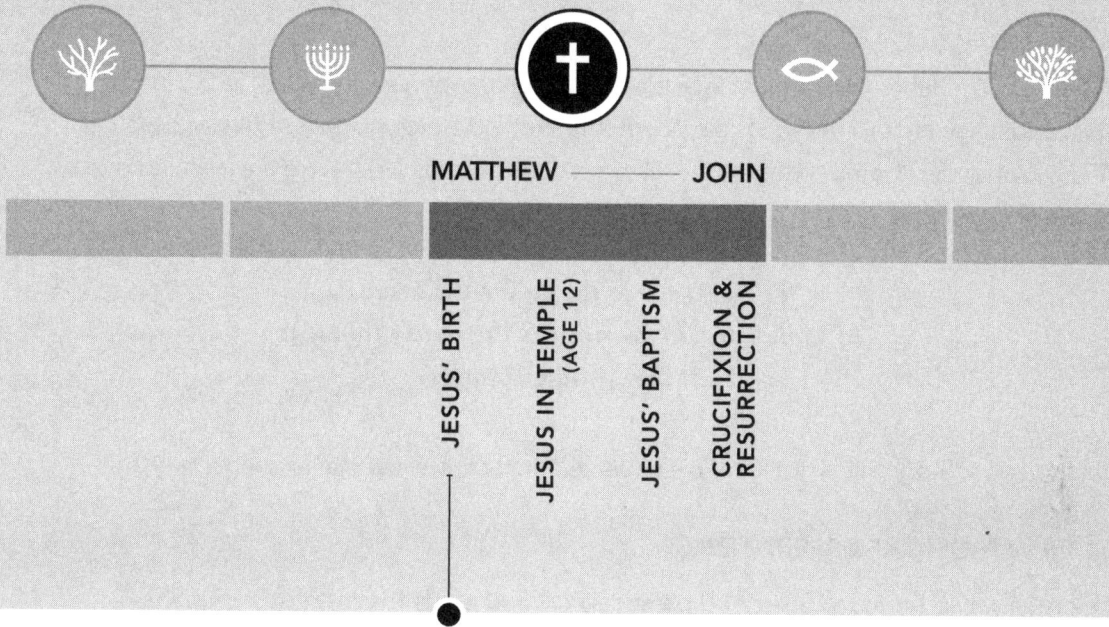

READ THE STORY | Follow this reading guide if you want to pace yourself this week:

○ Day 1: Luke 1:26–45

○ Day 2: Luke 1:46–56

○ Day 3: Luke 2:1–14

○ Day 4: Luke 2:15–21

○ Day 5: Matthew 2:1–12; Micah 5:2

A VIEW FROM THE LOWER STORY

You know the story. Nearly everyone does. Even though businesses try to avoid the word *Christmas* as they welcome us into their stores with "Happy Holidays." Even though municipalities do their best to replace manger scenes with Frosty, Santa, and Rudolph. Just about everyone can tell you what happened, at least in the Lower Story.

Mary and Joseph traveled to Bethlehem, the town of their ancestors, so they could be counted in the census Caesar Augustus, the emperor of Rome, ordered, even though her doctor likely told her donkey travel in the third trimester was out of the question. As they arrived in Bethlehem, Mary went into labor. Mention the phrase "no room in the inn" and just about anyone can tell you how Joseph tried to find a nice place for Mary to have her baby, but all the "hotels" where full—all they could find was a cave-like area behind one of the inns. Apparently . . .

The best we could do for the arrival
of God into our world was the barnyard suite
at the Manger Hotel.

In the Lower Story, this is not what we expected. In fact, it is just plain wrong.

A VIEW FROM THE UPPER STORY

More than two thousand years had passed since God made the promise to Abraham, more than a thousand years since he promised David that the solution to overturn Adam's fateful curse would come from his family. Every story of Israel points to this day. Many Old Testament prophecies, 353 of them, would be fulfilled to give us confidence that Jesus is the promised Messiah, including that Jesus would be born in Bethlehem. God orchestrated Caesar Augustus' decree for an empire-wide census to move Mary and Joseph to Bethlehem in time for the delivery.

From the Lower Story, Mary and Joseph were just a number in the census. To the world, they were poor and irrelevant. But they mattered to God and so do we! Why? Because he loves us. They were from the tribe of Judah, and they were chosen by God to bring Jesus into the world. Mary's response was like, "Yes, be born in me!" We are in the same position as Mary and Joseph. God wants to live in us.

Take down the No Vacancy sign and
say the same thing Mary did: "Yes, be born
in me. Make my heart your home."

Go ahead and "be counted" in the Lower Story, but also "be counted" in the Upper Story.

GOD'S STORY . . . MY STORY

1. Read Luke 1:26–38. Put yourself in Mary's shoes. Gabriel the angel appears out of nowhere and says that you have found favor with God and therefore you will give birth to the Son of God. What would be your response? What do you think of Mary's response in verse 38?

2. Read Luke 1:39–44. The first person to acknowledge Jesus was his cousin, who was still in the womb of Elizabeth. What do you think about that?

3. Read Luke 1:46–56. How does Mary's song reveal what she understood about God's Upper Story?

4. Read Matthew 2:3–6 and Micah 5:2. The chief priests and teachers quoted the prophecy of Micah from over seven hundred years earlier. This is just one of 353 prophecies Jesus fulfilled. Why do you think God went to this extent and precision in bringing us Jesus?

5. Read Luke 2:1–7. God used the census Caesar Augustus organized for his own purposes to get Mary and Joseph to Bethlehem just in time to have Jesus born there to fulfill the prophecy. Do you sense God still might be doing things like this today in our world and government?

6. Read Luke 2:19 and 2:51. On two occasions we find Mary stopping to treasure and ponder what was happening in her life. Maybe we miss what God is doing because we don't do this. Take some time to ponder and even journal what God is doing in your life right now.

SHARE THE STORY

Review the first four movements of the story from memory. Then fill in the blanks for the fifth movement—**The Story of the New Garden**. See page 11 for help.

God will one day create a new earth and a new _____ and once again come down to be with us. All who place their faith in _____ in this life will be eternal residents in the life to come.

The Desert Debut

The Story of Jesus

JOHN THE BAPTIST

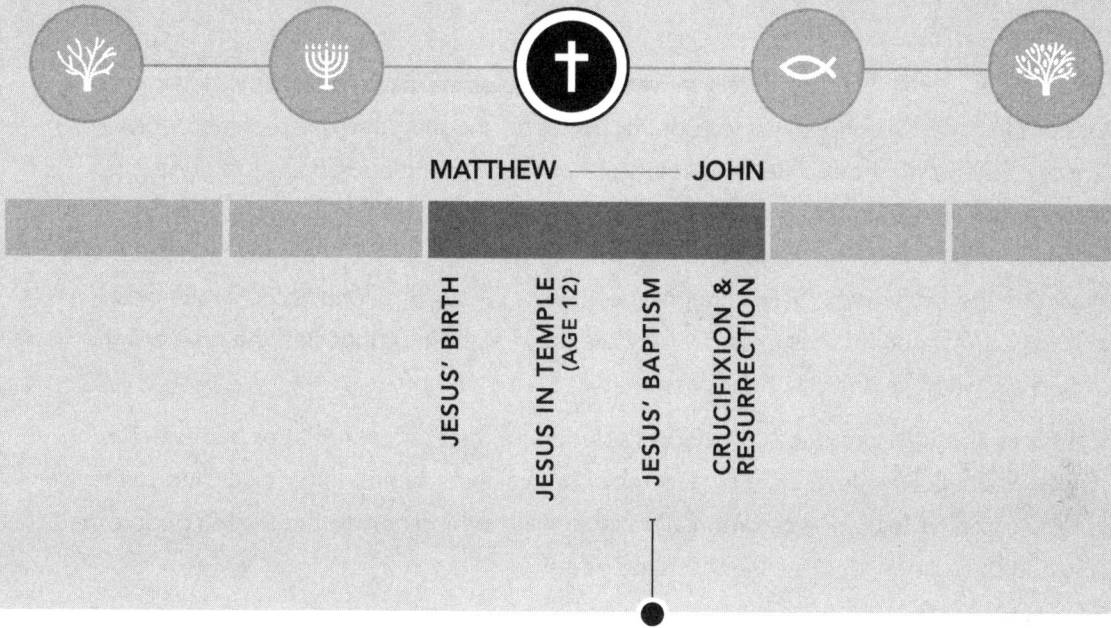

MATTHEW ———— JOHN

JESUS' BIRTH

JESUS IN TEMPLE (AGE 12)

JESUS' BAPTISM

CRUCIFIXION & RESURRECTION

🎵 **READ THE STORY** | Follow this reading guide if you want to pace yourself this week:

○ Day 1: Matthew 3:1–12; Mark 1:1–8; Isaiah 40:3

○ Day 2: Matthew 3:13–17; Mark 1:9–12

○ Day 3: Matthew 4:1–11

○ Day 4: Luke 3:1–6, 21–37; 4:1–13

○ Day 5: John 1:1–42

A VIEW FROM THE LOWER STORY

I hate to admit that whenever we are in the downtown area of a large city and see someone standing on a street corner shouting the good news of the gospel at the top of his lungs asking people to repent and be saved, the skeptic in me rises to the surface. The word lunatic may even cross my thoughts. However, when I read about John the Baptist, I become ashamed of my narrow-mindedness, because this is most likely how people in his day viewed him.

A scruffy, eccentric, hippie-type dude wearing wild clothes made from camel's hair, coming out of the desert picking locust legs out of his teeth, shouting at the top of his lungs to anyone who would listen, "Repent!" In the Lower Story, John appears as just another strange guy who thought he spoke for God, but the Jewish leaders knew his message had a familiar ring to it. When they asked him who he was, he replied, "I am the voice of one calling in the wilderness, 'Make straight the way for the Lord'" (John 1:23). At the close of the Old Testament this is exactly what Isaiah and Malachi prophesied the next prophet would say when he arrived on the scene.

John was about to introduce us to God's solution for restoring our relationship with him. Those who followed John were baptized by immersion as a ceremonial cleansing to prepare for the coming Messiah. A ceremonial washing was nothing new to the Jewish people, as this had been done for over one thousand years.

One special day, Jesus walked by as John was baptizing, and in true "street preacher" form John announced, "Look, the Lamb of God, who takes away the sin of the world!" (John 1:29). Surprisingly Jesus approached John and asked to be baptized. Stunned and a little overwhelmed, John replied to Jesus, "I need to be baptized by you, and do you come to me?" (Matthew 3:14).

But Jesus insisted. So, John baptized Jesus, the long-promised Messiah. At that moment, heaven opened, and God's Spirit descended on Jesus like a dove. Then a voice from heaven declared, "This is my Son, whom I love; with him I am well pleased" (verse 17). It's interesting to note here that God the Father declared he loves his Son and is proud of him before Jesus had even done one thing to begin his ministry. God demonstrated a principle every good parent should practice.

> *Our children need to know that we love them*
> *and are proud of them not because of*
> *what they do, have done, or will do,*
> *but because of who they are.*

Immediately after coming up from the baptismal waters, the Spirit of God led Jesus into the wilderness where for forty days and nights he went without food. It didn't take long for Jesus to become hungry and vulnerable. Satan seized the opportunity to meet Jesus in his fleshly weakness and tempted him three times. Although stones turned into bread would have been mighty welcome at this point, Jesus refuted each of the three enticements by quoting Scripture (Deuteronomy 8:3; 6:16; 6:13). Not a bad reason for us to memorize Scripture!

A VIEW FROM THE UPPER STORY

There are three very dynamic things happening in this single story from above.

First, this is one of the few times in the Bible we see all three persons of the Trinity revealed together. Jesus, God's Son, is baptized; God, the Father, speaks; and God, the Spirit descends in the form of a dove.

Second, John called Jesus out as the Lamb of God, taking us back to the Exodus when the children of Israel put the blood of the lamb on their doorposts. When God saw the blood, he passed over those homes during the tenth plague in Egypt when all the firstborn were killed. That blood was the only solution to their dilemma. In the same way, Jesus' blood is our only solution to get us out of the mess sin has gotten us into. We must believe he is who John says he is—God's Son.

Here's one more: Jesus' time in the wilderness to be tempted by Satan harkens us back to the garden of Eden. Adam was tempted by Satan just once and fell, catalyzing the human race into death and darkness. Jesus, referred to several times as the Last Adam (1 Corinthians 15:22, 44–49), began his ministry by being tempted not once but three times by Satan and did not fall. Jesus' first act following his baptism was a redo of the garden of Eden.

We now have the opportunity to disassociate ourselves from the first Adam that brings us death, and associate with the Last Adam who brings us life (Romans 5:12–21).

Think what you want about street preachers. They may be unconventional and take us out of our comfort zone, and yes, they may even be a little crazy, but they just might know the One who takes away the sin of the world. There's nothing crazy about that.

GOD'S STORY . . . MY STORY

1. Have you ever run into a street preacher? What were your thoughts? Do you believe you would have thought the same thing about John the Baptist?

2. Have you ever found yourself in a season of life you could call a desert? Describe what you were feeling.

3. Did your parents let you know they loved you unconditionally for who you are? Or did you feel as though you needed to perform to gain their love and respect?

4. If you are a parent, how are you doing letting your children know you love them because they are your son/daughter and not for how they perform?

5. Do you believe Jesus is the Son of God? Have you applied his blood to the doorposts of your heart?

SHARE THE STORY

Review the first four movements of the story from memory. Then fill in the blanks for the fifth movement—**The Story of the New Garden**. See page 11 for help.

God will one day create a new _____ and a new _____ and once again come down to be with us. All who place their faith in _____ in this life will be _____ residents in the life to come.

First Miracle

The Story of Jesus

JESUS, THE MIRACLE WORKER

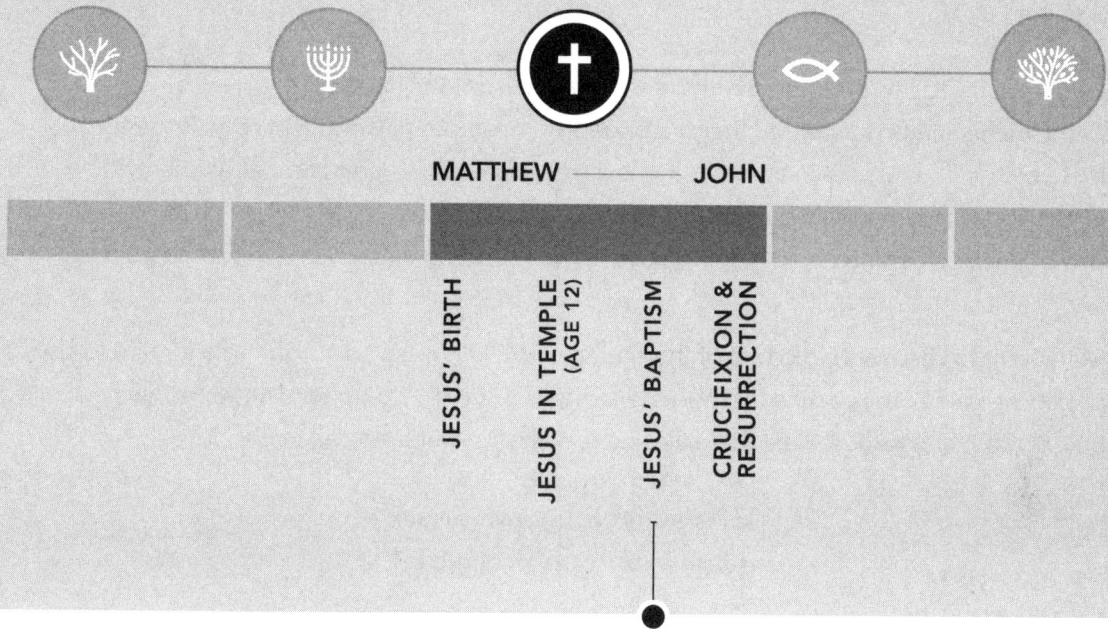

MATTHEW ——— JOHN

JESUS' BIRTH

JESUS IN TEMPLE (AGE 12)

JESUS' BAPTISM

CRUCIFIXION & RESURRECTION

READ THE STORY | Follow this reading guide if you want to pace yourself this week:

○ Day 1: John 2:1–5

○ Day 2: John 2:6–12

○ Day 3: Psalm 104:14–15; Proverbs 3:9–10; 9:1–6

○ Day 4: Isaiah 25:6–8

○ Day 5: Revelation 19:4–10

A VIEW FROM THE LOWER STORY

Jesus was at the beginning of his short three-year ministry. As we saw in our last study, everything kicked off with the baptism of Jesus. Immediately following the baptism, the Spirit led Jesus into the wilderness for a redo of the temptation of the first Adam (Genesis 3). Jesus emerged from this experience the victor.

Now, with the Spirit remaining with Jesus, he proceeded to do his first of thirty-five miracles recorded in the Gospels. No one could have guessed what it would be. Let's first take a look at it from the Lower Story.

Jesus was invited to a wedding with his mother and some of his disciples in a town called Cana. Immediately we are told that the bridegroom ran out of wine. This may not seem like a big deal for us, but in that day, it was a major faux pas, a great embarrassment. Now, it is believed that in the time of Jesus, Jewish weddings lasted for as long as seven days. It was a grand celebration, and running out of wine would be a real bummer for the guests and the host.

Mary went to Jesus and told him of the situation. While it wasn't the right time for him to go public, he quietly took action. He had the servants fill up six stone jars with water. Each jar held up to thirty gallons. Next thing we know, voilà, the water turned into wine.

*Jesus might be a great person
to invite to your next party!*

Here's the math: 180 gallons of water equals 900 bottles of wine. Holy Bordeaux, Batman . . . that's a lot of wine! But it wasn't just a wine you would drink on an average Tuesday; it was a great wine. Today it would be equivalent to serving nine hundred bottles of 2016 Harlan Estate Meritage at $1,800 a bottle. That's $1.6 million.

Jesus saved the day in the most extravagant manner and saved face for the bridegroom who never knew exactly what happened.

A VIEW FROM THE UPPER STORY

Two significant things were going on from the Upper Story. First, Jesus was interrupting the laws of nature. There is no chemical pathway that starts with water and ends up with wine. Here we see the Creator of the universe (John 1:3) showing his power by messing with the very laws he set in place. Over the course of the three years, he would show his power over nature eight more times.

But there was something else going on that is quite remarkable. The Old Testament prophets spoke of a time when God would send a Messiah and redeem his people. They prophesied that an abundance of wine would be a sign of God's future redemption. Jesus was fulfilling that prophecy at this joyous event (Hosea 2:18–23). This miracle at Cana signals to us that the Messiah had indeed come. An "abundance of wine" is an understatement!

Yet, there is still more.

> *This miracle is pointing us to another wedding party altogether where Jesus will one day step into the role of the bridegroom.*

It's called the wedding supper of the Lamb. It is an event yet to take place when those of us who believe in Jesus in this life (the bride of Christ) will be at a wedding feast hosted by Jesus (the Bridegroom). And this time, we won't be running out of any wine. Here is the prophecy Isaiah made seven hundred years earlier about this coming event:

> *On this mountain the LORD Almighty will prepare*
> *a feast of rich food for all peoples,*
> *a banquet of aged wine—*
> *the best of meats and the finest of wines.*
>
> *Isaiah 25:6*

When Jesus is involved, there is nothing but the best present. Isaiah goes on to tell us that at this event God will wipe every tear from our eyes (Isaiah 25:8).

John's revelation gives us greater insight into the banquet (Revelation 19:6–9). He also reminded us Jesus will be wiping every tear from our eyes (Revelation 21:4). I don't know about you, but I long for that day. The entire Bible ends with a wonderful invitation for all of us:

> *The Spirit and the bride say, "Come!" And let the one who hears say, "Come!" Let the one who is thirsty come; and let the one who wishes take the free gift of the water of life.*
>
> *Revelation 22:17*

Have you responded to this wonderful invitation?

GOD'S STORY . . . MY STORY

1. Read John 2:1–5. What do you think of the boldness of Mary to ask Jesus to deal with this problem? Do you feel comfortable bringing Jesus your problems and struggles? Why or why not?

2. Read John 2:6–11. It is impossible to take water and turn it into wine. Isn't that the point of miracles? Do you believe God is still doing miracles in our day?

3. Read Psalm 104:14–15, Proverbs 3:9–10, and 9:1–6. While the Bible gives several warnings about the abuse of wine and alcohol, what do you glean from these verses about the positive side of wine?

4. Read Isaiah 25:6–8 and Revelation 19:4–10. These verses speak to the coming wedding supper of the Lamb. Imagine yourself at this event. What emotions does this evoke in you?

5. What is a miracle you would love to see Jesus perform today in your life or in our world?

SHARE THE STORY

Review the first four movements of the story from memory. Then fill in the blanks for the fifth movement—**The Story of the New Garden**. See page 11 for help.

_____ will one day create a new _____ and a new _____ and once again come down to be _____ us. All who place their faith in _____ in this life will be _____ residents in the life to come.

Nic at Night

The Story of Jesus

NICODEMUS

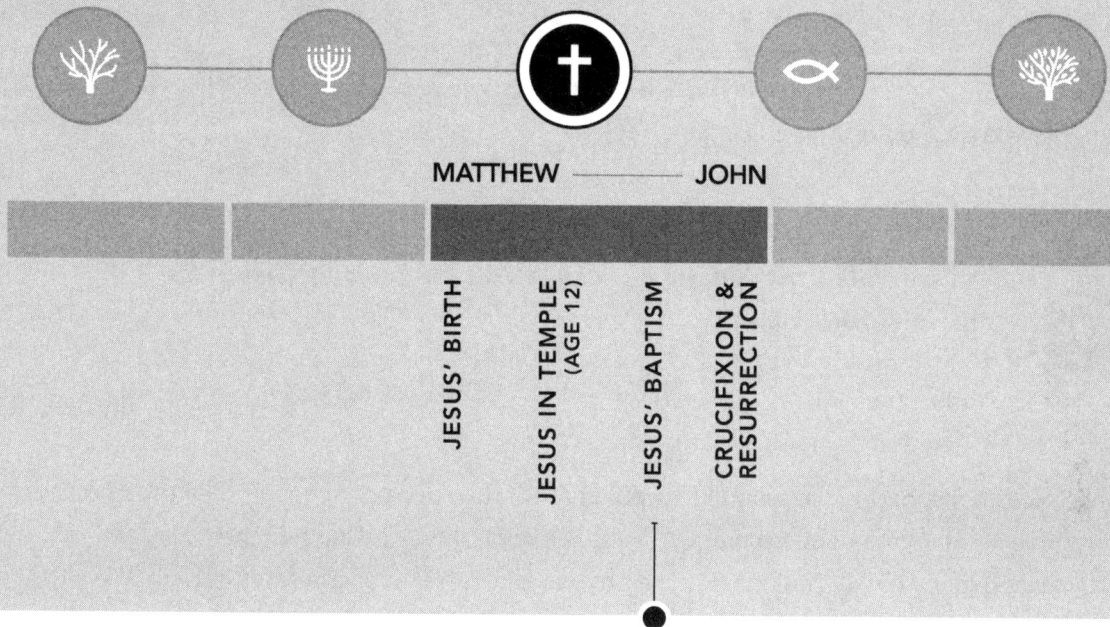

Timeline labels: JESUS' BIRTH | JESUS IN TEMPLE (AGE 12) | JESUS' BAPTISM | CRUCIFIXION & RESURRECTION

MATTHEW ———— JOHN

READ THE STORY | Follow this reading guide if you want to pace yourself this week:

- ○ Day 1: John 3:1–15
- ○ Day 2: John 3:16–21
- ○ Day 3: Genesis 22:1–19; Numbers 21:4–9
- ○ Day 4: Romans 5:12–21; 1 Corinthians 15:42–49
- ○ Day 5: John 19:38–42

A VIEW FROM THE LOWER STORY

There is a television program called "Nick at Nite" that is Nickelodeon's nighttime block of programming featuring family comedies. The Bible airs such a story, but it is not a television show. It centers around a man named Nicodemus who came to Jesus at night.

Nicodemus was a member of the Jewish ruling council. These are the people who would struggle the most with Jesus. Jesus was "moving their cheese," shifting their comfortable paradigms, and they didn't like it. But Nicodemus seemed terribly intrigued with the miracles of Jesus. His logic: For a human to pull this off it must mean that God was with him.

He called for an evening meeting with Jesus to get some answers and possibly to avoid negative chatter among his colleagues.

Jesus responded,

> **"Very truly I tell you, no one can see the kingdom of God unless they are born again."**
>
> **John 3:3**

Nicodemus responded precisely like I would have: "How does one reenter their mother's womb a second time to be born again?" Jesus responded by telling him there are two different kinds of births. The first one is a physical birth; the second, a spiritual birth. We all have experienced the first. What is this spiritual birth that Jesus talked about? Jesus told him that this is a birth that involves the very Spirit of God (John 1:13).

Nicodemus admitted he was clueless as to what Jesus was talking about. Jesus essentially said back to him, "Why, of course you are. I am speaking of things from the Upper Story in heaven. You've never been there, but I have. That is where I came from."

Then Jesus shared with Nicodemus how one is born again in what has become arguably the most popular verse in all the Bible:

> **For God so loved the world that he gave his one and only Son, that whoever believes in him shall not perish but have eternal life.**
>
> **John 3:16**

If one believes in Jesus, they will experience this "spiritual birth." And if you are "born again" you inherit eternal life! What on earth could possibly be better news than this?

It brings up the question:

> **Why would God do this for us? Jesus gives a singular answer: because God "so loved us." This is the ultimate encounter with God's love!**

I have always loved that John put the word "so" into this famous statement. It means that God's love is so magnanimous that he did the unthinkable—he gave his one and only Son to die to make a relationship with him possible—to get us back into the garden.

A VIEW FROM THE UPPER STORY

God has been offering us so many clues from the Upper Story it is hard to deny the veracity of what Jesus is offering us.

The first intimation harkens back to 2050 BC when God instructed Abraham to "Take your son, your only son, whom you love—Isaac—and go to the region of Moriah. Sacrifice him there as a burnt offering on a mountain I will show you" (Genesis 22:2). The language is so similar to John 3:16 it is hard to believe God did not intentionally orchestrate it. And Moriah is the city of Jerusalem where Jesus would be sacrificed. God provided a ram to spare Isaac, but there was no such ram available for God's Son.

God dropped us another clue somewhere between 1446–1406 BC through Moses. Jesus referred to the event in his conversation with Nicodemus. God sent venomous snakes to bite the children of Israel for their sins. The people came to Moses and confessed their sin. God instructed Moses to take a bronze snake and wrap it around a pole and lift it up. If the people looked at it, they would be healed. (By the way, to this day this is the key symbol for the medical profession.) Jesus foretold the day he would be "lifted up" on a pole. If people see him, believe in him, they will be healed.

Later in the writings of Paul, he clarified for us the importance of being born again (Romans 5:12–21; 1 Corinthians 15:42–49). Our physical birth connects us to Adam, which results in our death because of the sin virus we received from him.

*Our spiritual birth connects us to Jesus
and disassociates us from Adam.*

This new birth tethers us to a "new humanity" (Ephesians 2:15) founded in Jesus, who "knew no sin" (2 Corinthians 5:21 ESV). When we are baptized, it symbolizes that we have died to our association with our old life that leads to death, and we are raised to our new life in Christ, which leads to eternal life.

We are not told how Nicodemus responded to his evening conversation with Jesus. So, what happened to him? We later find him at the crucifixion and burial of Jesus. He accompanied Joseph of Arimathea, who offered his tomb to bury Jesus. Nic brought seventy-five pounds of spices to help Joseph properly wrap the body of Jesus for burial. This time he did it in broad daylight.

GOD'S STORY . . . MY STORY

1. In John 3:8, Jesus compared faith to the blowing of the wind. We can't see it, but that doesn't mean it isn't real. How does this help you with all the mysteries of a life of faith?

2. Read John 3:17–18. Many people think that God sends people to hell. How do these two verses help us understand this isn't true?

3. Do you think you better understand the difference and importance of spiritual birth and physical birth? Sometime this week, try to explain it to someone else.

4. If you called a meeting with Jesus, what question would you ask him?

5. At the end of the story in John 19:38–42, Nicodemus goes public with his faith in Jesus. Would you say you have a public faith or more of a private faith?

SHARE THE STORY

Review the first four movements of the story from memory. Then fill in the blanks for the fifth movement—**The Story of the New Garden**. See page 11 for help.

_____ will one day create a new _____ and a new _____ and once again come down to be _____ us. All who place their _____ in _____ in this life will be _____ residents in the _____ to come.

From the Revered to the Reviled

The Story of Jesus

THE WOMAN AT THE WELL

MATTHEW ——————— JOHN

JESUS' BIRTH

JESUS IN TEMPLE
(AGE 12)

JESUS' BAPTISM

CRUCIFIXION &
RESURRECTION

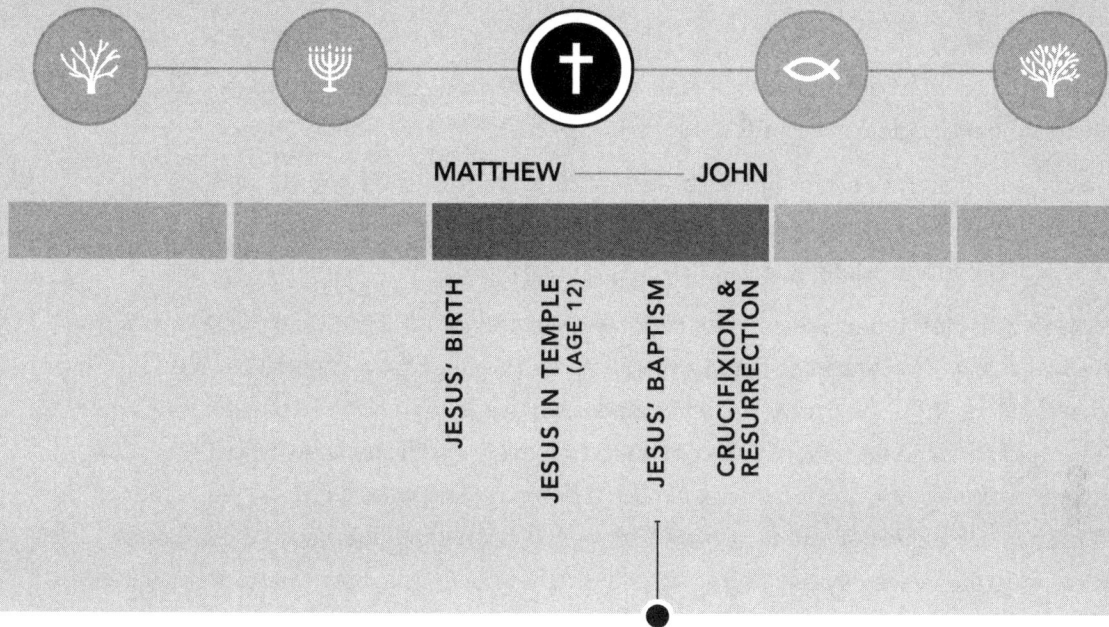

READ THE STORY | Follow this reading guide if you want to pace yourself this week:

○ Day 1: 2 Kings 17:18–40

○ Day 2: John 4:1–26

○ Day 3: John 4:27–42

○ Day 4: Matthew 18:20; Galatians 3:23–29

○ Day 5: Acts 8:1–25

A VIEW FROM THE LOWER STORY

After Jesus left Nicodemus in Judea, he heard through the proverbial grapevine the Pharisees knew he was gaining more and more followers, so he and the disciples scooted on back to Galilee through Samaria. Most Jews would have avoided Samaria and gone around the region, but not Jesus! It seemed Jesus had an appointment God the Father wanted him to keep with a certain woman at Jacob's well.

Jesus left Nicodemus, a revered Jewish leader and teacher, and met this woman, who would have been reviled by the Jews, as were her people. The Jews looked down on Samaritans because they were descendants of Jews who had married Assyrians. The Assyrians overtook the northern kingdom in 722 BC (2 Kings 17:18–40).

Jesus arrived at the well around noon and sat down to rest, and here she came to draw water. When Jesus asked her if she would draw some water for him to drink, she was taken aback and perhaps a little fearful.

Whether his clothing or accent gave him away, we are not told, but clearly, she recognized he was a Jew: "You are a Jew and I am a Samaritan woman. How can you ask me for a drink?" (John 4:9). She clearly knew her place. But Jesus, whom she had never met before, engaged her in conversation, and continued to explain that if she knew who it was who asked her for a drink, she would ask him for a drink of living water, and she would never thirst again. He had her attention now! She could not imagine not having the chore of coming to the well every day to get water in the heat of the day! She wanted this water! Of course, he was talking about eternal life.

Jesus still offers this water today,
and if we ask, he will give it to us.

Next, Jesus told her to go call her husband, and she said, "I have no husband" (John 4:17). And Jesus proceeded to tell her that she spoke truth, since she had had five husbands, and the man she was living with now was not her husband. Stunned, she perceived he was a prophet, and she had a question for him. The Samaritans worshiped on Mount Gerizim in Samaria, but the Jews declared the only place to worship was Jerusalem. She wanted to know which was correct. He told her the time would come when all people would worship in Spirit and in truth. She recognized the Messiah would come and when he came, she was looking forward to him explaining everything. Then for the grand reveal, Jesus said, "I, the one speaking to you—I am he" (John 4:26).

She dropped her water jug and ran back into town bringing everyone she could with her to meet a man who "told [her] everything she had ever done" (verse 29). They came and many believed!

A VIEW FROM THE UPPER STORY

Our "woman at the well," an outcast turned ambassador, enlightens us to certain aspects of Jesus' ministry and gives us insight as to what God was up to by heading straight through Samaria.

To begin with, when Jesus talked to this woman, he brought value to women in a culture where they were at best second-class citizens. He also used a woman who clearly lived a difficult life having had more than one husband and was living with a man who was not her husband, showing us God can use anyone no matter how culture may dismiss them.

Jesus also told the Samaritan woman the day had arrived when people didn't have to go to any temple to worship but would worship in Spirit. This is true for us today. We do not need to go to a church building to worship God but can worship anywhere twenty-four hours a day, seven days a week, 365 days a year because his Spirit is with us wherever we go.

However, the most significant thing we learn from this important appointment is that God's love goes beyond the Jewish people. As we take a view from the Upper Story, we see Jesus will remove the barrier between the Jews and Samaritans with the birth of the church (Acts 8:1–25). Followers of Jesus now have no problem stepping on Samaritan soil to share the good news.

Even though salvation (the Messiah—Jesus) came to us from the Jews,

> *God loves all people, the revered and reviled,*
> *male, female, Jew, and Gentile,*
> *regardless of their past, and wants*
> *a relationship with them.*

This means you!

GOD'S STORY . . . MY STORY

1. Why do you think the woman was going to the well alone at noon or in the heat of the day instead of earlier in the day when it was cool (John 4:6–7)?

2. Do you ever feel as though God cannot or will not use you because of your past or your status in society?

3. What was Jesus talking about when he referred to the living water he offers (John 4:9–14)?

4. How do you think this lady's life changed after her encounter with Jesus? If you have made a decision to follow Jesus, how has your life changed?

5. What does it mean to you that we worship in Spirit and in truth?

SHARE THE STORY

Recite the five movements of the story from memory. See page 11 for help.

No Ordinary Man

The Story of Jesus

JESUS, THE TEACHER

MATTHEW ———— JOHN

JESUS' BIRTH

JESUS IN TEMPLE (AGE 12)

JESUS' BAPTISM

CRUCIFIXION & RESURRECTION

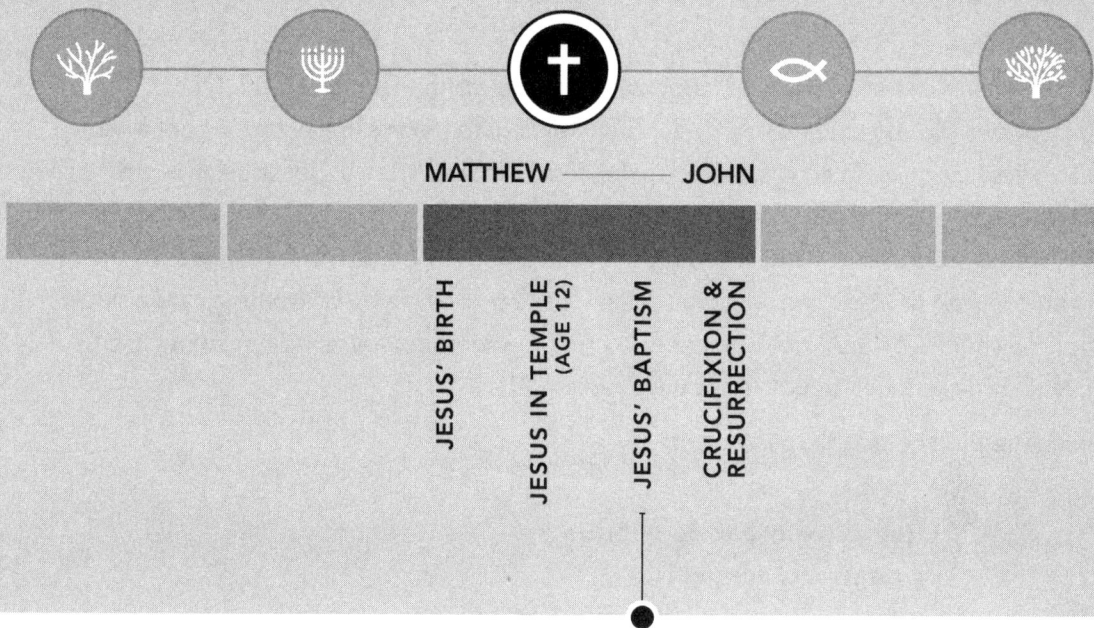

READ THE STORY | Follow this reading guide if you want to pace yourself this week:

○ Day 1: Matthew 5:1–20

○ Day 2: Matthew 5:21–48

○ Day 3: Matthew 6:1–24

○ Day 4: Matthew 6:25–34

○ Day 5: Matthew 7

A VIEW FROM THE LOWER STORY

Have you ever met someone and known almost immediately that he or she was somebody special? I'm talking about someone you meet for the first time who has an extraordinary personality—a commanding presence that draws you to them magnetically.

This is the effect Jesus had on people when he entered their towns or homes. It became clear early in his ministry that, even though he was a child of a humble carpenter from Nazareth, he was special. And one of those qualities that stood out and attracted attention was the way he taught people about God.

A prime example of this is Jesus' famous speech we call the Sermon on the Mount (Matthew 5–7). The entire talk is Upper Story wisdom to help us live better in our Lower Story lives. For example, he attacked materialism: "Do not store up for yourselves treasures on earth . . . . But store up for yourselves treasures in heaven" (6:19–20). He warned against the seductive power of money: "You cannot serve both God and money" (verse 24). He even coached us about the concerns of life: "Can any one of you by worrying add a single hour to your life? . . . Do not worry about tomorrow, for tomorrow will worry about itself. Each day has enough trouble of its own" (verses 27, 34).

In this sermon he teaches us to pray:

> *"'Give us today our daily bread.*
> *And forgive us our debts,*
> *   as we also have forgiven our debtors.*
> *And lead us not into temptation,*
> *   but deliver us from the evil one.'"*
>
> *Matthew 6:11-13*

This is Lower Story stuff. We need to eat. Pay the bills. Avoid the little voice that says, "Go ahead; do what feels good. No one will know." These are the groanings of daily life, the raw clay God uses to shape us as vessels on the potter's wheel. So, we cry out to God to meet us in our Lower Story, and he does. Not always according to our liking, but he is intimately involved and cares deeply about the details of our daily lives out of his deep love for us. He empowers us to live the Lower Story from an Upper Story perspective. When we do, it most certainly leads to a taste of the abundant life even as we meander in the Lower Story (John 10:10).

A VIEW FROM THE UPPER STORY

But there is more going on in the teaching of Jesus than Lower Story advice. Jesus casts a vision for the eternal kingdom to come where we will live in perfect harmony with God and other believers. His teachings encourage us not to settle for a Lower Story kingdom that doesn't last.

Jesus is demonstrating what life will be like in the Upper Story. He wants to give us a vision of how God's kingdom is different—how character is more important than possessions and circumstances. The kingdom of God he describes will be a new garden—a restored version of the garden we learned about in the beginning of this story—where God will once again come down and dwell with all who believe in him. His teaching creates a longing in us for this vision to come to fruition. A holy anticipation.

Let's take another look at the Lord's Prayer and how it starts:

> "'Our Father in heaven,
> hallowed be your name,
> your kingdom come,
> your will be done,
>   on earth as it is in heaven.'"
>
> Matthew 6:9-10

Jesus was telling them—and us—that the first priority of our prayer should be an acknowledgment of God's will—his master plot, as it were—above everything else. We should long for God's Upper Story to descend into our Lower Story lives because what God wants for us will always be the best. We will certainly not experience it perfectly here on this old earth, but it is precisely how things will be in the kingdom, the new garden to come.

This is how we should start every prayer. Once this is done, then we can move to our Lower Story request for things like bread.

It is not enough to think of Jesus as just a great man. In the Lower Story, we may meet some people who achieved great things—celebrities, politicians, actors, professional athletes. If we want to rise above the day-to-day circumstances of our lives, however, we must be prepared to meet someone who redefines the word extraordinary. Jesus is that person.

GOD'S STORY . . . MY STORY

1. Read Matthew 5:1–12. Which of the Beatitudes do you find the most challenging? Why? Which one inspires you the most? Why?

2. Read Matthew 5:21–48. In these verses Jesus takes six topics to a new level of application—from the "letter of the law" to the "spirit of the law." Which one do you find to be the most challenging?

3. In Matthew 6:19–24, Jesus tells us, "Where your treasure is, there your heart will be also." Look at your spending over the last month. What is this telling you about where your heart truly is?

4. Matthew 6:25–34 says, "Do not worry." What parts of Jesus' teaching provides you the most insight to keep you from worry and concern in your life?

5. Matthew 7:28 says "the crowds were amazed at his teaching." What amazes you about Jesus' teachings?

SHARE THE STORY

Share the five movements of the story with five people this week. See page 11 for help.

Liar, Lunatic, or Lord

The Story of Jesus

JESUS, SON OF GOD

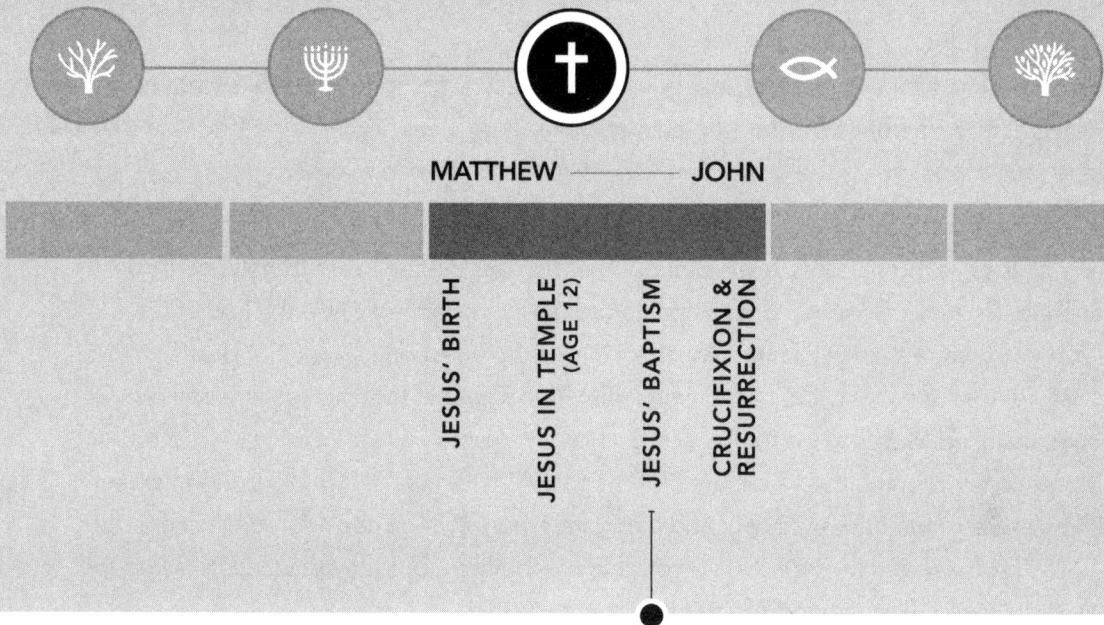

JESUS' BIRTH

JESUS IN TEMPLE
(AGE 12)

JESUS' BAPTISM

CRUCIFIXION &
RESURRECTION

MATTHEW ——— JOHN

READ THE STORY | Follow this reading guide if you want to pace yourself this week:

○ Day 1: Matthew 8

○ Day 2: John 7:1–52

○ Day 3: Zechariah 9:9–13

○ Day 4: Mark 8:27–38

○ Day 5: Mark 11

A VIEW FROM THE LOWER STORY

Here is one of the most important questions anyone can ask: Was Jesus who he said he was? No one disputes Jesus lived on this earth and left behind many great teachings. But the fact that he claimed to be the Son of God requires us to make a choice. C. S. Lewis, in his book *Mere Christianity*, gives us three choices: Jesus is either a liar, a lunatic, or Lord.[6]

In the Lower Story, Jesus is a historical figure who looked like a poor man from Galilee to some. To others, because of his teachings, he appeared to be a prophet. Jesus even asked those closest to him, his disciples, "Who do you say I am?" (Mark 8:29). They rightly

---

6   C. S. Lewis, *Mere Christianity* (HarperOne, 2009), chap. 3.

identified him as the Anointed One, but thought he was going to reestablish the throne of David at that time on this earth—an easy mistake. They were hoping for a king or a political leader who would help them overthrow the oppressive Roman rulers.

Jesus began dropping hints of who he truly was. People were impressed by his teaching and all the healing miracles Jesus did, but the religious leaders were threatened by Jesus and labeled him a blasphemer or imposter because he claimed to be the Son of God. "Are you greater than our father, Abraham?" was the question (John 8:53). Jesus replied, "Before Abraham was born, I am!" (verse 58). Remember in the Old Testament when God commissioned Moses to go to Pharaoh and take the Israelites out of Egypt? God told Moses to tell Pharaoh the "'I AM has sent me to you'" (Exodus 3:14). The Jewish leaders knew exactly what he was saying, and it angered them that he considered himself to be God. They knew the Messiah would come from Abraham, but they never considered the Messiah would have created Abraham.

Before Jesus went to Jerusalem for this celebration, he instructed his disciples to bring him a donkey. They thought it curious, but they ran off and soon returned with the donkey. Apparently, they were unfamiliar with the words of the prophet Zechariah of the Old Testament; otherwise, they would have caught this clue Jesus was giving them:

> *Rejoice greatly, Daughter Zion! Shout, Daughter Jerusalem! See, your king comes to you, righteous and victorious, lowly and riding on a donkey, on a colt, the foal of a donkey.*
>
> *Zechariah 9:9*

When Jesus rode into Jerusalem on that donkey everyone cheered. It must have felt like Inauguration Day. Surely, they thought, he would set up a throne and begin his reign. Instead, God had another plan they did not understand. Jesus tried to share it with his close buddies. He explained to them, the Messiah must suffer many things, be rejected by the chief priests and teachers of the law, and must be killed and rise again after three days.

Peter couldn't believe his ears, so he took Jesus aside and told him, "This shall never happen to you!" Jesus responded, "Get behind me, Satan! You are a stumbling block

to me; you do not have in mind the concerns of God, but merely human concerns"
(Matthew 16:22–23).

> *God does not do things the way*
> *we envision them, but in the end God's way*
> *is better because he has a bigger story*
> *in mind than we can fathom.*

It's one thing to believe Jesus is the Son of God when everything is going well. But when things don't go how we expect, who do we say Jesus is then?

A VIEW FROM THE UPPER STORY

In the Upper Story, the stage is being set for a dramatic event that will have eternal implications. A divine mission put in place back in the garden is about to be completed. Jesus will go from this triumphal entry to being arrested, chained, beaten, spit upon, and crucified. Could this actually be the Messiah? Why would God the Father allow anyone to be treated this way, let alone his own Son? There had to be a perfect sacrifice—someone with no sin to ensure the gap between God and man would be bridged once and for all.

> *God truly loves us so much he would give*
> *his only Son to suffer because he wants us*
> *to live with him forever in his eternal kingdom.*

Believing Jesus is who he said he is and accepting his sacrifice is the only way we get to do that.

If you go back to the Old Testament, you will find over three hundred prophecies about the coming Messiah. Jesus fulfilled every one of them—not just riding into Jerusalem on a donkey.

The question remains for you to answer—liar, lunatic, or Lord?

GOD'S STORY . . . MY STORY

1. Jesus said, "I am the way and the truth and the life. No one comes to the Father except through me" (John 14:6). What does this tell you about Jesus?

2. When circumstances in your life do not unfold as you expected, do you doubt God's plan is better for you?

3. Can you recall a situation in your life when you thought things would go a certain way, and they went "wrong," but in the end, it turned out better than you thought?

4. Ultimately it doesn't matter who anyone else says Jesus is except for you. So, who do you say Jesus is—liar, lunatic, or Lord?

5. If someone came to you today claiming to be the Son of God, you would think he was a lunatic? What made Jesus' claim more believable?

SHARE THE STORY

Review the five movements of the story from memory.

Now that you can share the story it is time to share your story—your personal journey to becoming a follower of the story. Each week you will be asked to think through the five movements of your story and put it in writing and then learn to share it with others. Let's begin below.

Movement 1 of Your Story

What was your story growing up in terms of faith (unchurched, Christian home, broken or blended family, addiction, normal, wonderful)? Write out your story below.

Pay It Forward

The Story of Jesus
A NEW COMMANDMENT

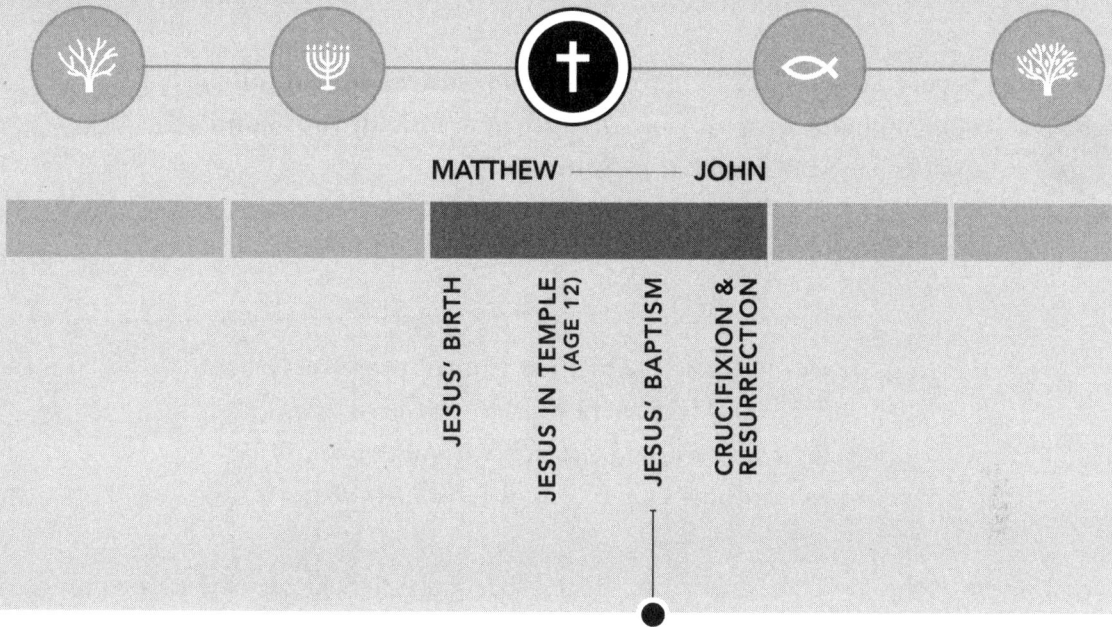

MATTHEW ———— **JOHN**

JESUS' BIRTH

JESUS IN TEMPLE (AGE 12)

JESUS' BAPTISM

CRUCIFIXION & RESURRECTION

READ THE STORY | Follow this reading guide if you want to pace yourself this week:

○ Day 1: Luke 10:25–37; Matthew 22:34–40

○ Day 2: Deuteronomy 6:4–6; Leviticus 19:9–18; Exodus 20:1–17

○ Day 3: John 13:31–38; 21:15–17

○ Day 4: James 2:8–11; Romans 13:8–13

○ Day 5: 1 John 21:7–21

A VIEW FROM THE LOWER STORY

In Luke 10, an expert in the Old Testament law approached Jesus and asked him a very good question: "What must I do to inherit eternal life?" Masterfully, Jesus threw the question back to him: "What is written in the Law? . . . How do you read it?" (Luke 10:25–26). The man answered:

"'Love the Lord your God with all your heart and with all your soul and with all your strength and with all your mind'; and, 'Love your neighbor as yourself.'"

Luke 10:27

It was well accepted by the tenured professors of the Old Testament that all 613 laws can be boiled down and categorized under one of two headings—Love God or Love Neighbor.

For example, in the Ten Commandments, the first four deal with our love for God and the remaining six deal with our love for our neighbor (Exodus 20:1–17).

Deuteronomy 6:5 lays out the commandment to love God. The man who approached Jesus recited it word for word. Leviticus 9:18 lays out the command to love our neighbor. Again, the expert in the law quoted it verbatim.

On Tuesday of the Passion week Jesus was questioned by another expert of the law, this time attempting to test him with the hopes he might slip up, but Jesus knew his scriptures. The lawyer asked him what is the greatest commandment? Jesus quoted the two commandments without missing a word. He then threw in that "all the Law and the Prophets hang on these two commandments" (Matthew 22:34–40).

A VIEW FROM THE UPPER STORY

But something is about to change from the Upper Story. It had been in the works all along, but its hour had not yet come. On Thursday, the night before the crucifixion, Jesus was going to introduce a powerful paradigm shift.

He issued a "New Commandment." What is it?

"A new command I give you: Love one another. As I have loved you, so you must love one another. By this everyone will know that you are my disciples, if you love one another."

John 13:34-35

From this point on you will never hear or see a reference to the Great Commandment—the coupling of these two great axioms of life. We are certainly encouraged to love God. And we even see reference to the royal command to love our neighbor in James's letter, but it stands alone (James 2:8–11).

What is going on here? Jesus was saying two things:

1. From now on, stop trying so hard to love God. Rather, receive God's love, and then pass it on to others.

   Jesus' brand of love is pure, not toxic. It is sacrificial and unconditional. Our love is filled with qualifiers and innuendos.

   > **We receive his love to the brim and then pour it out on others. The supply is unlimited as long as our heart receptors are open.**

2. The measure of our love for God will not be in our worship alone but in our voluntary sacrifice for others.

   When Jesus met up with Peter after his resurrection, he asked Peter three times if he loved him. Each time Peter responded: "Yes, Lord, you know that I love you" (John 21:16). Each time Jesus told him to "take care of and feed my sheep " (John 21:15–16, paraphrased). In essence he was inviting Peter to prove his love for him by paying it forward.

In 1 John, he continues this theme. He redefines love for us:

This is love: not that we loved God, but that he loved us and sent his Son as an atoning sacrifice for our sins. Dear friends, since God so loved us, we also ought to love one another.

1 John 4:10-11

This new command might actually be harder than the older one. I don't know about you, but I love pouring out my heart to God in worship. Most of the time it flows out of a place of gratitude for what he has done for me and my family. However, I think it may be more difficult for us to receive God's love, struggling to believe he really does love us considering all the things we have done or simply because we feel so puny in the world. Does God really notice me and like me? Hard to believe some days, but it turns out to be true.

GOD'S STORY . . . MY STORY

1. Read Luke 10:25–37. Why do you think Jesus told the Good Samaritan story to this expert of the Law?

2. Read Exodus 20:1–17. Can you see how the first four commands relate to our love for God and the next six relate to our love for our neighbor? Which of these commands comes the easiest to you? Which one causes you the biggest struggle?

3. Read John 13:31–38. How are you doing at receiving God's love for you?

4. Read Romans 13:8–13. What is the only debt God encourages us to have? What does this mean to you?

5. Read 1 John 21:7–21. Based on your relationship with others, could you conclude that you love God?

SHARE THE STORY

Review the five movements of the story from memory.

Movement 1 of Your Story

Share your answer to last week's question with another person: What was your story growing up in terms of faith?

The Hour of Darkness

The Story of Jesus
CRUCIFIXION

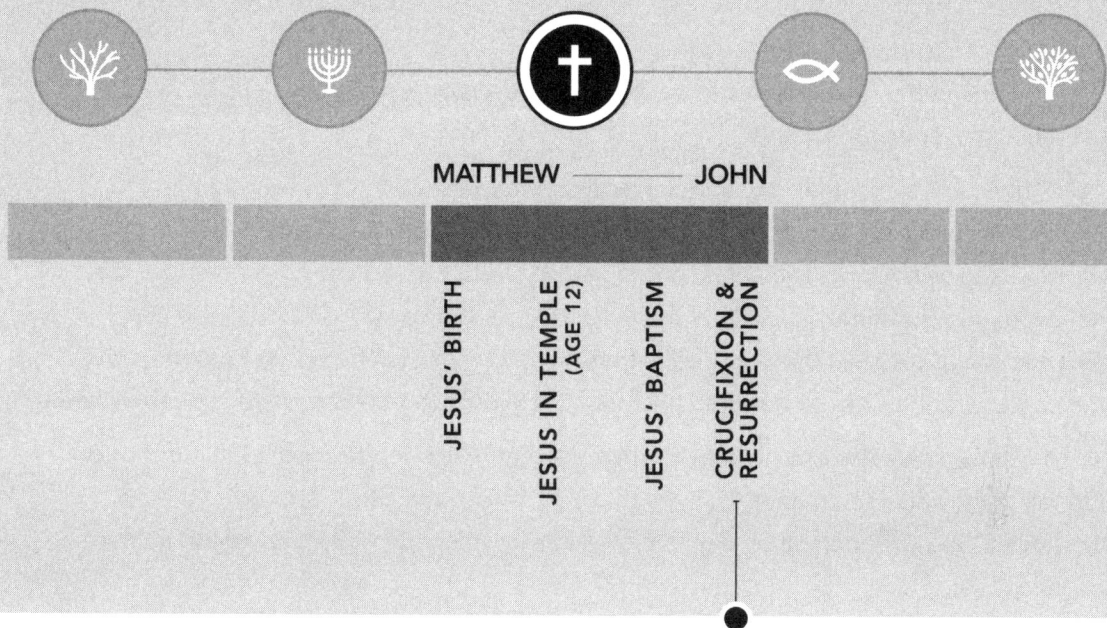

MATTHEW ——— JOHN

JESUS' BIRTH

JESUS IN TEMPLE
(AGE 12)

JESUS' BAPTISM

CRUCIFIXION &
RESURRECTION

🎵 **READ THE STORY** | Follow this reading guide if you want to pace yourself this week:

- ◯ Day 1: Matthew 26:31–75
- ◯ Day 2: Matthew 27:1–31
- ◯ Day 3: Matthew 27:32–66
- ◯ Day 4: Genesis 3
- ◯ Day 5: Hebrews 10:1–25

A VIEW FROM THE LOWER STORY

It all began with a betrayal! One of Jesus' closest friends, Judas, went to Jewish authorities and for a mere thirty pieces of silver the set in motion the plan for them to find and arrest Jesus. His modus operandi? A kiss! Of all things! By the way, in today's currency, it would have been around $260 to $530 to throw the Son of God under the bus.

Jesus had gone to the garden of Gethsemane to pray because his spirit was distressed. He knew what his next calling was—it was the gruesome death on a Roman cross. Crucifixion was the cruelest form of capital punishment, and Jesus knew what was coming. Leaving his band of ragamuffin followers to stay back and watch, Jesus went further into the garden to wrestle in prayer with his Father.

"My Father, if it is possible, may this cup be taken from me. Yet not as I will, but as you will" (Matthew 26:39). And as he prayed, he was so distraught that drops of blood were intermingled with his sweat that fell to the ground. Jesus prayed this prayer not one time, not two times, but *three* times. After the third time, he got up with a new resolve and returned to the disciples. He declared the hour had come when he would be betrayed into the hands of sinners. As he declared this, Judas approached and kissed Jesus on the cheek.

Jesus received an answer to his prayer, but it wasn't the answer he sought. Sold out to do the will of the Father no matter what, he moved forward with God's plan, even though he desired God to find another way. In the end Jesus conceded to whatever the Father deemed best.

> **Whenever we pray, no matter what the request, it would be fitting for us to always end our prayers with, "Nevertheless, God, not my will, but yours be done."**

The soldiers arrested Jesus, and the disciples scattered. Three times Peter, his right-hand man, denied he even knew Jesus. Jesus was left completely alone.

After a "kangaroo court" where Jesus declined to defend himself, a flogging with a cat o' nine tails, being spit upon, adorned with a crown of thorns that pierced his head, and being draped with a purple robe mocking his royalty, the wheels were set in motion toward a hill called Golgotha—"the place of the skull." It was there Jesus would be set up on a cross with nails piercing his hands and feet between two rightfully convicted criminals.

To everyone looking on, especially Jesus' followers, it looked as though all their hopes for this man to be their Messiah were also impaled by the nails. It seemed he was finished!

And right before he surrendered his spirit into the Father's hands, Jesus himself cried, "It is finished" (John 19:30). From the Lower Story it surely looked as though he was!

A VIEW FROM THE UPPER STORY

Hearing these words from the cross—"It is finished."—those standing by thought, *You're absolutely right. You are finished.* Some were elated, others were heartbroken. However, this is not even close to what Jesus meant when he uttered those words. He was not finished, but the work he came to do for the Father was finished. God's plan to get us back had now come to fruition! The enduring solution for covering sin that God indicated back in the garden of creation when he replaced Adam and Eve's fig leaves with the skin of an animal had now taken place. Our sin required the shedding of another's blood, but not that of animals (Hebrews 10:4). Jesus was sinless, therefore:

> ### Jesus' blood was the once-for-all covering our sin needs to get us back into a relationship with God, which is all he ever wanted.

The moment Jesus died, the enormous curtain in the temple, which quarantined the presence of God from us for all these centuries, was ripped open. This sixty-foot-high curtain was torn from top to bottom—not bottom to top as if a man could do it. Hebrews 10:20 tells us that in the Upper Story the curtain has always represented Jesus. Through faith in Christ, we can now enjoy a personal relationship with God without a priest, without sacrifices, without a Holy of Holies because the payment for sin has now been made.

No doubt, from the Lower Story the disciples and all who watched thought this was the end of Jesus' story. They must have had great doubts. But those doubts would soon be erased . . . in exactly three days!

GOD'S STORY . . . MY STORY

1. Have you ever been betrayed by a close friend? Describe what it feels like for you to know Jesus has experienced your pain.

2. Do you trust God enough to finish all your prayer requests with the phrase, "Not my will, but your will be done"?

3. When Jesus prayed, he didn't get the outcome he wanted. Have you ever prayed for something, but the answer didn't come as you hoped? Do you think God's Upper Story might have a better outcome in mind?

4. What does it mean to you that you have direct access to God?

5. Have you accepted Jesus' blood as covering for your sin? If not, why not now? And if so, when?

SHARE THE STORY

Review the five movements of the story from memory.

Movement 2 of Your Story

How did your environment growing up affect your faith development either positively or negatively? Write out your story below.

Not Forsaken

The Story of Jesus
CRUCIFIXION

JESUS' BIRTH

JESUS IN TEMPLE
(AGE 12)

JESUS' BAPTISM

CRUCIFIXION &
RESURRECTION

MATTHEW ——— JOHN

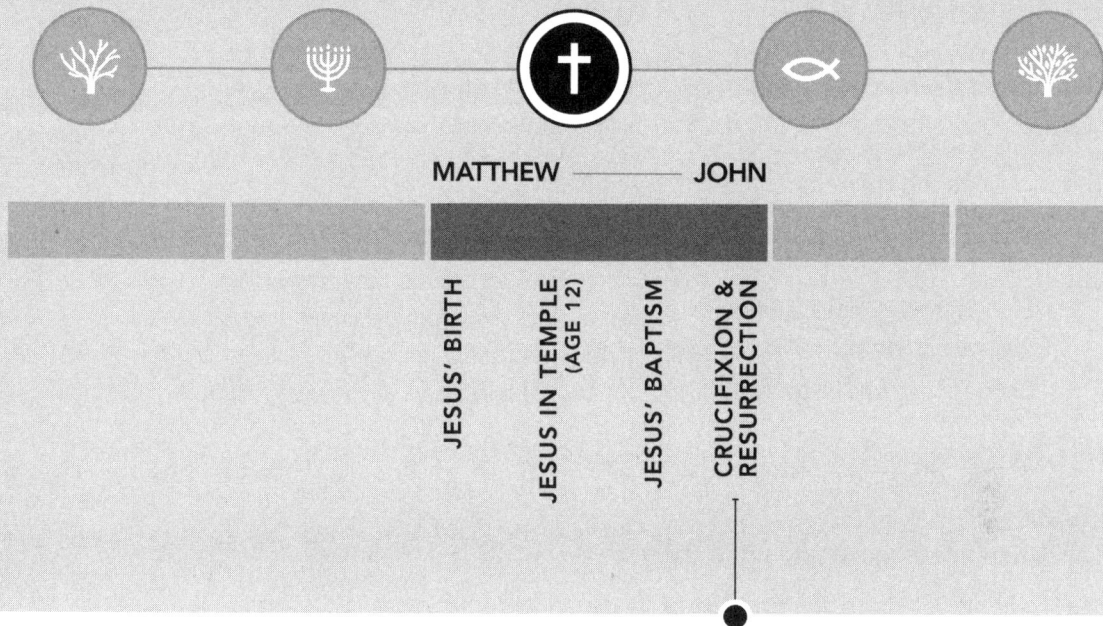

READ THE STORY | Follow this reading guide if you want to pace yourself this week:

◯ Day 1: Mark 15:21–32

◯ Day 2: Mark 15:33–47

◯ Day 3: Psalm 22:1–18

◯ Day 4: Psalm 22:19–31

◯ Day 5: Romans 8:35–39

A VIEW FROM THE LOWER STORY

Have you ever felt forsaken? Somebody you counted on turned their back on you? You were forgotten, left out, left alone, abandoned?

Jesus sure did. You may remember when he hung on the cross, he cried out:

> *"My God, my God, why have you forsaken me?"*
>
> *Matthew 27:46*

I was taught the moment Jesus took all our sins upon himself, the Father turned his face away from him.

There is a beautiful hymn that reinforces this idea:

> How great the pain of searing loss,
> The Father turns his face away
> As wounds which mar the chosen One
> Bring many sons of glory.

> ("How Deep the Father's Love for Us")

This is how things looked from the Lower Story.

A VIEW FROM THE UPPER STORY

But there is something very different going on from the Upper Story.

There is a teaching technique used among Jewish rabbis called Remez that exposes what Jesus was really doing on the cross. The rabbi basically gives the student the first line of a section of Scripture to help jog their memory and get them started.

Look at the first line of Psalm 22:

> My God, my God, why have you forsaken me?

Jesus wasn't crying out to God but leading the people back to Psalm 22. The people would have been prompted to say the second line of this petition:

> Why are you so far from saving me,
>   so far from my cries of anguish?
> (verse 1)

This would have led them deeper into the psalmist's lament. See if you recognize any of the lines and how they mirrored what Jesus was experiencing on the cross.

Psalmist: "All who see me mock me; they hurl insults, shaking their heads" (verse 7).
Gospels: "Those who passed by hurled insults at him, shaking their heads" (Matthew 27:39).

Psalmist: "'He trusts in the Lord,' they say, 'let the Lord rescue him'" (verse 8).
Gospels: "He trusts in God. Let God rescue him now" (Matthew 27:43).

Psalmist: "My mouth is dried up like a potsherd" (verse 15).
Jesus: "Later, knowing that everything had now been finished, and so that Scripture would be fulfilled, Jesus said, 'I am thirsty'" (John 19:28).

Psalmist: "They pierce my hands and my feet" (verse 16).
Thomas: "Unless I see the nail marks in his hands and put my finger where the nails were, and put my hand into his side, I will not believe" (John 20:25).

Psalmist: "They divide my clothes among them and cast lots for my garment" (verse 18).
Gospel: "And they crucified him. Dividing up his clothes, they cast lots to see what each would get" (Mark 15:24).

Jesus was pointing us to the psalm that was written over one thousand years prior that described everything that had just happened to him. In the Lower Story the Jews and Romans came together to kill Jesus. In the Upper Story, this was God's plan all along. He was fulfilling prophecy.

But the psalm doesn't end there. There is a declaration of praise for deliverance. Read carefully:

> For he has not despised or scorned
>   the suffering of the afflicted one;
> he has not hidden his face from him
>   but has listened to his cry for help.
> (verse 24)

Before they could do anything about it, Jesus declared with one more thrust of air through his worn and beaten frame,

"It is finished." With that, he bowed his head and gave up his spirit.

John 19:30

The Jewish audience knew how Psalm 22 ended.

> They will proclaim his righteousness,
>> declaring to a people yet unborn:
>> He has done it!
> (verse 31)

"He has done it!" Sound familiar? In Hebrew it's just one word as well, *hasah*, and it means "accomplished/finished." Jesus began Psalm 22 with the first line and then finished Psalm 22 with his last breath.

> *Jesus was not forsaken by the Father. Out of his deep love for us, even in intense anguish and pain, the Rabbi was teaching us, showing us the way to the new garden.*

GOD'S STORY . . . MY STORY

1. Have you ever felt forsaken? How did it or does it still affect you?

2. Read Psalm 22:2–5. Have you ever felt forsaken by God? How does David's words help us think this through and have a proper response?

3. Read Mark 15:33–37. What emotions stir in you knowing that the Father did not turn his face from Jesus?

4. Read Psalm 22:31. Who do you think the "people yet unborn" refers to in this passage?

5. Read Romans 8:35–38. The Father did not turn his face from Jesus and will not turn his face from us. Which statement in Paul's declaration speaks to you the most?

SHARE THE STORY

Review the five movements of the story from memory.

Movement 2 of Your Story

Share your answer to last week's question with another person: How did your environment growing up affect your faith development either positively or negatively?

Dawn of Hope

The Story of Jesus

RESURRECTION

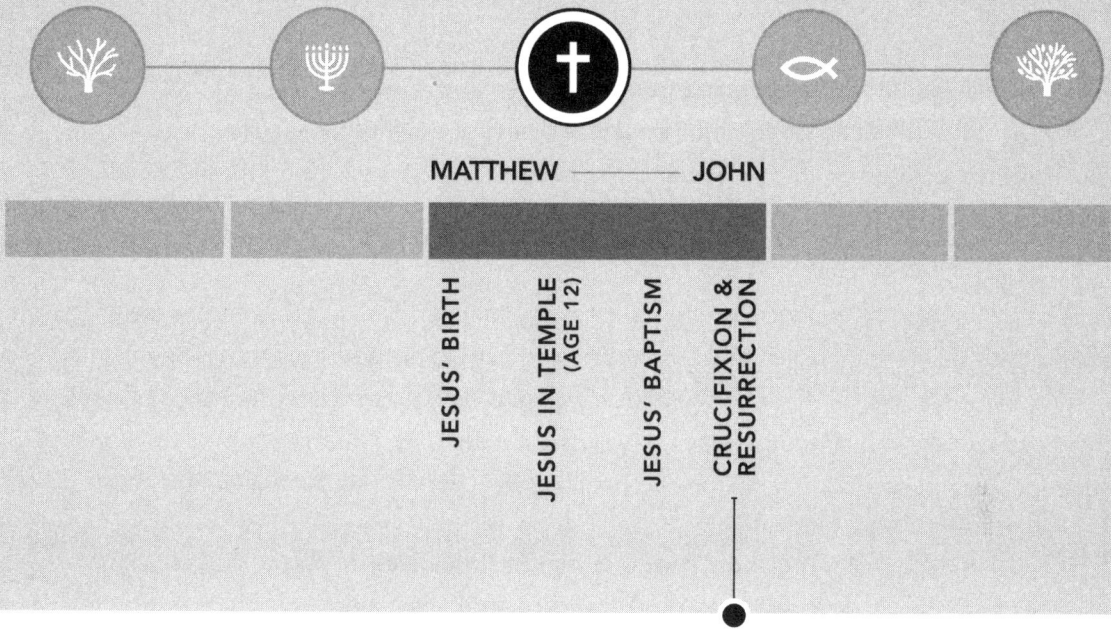

Timeline markers (left to right): JESUS' BIRTH · JESUS IN TEMPLE (AGE 12) · JESUS' BAPTISM · CRUCIFIXION & RESURRECTION

MATTHEW ———— JOHN

READ THE STORY | Follow this reading guide if you want to pace yourself this week:

- ◯ Day 1: Matthew 28
- ◯ Day 2: Mark 16:1–8
- ◯ Day 3: Luke 24:1–12
- ◯ Day 4: John 20
- ◯ Day 5: John 21

A VIEW FROM THE LOWER STORY

Many times, I have stood at the graveside of a loved one, and it always underscores the reality that for the deceased, life as we know it is over. I recall memories of the person, laughs we shared and tough times we faced together, but am always left with an empty feeling. That person is gone for good. Nothing I can do will bring them back. Even if they belonged to God, which fills me with hope, I cannot shake the feeling that our relationship is over. The followers of Jesus certainly knew this feeling.

You would think the religious leaders would have been satisfied that Jesus was dead and gone, would have felt as though the threat was over. But no, they were still worried about political insurrection from this small band of rabble-rousers. They worried these followers would stage a resurrection by stealing Jesus' body; therefore, the request was made to have a sentry posted at the tomb and a heavy stone to secure the entrance.

The disciples had just experienced the saddest day of their lives, and their hopes were exhausted. They were stuck in their Lower Story and could not see beyond it. They didn't remember Jesus' words: "The Son of Man is going to be delivered into the hands of men. They will kill him, and after three days he will rise" (Mark 9:31). There are times in all our lives when we cannot see God's hand moving because we can only see our Lower Story.

During these times, it would do us well to stop, remember God's promises, and trust that he will do what he said he will do.

All was quiet on Saturday after Jesus was buried, but on Sunday morning as the sun rose, two ladies both named Mary ventured to the tomb with spices to embalm Jesus' body. When they arrived, the stone had been rolled away from the entrance. As they looked in expecting a dead body, the ladies encountered an angel who told them, "He is not here; he has risen" (Matthew 28:6). The angel then directed them to hurry and go tell the disciples, which they did.

Of course, the disciples did not take their word for this. Peter and John took off to the tomb to see for themselves. They only saw burial clothes lying where the corpse had been.

Not knowing what happened to Jesus' body, these poor followers were just hanging together, grieving and scared in a locked room. The evening of the same day, Jesus appeared in the room. They did not let him in. He just appeared. Jesus showed them the scars on his hands and feet. Can you imagine the elation that replaced their fear? Their Messiah had truly risen from the dead!

A VIEW FROM THE UPPER STORY

In the Lower Story, death seems so final. From the Upper Story, however, it is only the beginning. Jesus' earthly body did die, but when he rose from the dead, he was raised with a new imperishable body. Obviously, it could penetrate locked doors. Jesus' death was final, but not for him—it was the final blow to death. When he rose from the dead, death was conquered once and for all.

Our earthly bodies must die as well because we have been contaminated with the sin virus. But because Jesus rose from the dead and conquered death, we have the promise that we, too, will be raised from the dead and receive a new body. I for one am hoping for a few nips and tucks, if you know what I mean.

Despite great efforts to discredit Jesus and keep him in the grave, he rose again just as the prophets said he would.

Jesus' own victory over death gives everyone the same opportunity to live forever with God.

Jesus' mission on earth was completed, but before he left his disciples to return to his heavenly Father, he gave his followers one more exhortation. It has become known as the Great Commission.

"Therefore go and make disciples of all nations, baptizing them in the name of the Father and of the Son and of the Holy Spirit, and teaching them to obey everything I have commanded you. And surely I am with you always, to the very end of the age."

Matthew 28:19 20

This is God's plan for those of us who have accepted Jesus as our Savior and are in a relationship with God—to continue to make disciples. How was Jesus going to be with them and us to the end of the age? Read on, my friend!

GOD'S STORY . . . MY STORY

1. Have you lost someone very dear to you that is keeping you "stuck" in your Lower Story? How does knowing Jesus was raised from the dead help reassure you that you will see that person again?

2. Have you ever been or are you now in a difficult situation where you were stuck in your Lower Story perspective that robbed your joy or your peace? How can remembering there is an Upper Story bring peace and joy back into your life?

3. What do you think your response would have been when Jesus magically walked into the room?

4. Do you share your faith on a regular basis? Why or why not?

5. Is there someone in your life who desperately needs Jesus? Write their name(s) down and begin praying for them right now. When the time is right, share your journey of trusting God, and see what happens.

SHARE THE STORY

Review the five movements of the story from memory.

Movement 3 of Your Story

Describe the day you turned your life over to Christ. What pushed you over the edge? Where were you? Who was with you? What did you do or say? Did you get baptized? Write your story below.

Same Power

The Story of Jesus
RESURRECTION

MATTHEW ——— JOHN

JESUS' BIRTH

JESUS IN TEMPLE
(AGE 12)

JESUS' BAPTISM

CRUCIFIXION &
RESURRECTION

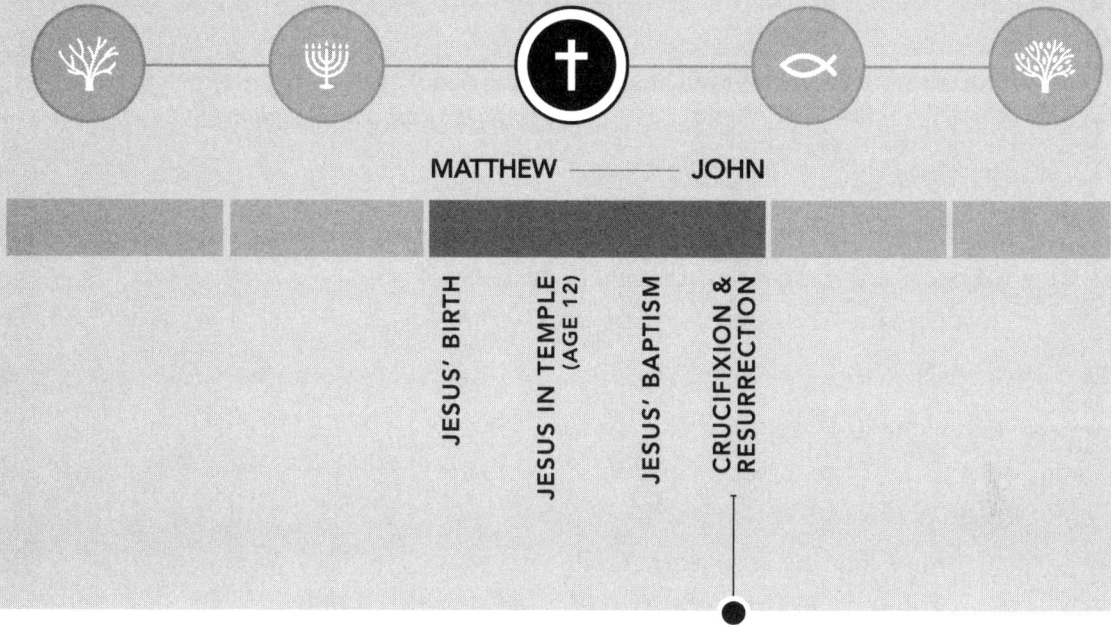

§ **READ THE STORY** | Follow this reading guide if you want to pace yourself this week:

○ Day 1: John 20:1–18

○ Day 2: John 20:19–31

○ Day 3: John 1:29–34; Philippians 2:5–11

○ Day 4: Ephesians 1:15–23; Romans 8:9–11

○ Day 5: 1 Corinthians 15:12–58

A VIEW FROM THE LOWER STORY

In Paul's letter to the believers at Ephesus, he offered this amazing prayer:

I pray that the eyes of your heart may be enlightened in order that you may know the hope to which he has called you, the riches of his glorious inheritance in his holy people, and his incomparably great power for us who believe. That power is the same as the mighty strength he exerted when he raised Christ from the dead and seated him at his right hand in the heavenly realms.

Ephesians 1:18-20

Did you notice that Jesus didn't raise himself from the dead? Huh—we know for a fact that he is God (John 1:1–2), so why did he not pull this off by and for himself?

God has three things we humans do not have:

- Omnipresence—the ability to be all places at the same time
- Omniscience—the capacity to know all things
- Omnipotence—the capability to be all powerful

So, what gives?

A closer look at the life and pattern of Jesus reveals that he left these three things behind when he came to earth to represent us. Paul's letter to the Philippians gives us this insight:

> *Who, being in very nature God,*
> *   did not consider equality with God something to be*
> *used to his own advantage;*
> *rather, he made himself nothing*
> *   by taking the very nature of a servant,*
> *   being made in human likeness.*
>
> **Philippians 2:6-7**

To not use these three superpowers to his own advantage and genuinely represent us, he decided to leave them behind. He didn't lose them; he just left them behind.

Consider this story to help us understand what Jesus did. Several years ago, when we were visiting Colorado, we made arrangements to meet up with some old friends. We secured a reservation at a very nice French restaurant. It was going to be our treat. However, when the check came, I quickly realized I had left my wallet back at the hotel. Our good friends were stuck with the entire bill! How humiliating.

I had the ability to pay . . . I just left that ability back at the hotel. Jesus did the same thing, except he knowingly volunteered to leave these powers behind. Now that he is back with the Father, he once again has possession of them.

*That means that for the thirty-three years
Jesus walked the earth, he was as
limited as we are.*

- He could only be in one place at a time. If he wanted to go somewhere he had to walk or ride a donkey.
- He didn't have knowledge about everything. He constantly had to go to the Father to find out what to do. Nineteen times in the gospel of John he is seeking the Father to discover direction for his life.
- He didn't have the power to perform miracles. There are an estimated thirty-nine miracles recorded in the gospels through Jesus, but it wasn't Jesus who pulled them off.

This includes the resurrection.

A VIEW FROM THE UPPER STORY

So, who did raise Jesus from the dead?

Remember when Jesus was baptized the Holy Spirit descended upon him like a dove and remained with him (John 1:32–34)? The Holy Spirit didn't just make a cameo appearance. He remained with Jesus. In the very next story, we find the Holy Spirit leading him into the wilderness (Matthew 4:1). After that, we see Jesus' first miracle—turning the water into wine. It was the Holy Spirit who was performing these miracles through Jesus.

What does this mean to us?

When we accept the forgiveness of our sins through the work of Jesus on the cross, we are told repeatedly that the same Holy Spirit descends on us and remains with us to give us access to supernatural power.

Paul not only mentioned this in his letter to the Ephesians, but he also alerted the Roman Christians of this truth:

> *And if the Spirit of him who raised Jesus from the dead is living in you, he who raised Christ from the dead will also give life to your mortal bodies because of his Spirit who lives in you.*

Romans 8:11

The implications to us are staggering. If we are believers in Jesus, we have the same Spirit in us. If we will align our lives, as Jesus did, to the Upper Story of God, the Spirit will give us all the power we need to accomplish it. And here is the big promise—when Jesus returns, the *same power* that raised Jesus from the dead will raise us from the dead to live with the Father, Son, and Holy Spirit forever in the new garden.

GOD'S STORY . . . MY STORY

1. Read John 20:1–31. Why is the resurrection of Jesus so critical to your story?

2. To tap into the same power that raised Jesus from the dead we must empty ourselves of the allusion of control. Do you believe you have turned over the control of your life to God? Explain.

3. To tap into the same power that raised Jesus from the dead we must align our lives to the will of the Father (the Upper Story). Do you believe your life is aligned to God's will for your life? Explain.

4. To tap into the same power that raised Jesus from the dead we must not try harder but yield harder to the Spirit's power in us. Do you believe you are letting the Spirit's power work through you or are you working from your own strength? Explain.

5. Read 1 Corinthians 15:12–20. What are your thoughts and hopes about your resurrection at the return of Jesus?

SHARE THE STORY

Review the five movements of the story from memory.

Movement 3 of Your Story

Share your response to last week's question with another person: What were the circumstances that led you to be open to becoming a follower of Christ?

The Church Is Born

The Story of the Church
THE HOLY SPIRIT

ACTS ———————— JUDE

BIRTH OF CHURCH
PETER
PAUL'S CONVERSION
PAUL'S JOURNEYS
DEATH OF PETER AND PAUL
JOHN EXILED TO PATMOS

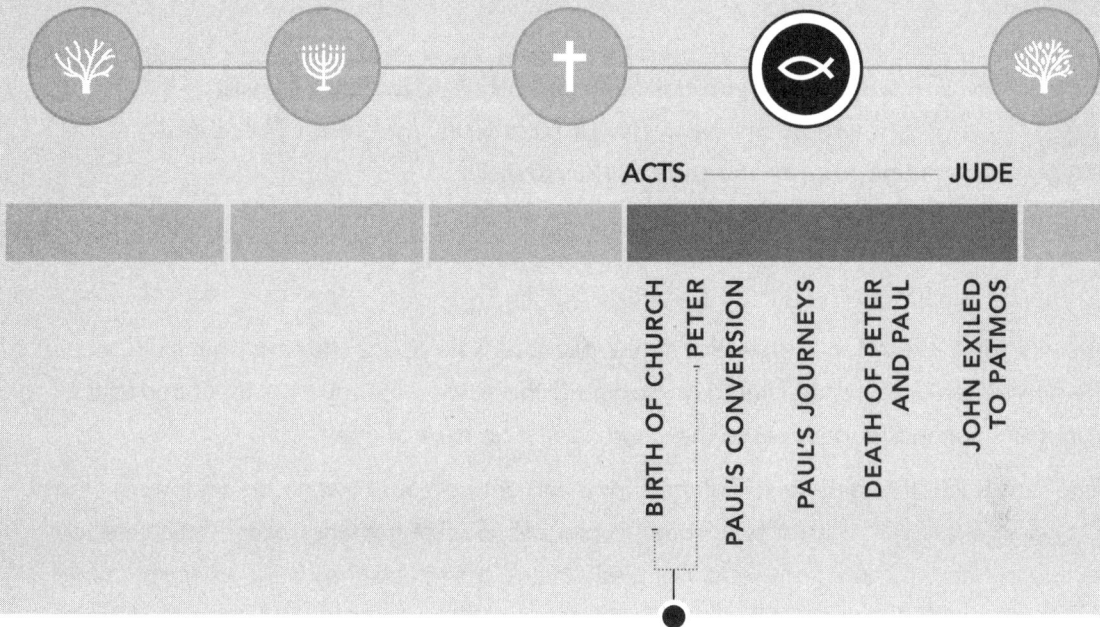

🎵 **READ THE STORY** | Follow this reading guide if you want to pace yourself this week:

○ Day 1: John 14

○ Day 2: Acts 1

○ Day 3: Acts 2:1–13

○ Day 4: Acts 2:14–41

○ Day 5: Acts 2:42–47; 4:32–37

A VIEW FROM THE LOWER STORY

By some estimations there have been more than two hundred specific predictions about when Jesus will return, and they have all been wrong. Of course, we would all love to know, but the Bible tells us that even Jesus did not know the time when he walked our earth. Only God the Father knows when it will be. If Jesus isn't concerned about the date, why should we be?

Before Jesus ascended to the Father, he assured his disciples and us he was going to return, but until that time he was not leaving them alone. He promised to send the Holy Spirit to fill his followers with power and courage to follow his challenge to go make other disciples by sharing the good news of Jesus' return.

"You will receive power when the Holy Spirit comes on you; and you will be my witnesses in Jerusalem, and in all Judea and Samaria, and to the ends of the earth."

Acts 1:8

Once again locked in the Upper Room, the disciples waited, not knowing what to expect next. After ten anticipation-filled days, suddenly there was a mighty wind that flooded the room and flaming tongues of fire that came to rest on each of them.

The Holy Spirit, the third person of the Trinity, had entered our Lower Story endowing these ordinary people with the ability to speak in tongues, or different languages. They were so overwhelmed they could not keep silent, so out into the streets they went, using this new gift to spread the gospel. God loved all people so much he wanted everyone to hear the good news in their own heart-language!

Their message? Repent, believe, and be baptized. Onlookers thought they must be drunk, although it was only mid-morning. If they were drunk, it was on the Spirit, capital S, but definitely not with spirits, small s. By the time they stopped talking, three thousand new followers were added to their number.

These new believers began meeting together in homes, seeing each other daily at the temple court. Each home could hold about thirty people. That means one hundred brand-new churches. They devoted themselves to four things: the apostles' teaching, fellowship, eating together, and prayer. These Spirit-infused converts reached out into the community and met the needs of those around them. As they met the needs in their community, the love of Christ shone through them, and we are told that God added to their number daily those who were being saved (Acts 2:47).

The church was born!

> *As believers, we need a fellowship of like-minded people who give themselves to reading God's Word, sharing meals, praying, and reaching out into our community to share Christ's love with those around us.*

God's plan is still for his people today to spread the good news about Jesus by sharing his love. To pull this off we need two things—the Holy Spirit and each other. We are better together!

A VIEW FROM THE UPPER STORY

While every story and character in the Old Testament points to the first coming of Jesus, every character and story in the New Testament points to the second coming of Jesus. This is where our lives intersect with God's Upper Story. The instructions in this part of God's Word provide us with our road map and marching orders.

> *Just as he used Israel to fulfill his plan to lead us to Jesus' first coming, God promises to use this new community of believers, the church, to bring us to Jesus' second coming.*

God loves all people and wants to have a relationship with them. If we share the love God has lavished on us with others, he will "draw all people to [himself]" (John 12:32).

Sharing Jesus with those around us can be a fearful task, but Jesus did not leave us to do this mission alone. We also have the transforming power of the Holy Spirit in our lives. The same Spirit who came upon those believers at Pentecost comes to reside in each of us when we accept Jesus as our Savior. This power is not to do our will, but to do God's will. Our job is to align our lives with God's desire. Everything these early followers experienced is available to us today.

He is always with you.

GOD'S STORY . . . MY STORY

1. What do you think are the primary drivers that caused the church to grow so rapidly? Do you see that happening in our day?

2. Have you found a church home where you can be challenged to grow spiritually? If not, this is your first step in aligning your life with God's plan.

3. Do you have a group of believers you meet with often where you can commit to doing the four things the believers in the New Testament devoted themselves to? Write their names down, and thank God for them (Acts 2:42).

4. Do you and/or your group regularly reach out beyond yourselves to help others experience the love of Jesus? If so, how? If not, this is probably your next step.

5. How does the anticipation of Jesus' return influence how you live today?

SHARE THE STORY

Review the five movements of the story from memory.

Movement 4 of Your Story

What were the circumstances that led you to be open to becoming a follower of Christ (a friend, a crisis, an invitation to church, a Bible study, a book or movie)? Write your answer below.

Blinded by the Light

The Story of the Church

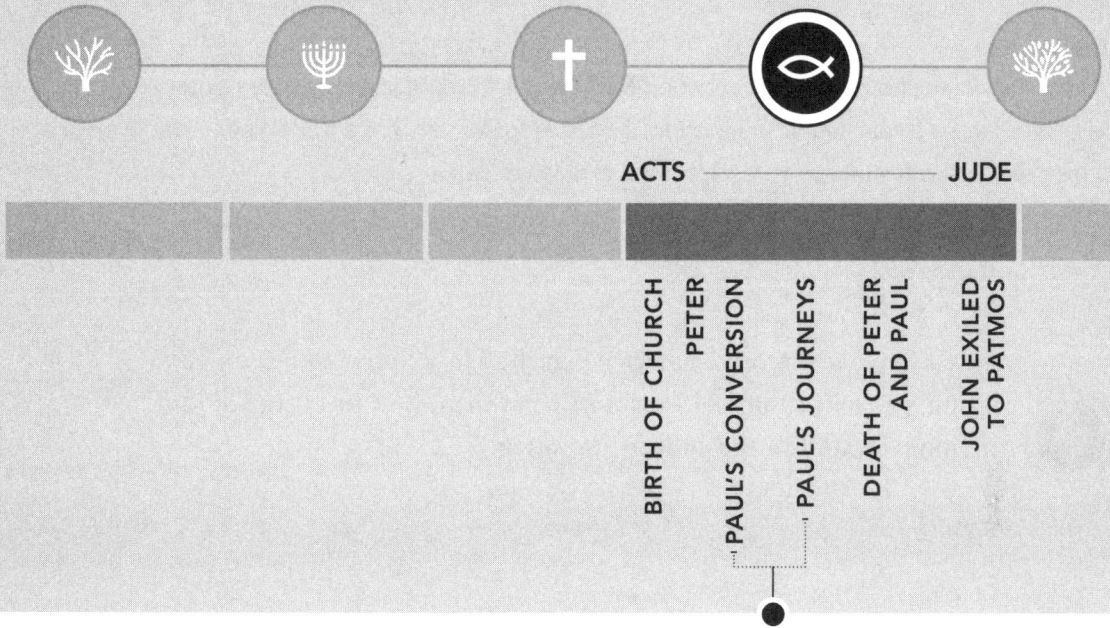

ACTS ———————— **JUDE**

BIRTH OF CHURCH
PETER
PAUL'S CONVERSION
PAUL'S JOURNEYS
DEATH OF PETER AND PAUL
JOHN EXILED TO PATMOS

READ THE STORY | Follow this reading guide if you want to pace yourself this week:

○ Day 1: Acts 7:51–8:3

○ Day 2: Acts 13:13–52

○ Day 3: Acts 9:1–31

○ Day 4: Acts 18:1–27

○ Day 5: Acts 21:1–26

A VIEW FROM THE LOWER STORY

Way back buried in the Old Testament, God told Abraham "all peoples . . . will be blessed" through him (Genesis 12:3). This promise was fulfilled in Jesus, Abraham's offspring, forty-two generations later. Now it is time for God to make good on his promise.

For this task, he selected probably the most unlikely candidate he could have found—Saul. Why was Saul an undesirable choice in our eyes? We are introduced to Saul, a young, zealous Jewish leader, for the first time as he was standing by holding the coats of the men stoning Stephen. Stephen was being martyred for teaching about Jesus. It was Saul who gave the crowd his approval for this act. From that point on Saul began to roam like a bounty hunter breathing out murderous threats against Jesus' followers. Houston, we have a problem—not even close to a good resumé to spread the good news of Jesus.

As a result, the church was scattered into Judea and Samaria. Remember the Great Commission?

> *"But you will receive power when the Holy Spirit comes on you; and you will be my witnesses in Jerusalem, and in all Judea and Samaria, and to the ends of the earth."*
>
> *Acts 1:8*

One of Saul's missions was to track down followers of Jesus, but he experienced a major roadblock, literally. This was a high-voltage smack-down that knocked him to the ground and left him blind. A voice called out to him, "Saul, Saul, why do you persecute me?" (Acts 9:4). This is literally his "come to Jesus" meeting.

After this encounter, Saul took on a new name and got a new assignment. He was given two names at birth. His Jewish name was Saul. Because he was also a Roman citizen, he received a Latin name at birth—Paul. Now that his new mission was to take the good news to Gentiles (aka anyone not Jewish), he began using his Latin name rather than his Hebrew name.

It doesn't matter if we have a lightning bolt stop us in our tracks, or if we have a less spectacular event when we accept Jesus' free gift of salvation, the miracle is that we are no longer focused on what we want, but we concentrate on what God wants.

> *Like Paul, having an encounter with Jesus and coming to faith gives us a new perspective, a new way to live and a new focus.*

By way of three missionary journeys, Paul started numerous churches for the Gentiles, encouraged and strengthened many of the existing churches, and wrote thirteen of the twenty-seven books of the New Testament.

A VIEW FROM THE UPPER STORY

Paul was the fulfillment of a prophecy from Isaiah: "I will also make you a light for the Gentiles, that my salvation may reach to the ends of the earth" (Isaiah 49:6).

Paul began as an antagonist of Jesus and the church. The persecution of believers in Jerusalem caused them to leave their homes and run for their very lives. God used the oppression and tyranny at the hand of Saul in the Lower Story to accomplish his Upper Story plan of spreading the good news from Jerusalem to Judea and Samaria (Acts 1:8).

As with the early church, persecution often causes us to draw closer to God and depend on him more than during times of comfort and prosperity.

Now that Paul became a protagonist, God used him to take his message of love to the ends of the earth—and it is still going today!

GOD'S STORY . . . MY STORY

1. What was your first encounter with Jesus/salvation like?

2. How has your focus changed since that encounter?

3. Thinking about your life before you became a believer in Christ and now, what "name" would you use to characterize your life before Christ, and what "name" would you use now? (Examples: melancholy/joy-filled; sick/healed; fearful/trusting; floundering/steady)

4. Have you experienced a difficult season in your life that caused a reaction toward God? Did it draw you to depend on him more, or did you abandon your faith?

5. Just as Paul had a God-given mission, so does every one of us. Do you have a clear idea of what yours is? If not, pray and ask God for clarity as to what he wants you to do with your life.

SHARE THE STORY

Review the five movements of the story from memory.

Movement 4 of Your Story

Share your response to last week's question with another person: What were the circumstances that led you to be open to becoming a follower of Christ?

You've Got Mail

The Story of the Church

PAUL'S FINAL WORDS

ACTS —————— JUDE

BIRTH OF CHURCH
PETER
PAUL'S CONVERSION
PAUL'S JOURNEYS
DEATH OF PETER AND PAUL
JOHN EXILED TO PATMOS

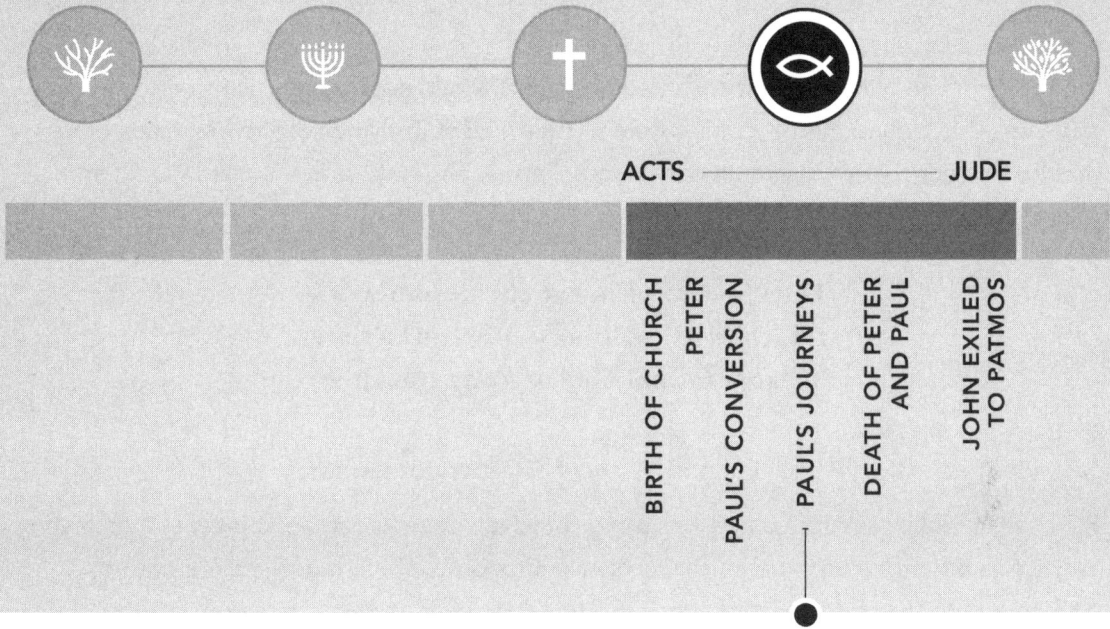

READ THE STORY | Follow this reading guide if you want to pace yourself this week:

○ Day 1: Acts 20:15–38

○ Day 2: Acts 21

○ Day 3: Acts 22:1–23:11

○ Day 4: 1 Timothy 6:11–21; 2 Timothy 4

○ Day 5: Acts 27:1–28:30

A VIEW FROM THE LOWER STORY

I love it when I get a real letter! Not an email, not an instant message or a Snapchat, but a real handwritten letter through "snail mail." It doesn't happen often, but every now and again, among my junk mail and bills, I find a hand-addressed envelope. My heart jumps for joy when I see it addressed to me. I feel amazingly special!

It is just that kind of real mail Paul sent to help the new followers at the churches he planted on his journeys. In fact, we still use the Epistles, as they are called, to guide us on how to live out our faith in a corrupt and fallen world. Paul knew if people believed in Jesus but did not live amazingly different lives, their friends and neighbors would not be particularly motivated to join them in adopting this new belief system (John 13:35). They needed to treat each other and those around them differently than non-believers. The way we live is often our most convincing message.

How we live when our circumstances are at their worst will cause others who see us to move toward God or away from him.

Someone once said, "Preach the gospel, and if necessary, use words."

Paul had tremendous success in establishing churches, training people to grow in their faith and live so others would experience God's love through them. However, his life was not all honey and roses. People were after him to snuff him out and keep him from sharing the good news about Jesus.

Several times Paul was beaten and thrown in prison. Some of these letters were written from his prison cell. Interestingly enough, the book of Philippians, one of these letters, is known as the treatise on joy. Who writes about joy from prison?

In other letters Paul warned against kinds of behaviors that don't reflect the values of God's community: falsehood, bitterness, anger, slander, sexual immorality, greed, foolish talk, and drunkenness.

All too soon, Paul's mission on earth came to an end. During Paul's third and final visit to Rome, he was arrested and flung into a wet, dark dungeon. He knew he wasn't going to make it out; it was time to pass the baton to the next generation. Timothy received two letters from Paul, preserved as two short books that bear his name. In these letters, Paul mentored this young lad to fight the good fight, finish the race, and keep the faith (2 Timothy 4:7).

One of the great tragedies of the early church is that so many of its pioneers were killed because of their beliefs. Most of the disciples were martyred for teaching others about Jesus. In the end, Paul was beheaded in Rome, but he successfully spread the church to the ends of the earth and prepared the next generation to continue his quest.

A VIEW FROM THE UPPER STORY

From the Lower Story perspective, following Jesus can be risky. Even today, people who follow Jesus face persecution, imprisonment, and even death. Paul persevered because he knew what was waiting for him in the Upper Story. He kept his eye on the end game. He had an Upper Story standpoint from his Lower Story shoes.

All of us who have embraced the gospel of Jesus Christ have become part of this new community, the church, and need to continue serving God no matter our circumstances by keeping our eye on the prize God has for us in his Upper Story.

In one of the most moving passages in his second letter to Timothy, Paul wrote:

> *I am already being poured out like a drink offering, and the time of my departure is near . . . . Now there is in store for me the crown of righteousness, which the Lord, the righteous Judge, will award to me on that day—and not only me, but also to all who have longed for his appearing.*
>
> *2 Timothy 4:6, 8*

Paul compared his life to a bottle of wine being poured out as a sacrificial offering to God. His heartfelt desire was that not one drop be left in the bottle when he departed this world.

The height and depth of God's love is so much he sent his only Son, Jesus, to die so we could get back into a relationship with him. Then he had men through the inspiration of the Holy Spirit pen the words in the Bible to create a love letter addressed to each of us. The Bible outlines the extent he was willing to go to work the countless details and millions of threads to knit our Lower Story with his Upper Story. How could we not desire to be like Paul—poured out like a drink offering until the very last drop is gone from our bottle? You've got mail!

GOD'S STORY . . . MY STORY

1. When was the last time you wrote or received a "snail mail" letter? Who was it from? How did it make you feel?

2. How do you respond when your circumstances are less than desirable? Would your response draw others toward God or repel them away from God?

3. Do you have a plan to pass your faith on to the next generation?

4. Have you surrendered to serve God until your very lost drop has been poured out?

5. Do you approach the Bible as God's love letter to you?

SHARE THE STORY

Review the five movements of the story from memory.

Movement 5 of Your Story

Describe the day you turned your life over to Christ. What pushed you over the edge? (Where were you? Who was with you? What did you do or say? Did you get baptized?)

I Stand at Your Door

The Story of the New Garden

LETTERS TO THE SEVEN CHURCHES

REVELATION

JOHN WRITES
REVELATION

US!

2ND COMING
GREAT WHITE THRONE

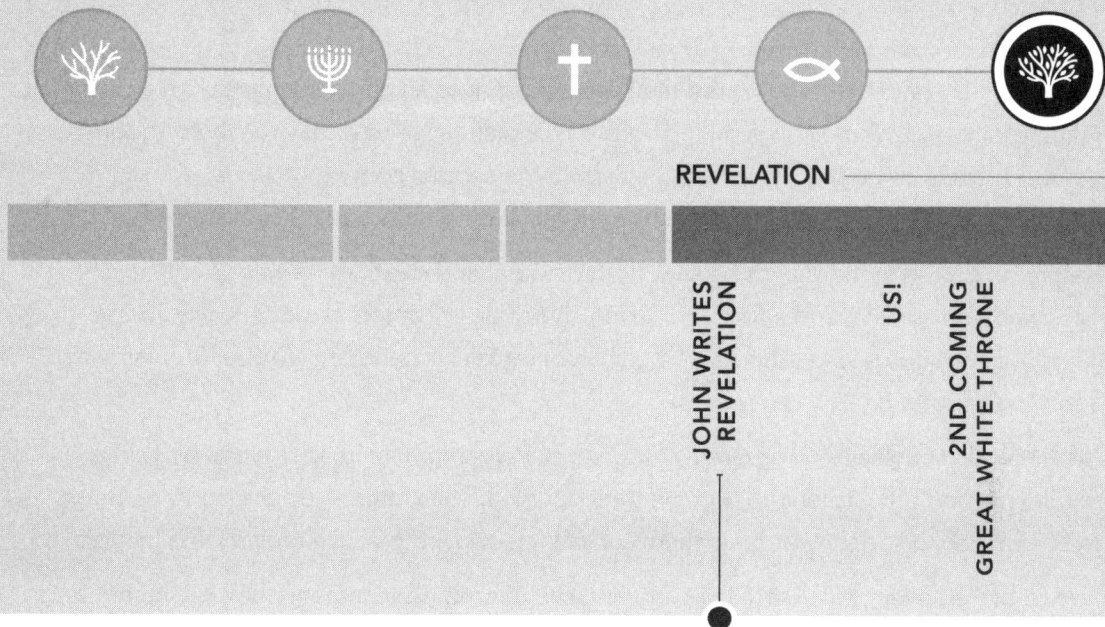

❧ **READ THE STORY** | Follow this reading guide if you want to pace yourself this week:

○ Day 1: Revelation 2:1–7, 12–17

○ Day 2: Revelation 2:18–29; 3:1–6

○ Day 3: Revelation 3:7–10

○ Day 4: Revelation 3:8–13

○ Day 5: Revelation 3:14–22

A VIEW FROM THE LOWER STORY

John is the disciple of Jesus who wrote the last book in the Bible—the book of Revelation. Historians tell us that he is the only apostle who was not killed for professing his faith in Jesus Christ. Instead, he was banished to the small island of Patmos (only four by eight miles) to spend his remaining days, completely isolated and surrounded by water. It is like being on the set of a spiritual *Cast Away*. The religious and political leaders thought his ability to do further damage would be controlled if they kept him far from everyone. Wow, did they ever miscalculate!

It was on this island that God visited the beloved John via an angel and gave him a clear vision of what was yet to come, including the best picture we have of what the kingdom of God is going to be like. This book is all about the second coming of Jesus, who John reminded us, "Loves us and has freed us from our sins by his blood" (Revelation 1:5).

Before he dove into the visions he saw, both dreadful and exciting, he went a little local, or Lower Story gazing, and addressed seven churches all located in modern-day Turkey. Actually, it was Jesus who addressed the churches from his panoramic Upper Story view as John took dictation.

Of the seven churches, there were two (Ephesus, Pergamum) to which he offered partial commendation but challenged them in their doctrine. They intermixed the purity of God's truth with pagan society that gave them sufficient leeway to practice idolatry and immorality.

To two of the seven churches (Sardis, Thyatira) he offered no commendation but recognized there was a remnant within the congregation who were trying to stay pure to Christ.

Two churches received full commendation by Christ (Smyrna, Philadelphia). They received the full respect of Jesus for enduring under persecution and suffering. Imagine the smile on their faces when they received this recognition.

Only one church (Laodicea) received absolutely no approval because they were totally lukewarm. They were neither *hot* (referring to the medicinal hot springs of nearby Hierapolis) nor *cold* (referring to the cool mountain streams of nearby Colossae).

> **They neither provided healing for the spiritually sick (hot water) nor refreshment for the spiritually weary (cold water). They were useless, so God wanted to spit or vomit them out of his mouth.**

Divine heaving—yikes!

A VIEW FROM THE UPPER STORY

Before we get transported to the Upper Story vision, Jesus wrapped up his report card of the churches living in the Lower Story with an important reminder and then an invitation. Here is the reminder:

> *"Those whom I love I rebuke and discipline. So be earnest and repent."*
>
> *Revelation 3:19, emphasis added*

Just as we learned with the community of Israel, so we now learn with the community of the church, God loves us too much to leave us alone, running astray to our destruction. He intervenes, he warns, he issues clear disciplinary actions, and invites us to turn around and move the direction that leads to life and peace.

Then this amazing invitation is offered:

> *"Here I am! I stand at the door and knock. If anyone hears my voice and opens the door, I will come in and eat with that person, and they with me."*
>
> *Revelation 3:20*

The image here is of Jesus standing outside the door when he should already be inside. He's been pushed out. Now, he is not only knocking but he is calling out their name. He wants to come in and share a meal with them. Conviviality is an act of deep fellowship.

> *Jesus is telling them and us that we can be fully restored to an intimate, loving, life-giving relationship with God.*

But . . . we must open the door!

GOD'S STORY . . . MY STORY

1. Read Revelation 2:1–7, 12–17. Do you feel you have a firm grasp on the essential teaching of Scripture? In what areas do you feel today's Christians and churches may be losing their way?

2. Read Revelation 2:18–29 and 3:1–6. Do you feel your faith is strong enough not to veer away from it when others do?

3. Read Revelation 3:8–11. If you received a letter from Jesus, do you feel you and the church you attend would receive a full commendation like the churches in Smyrna and Philadelphia? Explain your answer.

4. Read Revelation 3:7–13. Do you feel right now your faith is hot, cold, or neither? What is one thing you could do to change the temperature of your faith?

5. Read Revelation 3:14–22. Imagine Jesus standing outside your door knocking and calling out your name. Are you going to let him in? What do you think it would be like to share a meal with Jesus?

SHARE THE STORY

Review the five movements of the story from memory.

Movement 5 of Your Story

Share your response to last week's question with one person: How has your life been since accepting Christ?

The Tale of Two Arrivals

The Story of the New Garden

THE SECOND COMING

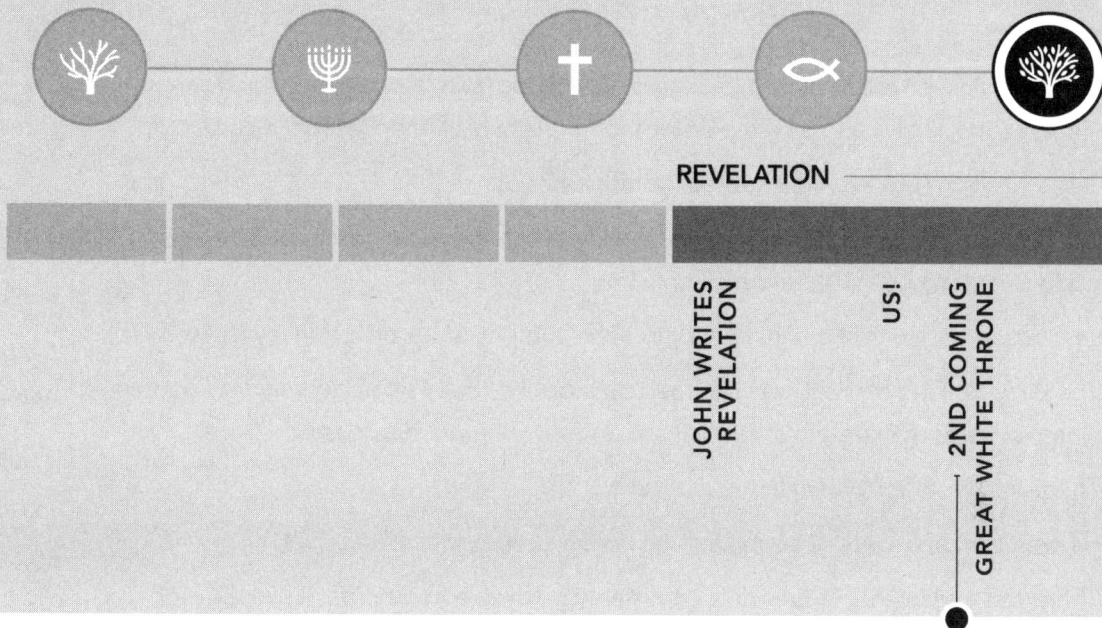

JOHN WRITES REVELATION

US!

2ND COMING

GREAT WHITE THRONE

REVELATION

READ THE STORY | Follow this reading guide if you want to pace yourself this week:

○ Day 1: Revelation 5:1–11

○ Day 2: 1 Thessalonians 4:13–18

○ Day 3: 1 Thessalonians 5:1–11

○ Day 4: Revelation 19:11–17

○ Day 5: Revelation 19:18–21

A VIEW FROM THE LOWER STORY

Jesus came down from the Upper Story into our Lower Story the first time around 5 BC. Here is what it looked like:

The first time Jesus came, he came *to represent us* (Philippians 2:6–7).

A broken people in need of redemption. He came as the Son of Man. He is called the second Adam, with the hopes that this redo, this mulligan, would get it right this time and provide a way back to God (1 Corinthians 15:45).

The first time Jesus came he was *poor* (Luke 2:24).

Mary and Joseph didn't have a lot. Jesus wasn't born with a silver spoon in his mouth but a wooden one, likely carved by the calloused hands of his father Joseph, a carpenter.

Jesus was from the town of *Nazareth* (Matthew 2:23).

Nazareth was on the wrong side of the tracks. It was common to hear people say, "Nothing good can come out of Nazareth" (John 1:46).

Jesus rode into Bethlehem in the womb of his mother, Mary, on a donkey (Luke 2:4–5).

The Bible doesn't explicitly say she road on a donkey but it's hard to imagine she walked ninety miles from Nazareth to Bethlehem on foot in her third trimester.

There was *no room* for him in the inn (Luke 2:7).

He was *born in a feeding trough* among smelly farm animals (Luke 2:7).

There was no fanfare, no fireworks on his arrival. It was a *silent night* (Luke 2:8–14).

There was the host of angels who said three lines of a great song but the only audience besides Mary and Joseph were some nearby shepherds.

Soon after his birth his family went on the run, *on defense* from King Herod who wanted to kill him (Matthew 2:13–15).

He came to us the first time as a baby wrapped in swaddling clothes (Luke 2:12 KJV).

He was an innocent, vulnerable, dependent, spotless *Lamb* (John 1:29).

> **He came the first time as a Lower Story dweller in all its limitations for our sakes.**

A VIEW FROM THE UPPER STORY

But . . . when he comes the second time things will be different.

He will not be *representing us but himself*—God, in all his glory, power, and splendor.

The first time he came he was poor and lived in humble circumstances; the second time he comes he will *show off his vast riches*—flaunting it in a righteous sort of way.

Jesus will not be coming from the lowly city of Nazareth but from sitting on a *throne* (Revelation 4:2–3).

Nothing but good can come out of heaven.

He will not be riding into town on a donkey tucked in the womb of his mother but on a *white stallion* (Revelation 19:11).

This time he will not be denied a room in the inn but will declare that the whole earth was created by him and belongs to him. He is the *owner*, and we are the guests (Revelation 4:11).

The first time he was born in a stable; the second time he will declare he is the *Alpha and Omega*, the beginning and the end; the great "I AM" who was and is and will always be (Revelation 22:13).

Turns out there is no BC—Before Christ. He has always existed (John 1:1–4).

The first time he came the audience was small; this time it will be a *global audience* (Philippians 2:10).

This time there will be fanfare. It will not be a silent night. Trumpets will blow for all to hear (1 Thessalonians 4:16). Following right behind him will be the armies of heaven also riding white horses and dressed in fine linen, white and clean—that would be us, by the way (Revelation 19:14).

The first time he came to us, he came as a baby; this time he will come as a *warrior* (Revelation 19:15).

He will be wearing a white robe, dipped in blood. His eyes will be like blazing fire and on his head will be many crowns (Revelation 19:12–13).

The second time he comes he will not be on the defense, running from a king who wants to kill him. No, he will come as the *King of kings on the offense* to bring justice and life (Revelation 19:16).

> *The first time he came as a lamb to be sacrificed for us; the next time he will come as a lion to rescue us from death (Revelation 5:5).*

GOD'S STORY . . . MY STORY

1. What contrast between Jesus' first coming and second stands out to you the most?

2. Do you sense Jesus' second coming is soon? Explain your thinking.

3. What excites you about Jesus' second coming? What overwhelms you?

4. If you knew that Jesus was coming back at the end of the week, what would you do differently today?

5. Share this week's study with two or three people and ask them what they think about the idea of Jesus' second coming. Record their responses.

SHARE THE STORY

Review the five movements of the story from memory.

The Five Movements of Your Story

Look back over your responses to the five questions pertaining to your story and write out a summary in the form of a letter to a friend. Think of writing five paragraphs, one for each question.

Love Honors Your Choice

The Story of the New Garden

HELL

REVELATION

JOHN WRITES
REVELATION

US!

2ND COMING
GREAT WHITE THRONE

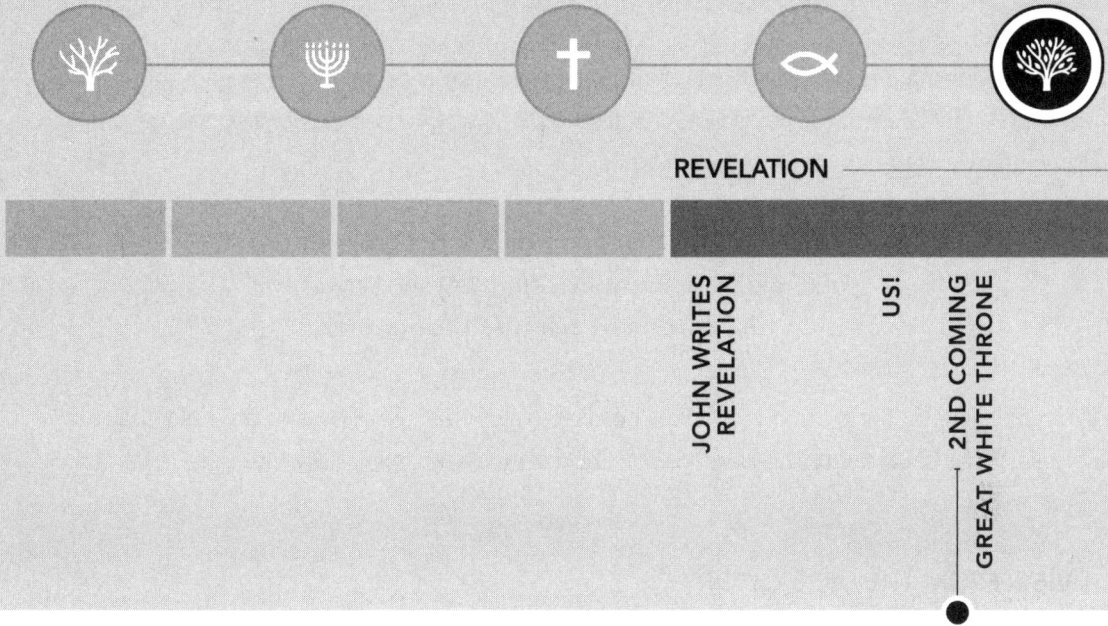

❧ **READ THE STORY** | Follow this reading guide if you want to pace yourself this week:

◯ Day 1: Luke 16:19–24

◯ Day 2: Luke 16:25–31

◯ Day 3: Revelation 20:1–6

◯ Day 4: Revelation 20:7–10

◯ Day 5: Revelation 20:11–15

A VIEW FROM THE LOWER STORY

Jesus came into our Lower Story to do for us (all of us) what we could not do for ourselves—to provide sufficient payment for our sins so we could be forgiven. This scripture exposes the heart of God:

> *The Lord is not slow in keeping his promise, as some understand slowness. Instead he is patient with you, not wanting anyone to perish, but everyone to come to repentance.*
>
> *2 Peter 3:9*

Jesus provided a payment to cover us all. All we must do is believe and receive this gift before our time in the Lower Story runs out. Just like Adam and Eve had a choice in the garden between two trees, so we have a choice.

> *God is wanting us to choose the tree that*
> *his Son hung on so he can grant us eternal life*
> *and entrance back into the garden.*

What happens to the person who takes hold of this choice? That is what our next chapter reveals. What happens to the person who chooses to reject this offer? Scripture is painfully clear below.

A VIEW FROM THE UPPER STORY

Luke 16 records Jesus telling us a parable of two guys that we can easily imagine literally. One guy is Lazarus, whose name means "God, the Helper," signaling he took God up on his offer. The other guy is simply called a "rich man." This guy lived a life of self-consumption and hedonism and ignored God and his neighbors.

Lazarus's body was buried, and his spirit went to a place called Abraham's side (Luke 16:20–22). I believe this is a peaceful place all people of faith went before the work of Christ on the cross. After Christ's finished work on the cross, he descended into Abraham's side and retrieved all these souls and took them into the presence of God now that the blood of Christ had been applied to their lives (Ephesians 4:8–9).

The rich man went to a place called hell. It is a place of torment for sure, but it is more than that. It is like sitting in prison on death row awaiting your day of execution. Could anything be more horrifying?

Fast-forward to Revelation 20. Jesus will return and set up court. He is the judge and the jury. All those who have rejected the offering of salvation will receive a resurrected body of some sort and stand before what is referred to as the Great White Throne Judgment Seat. There will be two books. The first will be a catalogue of every work done on earth. This will be entered as evidence and will quickly determine that logged sins have disqualified this person from entrance into the new kingdom.

Then a second book will be opened, called the Book of Life. This book contains all the names of people who received the gift of salvation in Jesus. For those who believed, their sins will not be remembered because they were given to Jesus—put on his account. Their names are listed in the Book of Life. Since the unbelievers did not choose to receive the gift while living in the Lower Story, their names have been blotted out of the Book of Life. They must give account for their sins, which will keep them from gaining entrance into the New Garden, the eternal kingdom of God.

We are told they will be cast into the lake of fire, a place originally designed for Satan and death, eternally separated from God.

Here's the bottom line:

God does not send anyone to hell;
he merely honors their choice.

True love does not force another to love him back. He loves you enough to have given his one and only Son to provide a way back into a relationship with him. He simply wants to know how you feel about him. He will honor your decision.

C. S. Lewis, well-known author, Oxford professor, apologist, and philosopher, said:

> I willingly believe that the damned are, in one sense, successful, rebels to the end; that the doors of hell are locked on the inside. They enjoy forever the horrible freedom they have demanded and are therefore self-enslaved: just as the blessed, forever submitting to obedience, become through all eternity more and more free.[7]

In his book *The Great Divorce*, he tells it like it is:

> There are only two kinds of people in the end: those who say to God "Thy will be done," and those whom God says . . . "Thy will be done."[8]

Christ's sacrifice has given all of us the opportunity to overturn Adam's sentence of death upon us. Just like Adam and Eve had the freedom to choose, God, out of his love for us, gives us the freedom to choose.

So, what will it be for you?

[7] C. S. Lewis, *The Problem of Pain*, in *The Complete C. S. Lewis Signature Classics* (HarperOne, 2002), 416.
[8] C. S. Lewis, *The Great Divorce*, (HarperOne, 2010), chap. 9.

GOD'S STORY . . . MY STORY

1. For your friends and family who don't believe, do you think their primary objections or hang-ups have to do with who God is? Or does it have less to do with God and more to do with them?

2. Do you believe that God should take away our choice and treat us more like robots?

3. Read 2 Peter 3:9. How does this verse speak to God's mercy?

4. Why do you think God doesn't just let everyone into heaven at the end of the day?

5. Does this create in you a sense of urgency to talk with your friends and family about Jesus?

SHARE THE STORY

Rehearse the five movements of the story and the five movements of your story. Pray about who you will share this with next week. It can be a single individual or a small group of people.

The Beginning

The Story of the New Garden

THE NEW GARDEN

REVELATION

JOHN WRITES
REVELATION

US!

2ND COMING
GREAT WHITE THRONE

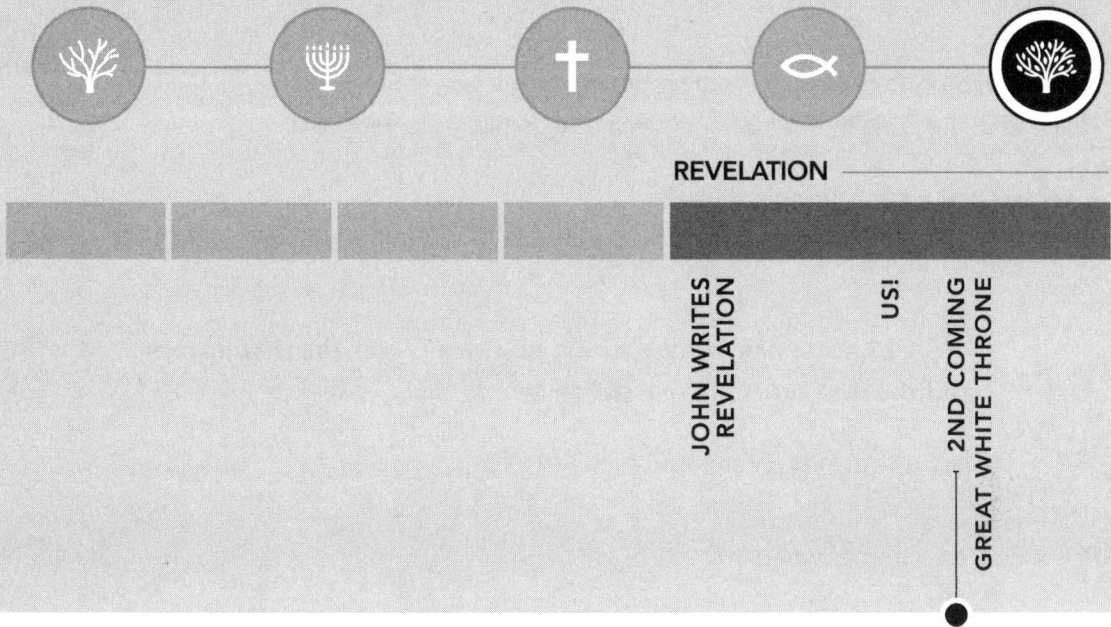

READ THE STORY | Follow this reading guide if you want to pace yourself this week:

○ Day 1: John 14:1–6

○ Day 2: Revelation 21:1–8

○ Day 3: Revelation 21:9–27

○ Day 4: Revelation 22:1–11

○ Day 5: Revelation 22:12–21

A VIEW FROM THE LOWER STORY

If you are a follower of Jesus Christ, no matter how difficult your life has become, no matter how dark your pathway, no matter how intense your weariness, take courage. Your Lower Story doesn't end there.

Because you have believed in Jesus, your story has just begun, and it will be a phenomenal one.

The Upper Story is once again coming down into our Lower Story. John took the last two chapters of the Bible to describe this place to us. Hold on to your seat.

A VIEW FROM THE UPPER STORY

John began Revelation 21 with these words:

> *Then I saw "a new heaven and a new earth," for the first heaven and the first earth had passed away.*
>
> *Revelation 21:1*

Remember how the story began?

> *"In the beginning God created the heavens and the earth."*
>
> *Genesis 1:1*

We have come full circle. Our future home will be a whole new earth—one that is not groaning or dying anymore because of the curse of sin (Romans 8:22–23).

John continued describing the glimpse into the future God gave him:

> I saw the Holy City, the new Jerusalem, coming down out of heaven from God, prepared as a bride beautifully dressed for her husband.
>
> (Revelation 21:2)

So, we will have a brand-new place to live on a brand-new earth, but this is not enough for God. Do you remember why he created us in the first place? Do you remember the one major theme of the Upper Story? Maybe what John described next will refresh your memory:

> And I heard a loud voice from the throne saying, "Look! God's dwelling place is now among the people, and he will dwell with them. They will be his people, and God himself will be with them and be their God."
>
> (verse 3)

Wow! God is coming down again into the Lower Story to be with us, just as he was with Adam and Eve. Not in a tabernacle with a curtained room to separate him from us, but right there with us, as in the original garden. Walking with us. Talking with us. This is all God has ever wanted. In this community that God has been building, there will be no more tears. No need for them, because there will be no death, no pain, no sadness. That is all Lower Story stuff.

Remember the garden at the beginning of the story? God is reconstructing it for us—with a few minor changes to make it even better. Imagine with me—there is a river that contains the water of life flowing from the throne of God down the middle of the city. On each side of the river are two trees of life bearing fruit every single month. Listen to this: We will not need any lamps or even the sun because God will provide all the light we need. John told us this will be our life forever and ever (Revelation 22:1–5).

There is that tree of life again. It was in the garden of Eden the last time we saw it. It was the tree that bore fruit to eternal life. Adam and Eve—and consequently all humanity—were banished from that garden, but now we have unguarded access to it again. And there is not just one tree, but two trees along a crystal-clear, life-giving river. Everything about this new community is zeroed in on abundant, eternal life.

One tree, however, is missing from this reconstructed garden—the Tree of the Knowledge of Good and Evil. It is the tree that God placed in the first garden for Adam and Eve so they could choose whether or not to embrace God's vision of life. Why isn't it in this new garden? Because it isn't needed. You have already made the life-giving choice when you accepted Jesus' offer for forgiveness.

Most importantly of all, when we return to this garden, we will see the face of our Lord God.

We will see the intense love in his eyes that went to such a great extent to get us back.

It will overwhelm us every day for eternity.

Once you see this vision, you can't unsee it. Like John, we, too, whisper under our breath, "Come, Lord Jesus."

GOD'S STORY . . . MY STORY

1. Read John 14:1–6. Jesus is preparing a place for you in the New Jerusalem to present to you after he returns. Describe the ideal place for you.

2. Read Revelation 21:4. Jesus will take his finger and once and for all wipe every tear from your eyes. What is the story that triggers your most intense tears you are looking to put behind you?

3. Read Revelation 21:27. What excites you the most about living in a world with absolutely no sin?

4. Read Revelation 22:4. What is the first thing you think you will do or say when you see God the Father and Jesus face-to-face?

5. Read Revelation 22:17. Who is the one person you are looking forward to seeing again in the new kingdom?

SHARE THE STORY

Share the five movements of the story and the five movements of your story with a friend.

WEEK
52

Your Place in the Story

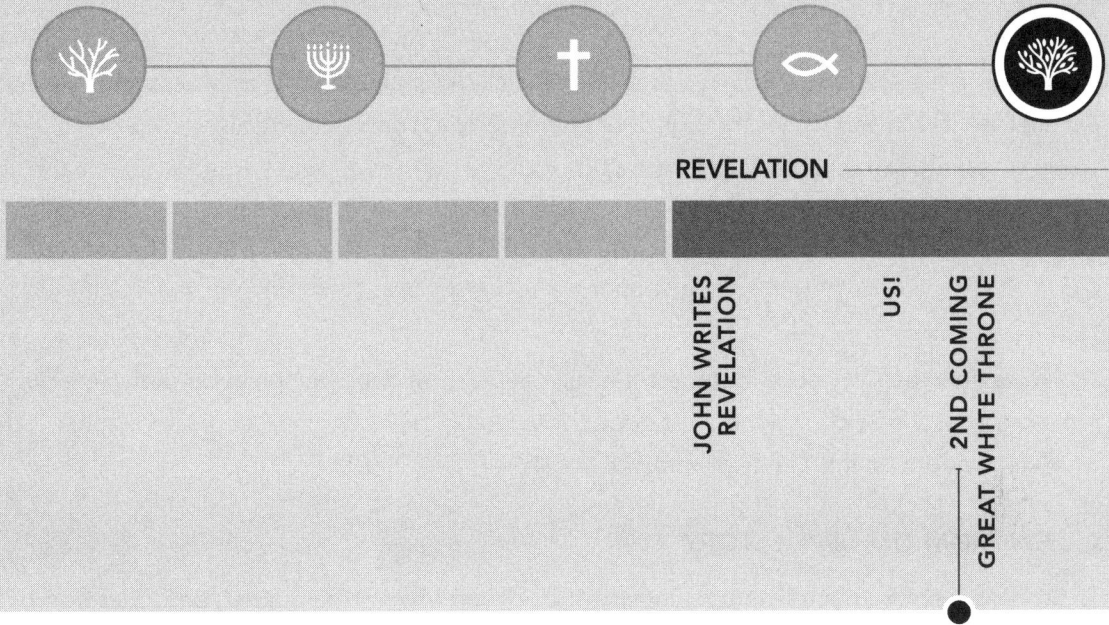

REVELATION

JOHN WRITES REVELATION

US!

2ND COMING

GREAT WHITE THRONE

❧ **READ THE STORY** | Follow this reading guide if you want to pace yourself this week:

○ Day 1: Jeremiah 1:1–9; Psalm 139:13–16; Acts 9:15–16

○ Day 2: Romans 8:29; Ephesians 2:10; Galatians 5:22–23

○ Day 3: Matthew 6:24–34

○ Day 4: Romans 12:3–8

○ Day 5: 1 Corinthians 6:20; 10:31

A VIEW FROM THE LOWER STORY

Let's go back to the breathtaking Sistine Chapel in Rome where we began our journey together on week one. You have now read the backstory of the three hundred characters Michelangelo painted on the ceiling and how they fit together to tell the one love story of God. You know how each played a part in the unfolding of God's Upper Story plan to get us back.

You look up, and over in the corner, much to your surprise, you see the back of a man who looks like Michelangelo. He is painting a scene on a blank spot on the ceiling. As you hone in on the painting in progress, you quickly recognize that it is a rendering of our current day. As you look a little closer, the scenery seems all too familiar. It includes places and faces of *your* world. Adrenaline kicks in and rushes through your entire body as soon as the reality dawns on you—this famous artist is painting a portrait of you!

You are a character in the
grand story of God.

You know how the story ends, but there are still things to be done, things to be said. Here is the big question—how will the artist depict your life on the ceiling amidst of all the folks we've read about on this fifty-two-week adventure?

A VIEW FROM THE UPPER STORY

To properly identify your role in the tapestry of God, you need some guiding principles from the Upper Story.

① *He has a plan for your life already set out.*

Read what God said to Jeremiah:

> "Before I shaped you in the womb,
>   I knew all about you.
> Before you saw the light of day,
>   I had holy plans for you:
> A prophet to the nations—
>   that's what I had in mind for you."
> (Jeremiah 1:5 MSG)

Check out David's discovery:

> Like an open book, you watched me grow from
> conception to birth;
>   all the stages of my life were spread out before you,
> The days of my life all prepared
>   before I'd even lived one day.
> (Psalm 139:15–16 MSG)

The same is true for you. Paul stated it clearly to us:

> For we are God's handiwork, created in Christ Jesus to do good works, which God prepared in advance for us to do.
> (Ephesians 2:10)

② *The foundational mission for every believer is to become like Jesus.*

Romans lays it out in plain language:

> For those God foreknew he also predestined to be conformed to the image of his Son, that he might be the firstborn among many brothers and sisters.
> (Romans 8:29)

The outcome of our lives is more about who you are becoming than what you do. Followers of Jesus don't just have a to-do list, but more importantly a to-be list. Traits like love, joy, peace, patience, kindness, gentleness, goodness, faithfulness, and self-control (Galatians 5:22–23). This is your "pre-destiny."

③ *The primary driver is to serve God not money.*

Heed the words of Jesus:

> "No one can serve two masters. Either you will hate the one and love the other, or you will be devoted to the one and despise the other. You cannot serve both God and money."
> (Matthew 6:24)

It is so easy to make the pursuit of money the priority of our lives—either to get rich or simply pay the bills. Jesus tells us just a few verses down if we put God first, he will throw in all the other things we need (Matthew 6:33). You've got to believe he will make good on his promise to move in this direction.

4 *It has something to do with the way God has wired you.*

Paul offered us this spiritual axiom:

> We have different gifts, according to the grace given to each of us.
>
> (Romans 12:6)

He then went on to admonish us to work in the area of our giftedness. Makes total sense. It's sad when a duck tries to climb a tree or a giraffe tries out for the swim team.

5 *It has something to do with the opportunity right in front of you.*

Many people try to think of a huge thing to give their life to. That is noble but very seldom how God works. God usually puts something good to do right in front of us. We take the first step and walk into that opportunity and see where it takes us.

6 *It's not about you.*

Paul laid down this principle succinctly in his letter to the Corinthians:

> So whether you eat or drink or whatever you do, do it all for the glory of God.
> (1 Corinthians 10:31)

Jesus set the example when he said:

> "For even the Son of Man did not come to be served, but to serve, and to give his life as a ransom for many."
> (Mark 10:45)

Jesus also told us if we truly want to find our lives we can't focus on ourselves but must lose ourselves in the service of God and others (Matthew 10:39). The decisions you make today provide the content the artist will use to create your portrait in the mural of God's story. I encourage you not only to love God but to receive his love for you and to align your life to his Upper Story plan. If you do this, God promises that all the events in your life will turn out for the good (Romans 8:28).

But the most important picture of all is the painting of you and God taking a walk in the cool of the day in the garden to come. If this painting is drawn of you, then it means you have truly captured God's big idea—he loves you and wants to be with you!

GOD'S STORY . . . MY STORY

1. Read Jeremiah 1:1–9; Psalm 139:13–16; Acts 9:15–16. Do you have a sense of why God has you here on earth?

2. Read Galatians 5:22–23. Of the nine virtues listed in this passage, which two are the strongest for you? Which two need a little more work? This becomes your to-be list.

3. Romans 12:3–8. What do you think your primary gifts are? Maybe ask a few people who know you what they think they are.

4. Read Matthew 6:24. Is God or money the primary driver of your life?

5. What are the opportunities to do good that are right in front of you? Do you think you could find your sense of mission by walking into this opportunity?

6. Write out a description of the painting of you that you would love to see on the ceiling of the Sistine Chapel. Or better yet, take a stab at drawing or painting it.

SHARE THE STORY

Spend some time writing and reflecting on how this encounter with God's love has helped shaped your life and drawn you closer to God.